Indigenous American Women

CONTEMPORARY INDIGENOUS ISSUES

*Series Editor*
Devon A. Mihesuah

# Indigenous American Women

Decolonization, Empowerment, Activism

Devon Abbott Mihesuah

University of Nebraska Press
Lincoln and London

Acknowledgments for the use of previously published material appear on pages ix–x, which constitutes an extension of the copyright page.

© 2003 by Devon Abbott Mihesuah

Manufactured in the United States of America

⊗

Library of Congress Cataloging-in-Publication Data
Mihesuah, Devon A. (Devon Abbott), 1957–
Indigenous American women: decolonization, empowerment, activism / Devon Abbott Mihesuah.
p.   cm.—(Contemporary indigenous issues)
Includes bibliographical references and index.
ISBN 0-8032-3227-6 (cl.: alk. paper)—ISBN 0-8032-8286-9 (pbk.: alk. paper)
1. Indian women—United States—Social conditions.   2. Feminism—United States—History.
I. Title.   II. Series.
E98.W8M54   2003
305.48'897073—dc21
2002028767

To Alli Abbott Wilson

# Contents

# Acknowledgments

Thank yous to family, friends, and colleagues who have assisted, inspired, and encouraged me in the writing of these essays: Olyve Hallmark Abbott, Rebecca Allahyari, Linda Beaverson, Mary Best, Joseph Boles, James F. Brooks, Elizabeth Castle, Duane Champagne, Diana Collier, Shannon Collins, Elizabeth Cook-Lynn, Gary Dunham, Clyde Ellis, Victoria Enders, Vicki Green, Curtis M. Hinsley, Eric Luke Lassiter, Deborah Maloney-Pictou, Denise Maloney-Pictou, Judith Michener, Billie Mills, Theda Perdue, Robert A. Pictou-Branscombe, Harald Prins, James Riding In, Victoria Sheffler, Delores Sumner, William Welge, Angela Cavender Wilson, Taryn Abbott Wilson, Terry P. Wilson, Donald Worcester, and Michael Yellow Bird, in addition to the everlasting patience of my husband, Joshua, and my children, Tosh and Ariana, and the Ford Foundation, Northern Arizona University's Office of Grants and Contracts, and the Smithsonian Institution.

The following chapters and essays have been reprinted or excerpted here or have been significantly revised: "Commonalty of Difference: American Indian Women in History," *AIQ* 20:1 (1996): 15–27, reprinted from the *American Indian Quarterly* by permission of the University of Nebraska Press. Copyright (c) 1996 by the University of Nebraska Press; "A Few Cautions at the Millennium on the Merging of Feminist Studies with American Indian Women's Studies," *SIGNS* 25:4 (2000): 1247–52, (c) 2000 by The University of Chicago. All rights reserved; "Research Guidelines for Institutions with Scholars Who Study American Indians," reprinted from the *American Indian Culture and Research Journal* 17:3 (fall 1993): 131–39 by permission of the American Indian Studies Center, UCLA, (c) Regents of the University of California; "Too Dark to Be Angels": The Class System among the Cherokees at the Female Seminary," reprinted from the *American Indian Culture and Research Journal* 15:1 (1991): 29–52 by permission of the American Indian Studies Center, UCLA, (c) Regents of the University of California; "American Indian Identities: Issues of Individual Choices and Development," reprinted from the*American Indian Culture and Research Journal* 22: 2 (1998): 193–226 by permission of the American Indian Studies Center, UCLA, (c) Regents of the University of California; "Anna Mae Pictou-Aquash: An American Indian Activist," in Theda Perdue, ed., *Sifters: Native Women's Lives* (New York: Oxford University Press, 2001), 204–22, copyright (c) 2001 by Oxford University Press, Inc. Used by permission of Oxford University Press, Inc.; "Interview with Denise Maloney-Pictou and Deborah Maloney-Pictou," *AIQ* 24:2 (spring 2000): 264–78, reprinted from the *American Indian Quarterly* by permission of the University of Nebraska Press. Copyright (c) 2000 by the University of Nebraska Press; "Infatuation Is Not Enough: Review of Ian Frazier's *On the Rez*," *AIQ* 24:2 (spring 2000): 283–86, reprinted from the *American Indian Quarterly* by permission of the University of Nebraska Press. Copyright (c) 2000 by the University of Nebraska Press; "Comment on 'Indian Girls,'" *HEArt* 5:1 (fall 2000): 18–20.

The epigraph in chapter 9 is an excerpt from the song "I'd Do It Again in a Heartbeat," music and lyrics by Shannon M. Collins, executive director of the ANNA Foundation. Used with permission.

# Introduction

I have written these essays because of my concern about tribal America. Today, American Indians of 557 tribes number approximately 2.4 million. Many of these people face numerous problems: unemployment is 90 percent on some reservations; 65 percent of American Indigenes aged twenty-five or older are high school graduates (compared to 75 percent of the total U.S. population), and the rate goes down for Indians on reservations; the median household income for Natives on reservations is less than twenty thousand dollars compared to thirty thousand dollars for the U.S. population, and 31.6 percent of Natives live below the poverty line, compared to 13 percent for the U.S. population; many Natives cannot purchase homes because tribal land cannot be used as collateral for loans; Natives suffer from diabetes, alcoholism, suicide, and infant mortality at higher rates than the rest of the U.S. population, and Indians report more spousal and child abuse than before; Natives have a lower life expectancy than any population in the New World; the Natives languages are dying— of 175 languages, 50 are spoken by two or more generations, 70 are spoken only by elders, and 55 are spoken by less than ten persons.[1]

In addition, Natives are still stereotyped in movies, on television, in literature, and as sports team mascots.[2] Indigenous skeletal remains and sacred cultural objects are still stored in archives and museums, pot hunters and many archaeologists continue to collect these items in the name of academic freedom, and portions of living Natives are harvested and kept for research for the "human genome project."[3] Lands inhabited and used by Indians are polluted and overused, affecting tribe members' health and tribal economies.[4] Natives are often ignored as authorities on their own histories and cultures, resulting in thousands of books and essays written about Natives from non-Natives' viewpoints, and Native scholars often are accused of achieving their university positions because of their race, not on the basis of their merits or accomplishments.[5] Negative terminology, such as the term "squaw," is still in use, despite objections by many Natives.[6] Many tribes contend with non-Indians and other Natives who appropriate their art and symbols.[7] The effects of colonialism have indeed been devastating, prompting the use of terms such as "holocaust" and "genocide."

Although many of the effects of colonialism have been negative, depressing facts and figures are not the focus of these essays. Tribes—often with the aid of non-Indians—have found ways to adapt and survive. Reverence for the roles females play within cultures has been decimated among some tribes, but among many groups Natives are vocal and active in their concern for keeping those traditional female roles and ideologies alive. Tribal spirituality has thrived despite missionaries' attempts at subsuming tribal religions and the federal government's policies of assimilating Natives by confining tribes to reservations, forcing education on their children, and terminating tribes' status with the federal government. Native women have survived the "good intentions" of women reformers in organizations such as the Women's National Indian Association and the Women's Home Mission Circle, groups that attempted to "help Indian peoples by pushing for assimilation, education, and Christianization," and Indigenous women continue to fight against stereotypes, abuse, and cultural appropriation.[8]

The essays in part I deal with issues related to research and writing about Native women. The public's ideas about Natives are in large part formulated by books and essays written by non-Indians. Policies pertaining to Indians are formulated by persons educated in the academy. Because standards for curriculum development, writing, and research, promotion, and tenure decisions are firmly in the hands of non-Indians, it is important to discuss how Indigenous women have been portrayed in literature, how non-Natives perceive them, and how they place themselves in the scholarly setting.

"A Few Cautions on the Merging of Feminist Studies with Indigenous Women's Studies" discusses topics that must be addressed when writing about Native women, including the need to recognize the heterogeneity among Native women through sensitive research methodologies. "Writing about Anna Mae Pictou-Aquash" reveals the perils one may encounter when researching and writing about a murder victim whose killers are still living and watching to see who emerges on the scene with new information. The next two pieces critique work by prominent writers Ian Frazier and Linda McCarriston, who have produced a book and poem, respectively, that have the potential to do much harm to Natives. I have included my commentary on Frazier's *On the Rez* here not only because it is an example of opportunism on the part of a non-Native writer, realizing financial gain at the expense of his subjects, but also because he idolizes leaders of the American Indian Movement (AIM) and is ignorant of the historic and modern roles females play in Oglala society.

"In the Trenches of Academia" emphasizes that the roles we play as educators, writers, and mentors are crucial. Interest in Indigenous histories, cultures, and literature is increasing, yet there are relatively few Indigenous professors to teach these topics. According to U.S. Department of Education statistics for 1997 listed in the *Chronicle of Higher Education*'s "2000–2001 Almanac," of 553,171 full-time teachers in the United States, only 0.4 percent are Indians. Yet there are more Native women in academe than ever before, and a good many of us use our credentials to assist tribal nation-building. At Northern Arizona University (NAU), where I have taught since 1989, every one of the thirteen courses I have taught on Indigenous history and culture has had at least 30 percent, often 40 percent or more, Natives in attendance. NAU currently has approximately fourteen hundred Natives enrolled, the second highest enrollment in the country (after Northeastern State University in Tahlequah, Oklahoma), and currently 71 percent of those Natives are female. They are enthusiastic and willing to become formally educated so they can become advocates for their tribes. In order to accommodate those students who desire to use their education to assist their tribes, in 2000 NAU approved the new Applied Indigenous Studies degree that allows students to focus on issues that are of vital importance today, such as policy, economic development, environmental protection, and recovering Indigenous knowledge.[9]

The methods Indian women in the academy use to teach and write are often different from the mainstream. Many Indigenous women scholars take issue with how we have been presented in works of history and anthropology, in the media, and in "postcolonial theories," mainly because tribes are still attempting to deal with the very real effects of colonialism. We sometimes write subjectively and are interdisciplinary in our approaches in order to find data, even though using information from more than one field often is not acceptable to those in academic power positions. Although Indigenous scholars do not always agree with each other, it is critical that we present our opinions and concerns not only to Natives but also to non-Natives. How else can we correct misconceptions about ourselves and seriously face tribal matters that need attention?

Like Indigenous women unconnected to higher education, Indigenous scholars disagree over how we should write, how we present ourselves, and what we should not reveal to non-Natives. For example, few Native women write about feminism, mainly because when we do we are criticized for being "divisive" and not "tribal" enough. My position as a Native female who has observed and encountered these relationships is that we are not being divisive; we are being realistic. Misogyny, colorism, ethnocentrism, and physical abuse are sad realities among Native people, and unless Natives do something about these problems, no one else will.

This essay also includes discussion about our roles as participants in creating and maintaining research guidelines and about ethics in researching and writing about Natives. It is frustrating to repeatedly write and vocalize our concerns about how scholars should behave in Indigenous communities when seeking research, because numerous scholars persist in writing about sensitive issues despite tribes' protests. Many unethical writers skirt Institutional Review Board procedures. We must, therefore, find ways to become part of committees that oversee scholarly and ethical behavior.

Part 2, "Colonialism and Native Women," focuses on how colonialism and patriarchal thought have affected—and still affect—Native women. Political policies, forced removal, physiological changes, psychological stress, and population and land loss from warfare and disease are most commonly addressed in the literature. Only in the past decade have scholars focused on how the introduction of Christian ideologies and patriarchal ideologies disrupted traditional gender roles. Indeed, women's powerful economic, political, social, and religious positions within most tribes are not honored as they once were, violence against Indigenous women has escalated, and many women suffer from psychological stress brought on in part by identity confusion.

These are complicated topics that cannot be addressed thoroughly in this book. James Axtell, Francis Jennings, David Stannard, and others have already written about the results of contact, although they do omit discussions of how these changes affected women specifically.[10] Perhaps in response to Bea Medicine's call to find out "what happened in the past between the sexes that determined the role-playing in the various cultures now . . . [that] the roles of women in our societies are very different," numerous other scholars (females, mainly) have analyzed Native women's traditional tribal roles, debated whether women had power, posited how patriarchal thought affected Native women, and speculated about how and why tribal changes occurred.[11]

"Colonialism and Disempowerment" attempts to bring home the points that Native women did have various degrees of power, equality, and prestige within their traditional tribal structures; the philosophies and policies of colonialism changed that status for many women; and Indigenous women still feel the effects of colonialism. The past does impact the present. Although one of my male colleagues prefers to describe NAU's new Applied Indigenous Studies Department as "looking only to the future, not focusing on the past," this is not the best catchphrase for a program designed to provide students with tools to assist their tribes in developing policy and addressing environmental, economic, and cultural issues. Knowing tribal traditions (including women's places in tribal traditions) can help modern Natives cope with the complex—and impersonal—world by offering them foundations to form their identities and to create strategies for dealing with adversity.

The essay "Culturalism and Racism at the Cherokee Female Seminary" discusses intratribal racism and "culturalism" within a tribe. There was and is no such thing as a monolithic, essential Indigenous woman.[12] Nor has there ever been a unitary "worldview" among tribes or, especially after contact and interaction with non-Natives, even among members of the same group.[13] Cultural ambiguity was and is common among Natives. Traditional Native women were as different from progressive tribeswomen as they were from white women, and often they still are.[14] Even within a single tribe (and sometimes within the same family), females possess a range of degrees of Native blood, of skin and hair color, and of opinions about what it means to be Native.

Authors can challenge notions of fixed identity among Indigenous women by investigating their subjects' allegiances to tribal traditions, their definitions of ethnicity and self, their emotions, and their physical appearance.[15] Reconstructions of the intricacies of Indigenous women's lives must be specific to time and place, for tribal values, gender roles, appearances, and definitions of Natives identity have not been static. Shortly after tribes' contact with Euro-Americans, a generation of mixed-race Natives emerged. Some of these individuals still appeared phenotypically Native and retained their cultural values. Others may have adopted the ways of their non-Native parent (almost always their father, initially) but appeared to be Native. Continued intermarriage with Euro-Americans and other mixed-bloods resulted in multi-heritage women whose appearances and cultural adherences were often indistinct, not only to themselves but also to researchers.

We know of the oppression of Native women at the hands of non-Natives, but what about inter- and intratribal racism and sexism among Natives? Tribes have long experienced factionalism between those who cling to tradition and those who see change as the route to survival, whether tribal, familial, or personal. Some intratribal factionalism might be termed "culturalism," a form of oppression that dovetails with racism. Natives in tribal power positions—political, economic, or social—often use expressions of culturalism against those who do not subscribe to their views. After Natives adopted new value systems, members of a single tribe often viewed each other as being from different economic and social "classes." Natives with a high "level of acculturation" might view themselves as "more enlightened" than others whom they deem "less enlightened," "uncivilized," or "heathen."[16] Usually, but not always, mixed-bloods had more money and material goods than full-bloods, and they maneuvered themselves into tribal leadership positions. These wealthy families often were educated, progressive, and Christian and did not value tribal traditions. Many saw themselves as morally superior to the uneducated, non-Christian, and less wealthy traditionalists (usually, but not always, full-bloods). Their "white blood" also contributed to their feelings of importance. From their point of view, they were in the superior "class."

Women situated in the upper level of one "class" did not necessarily belong to the higher echelon of the other. Lack of wealth placed some Indigenous women in a low economic category, but as far as they were concerned, their cultural knowledge put them in a higher social grouping. Those who valued tribal tradition and resisted acculturation believed themselves to be "more Indian" than the "sellouts." Many biracial Indigenes may have been more wealthy and educated than full-bloods, but among traditionalists these were not enviable social traits. LaVera Rose, a Lakota, makes the observation in her master's thesis on biracial Lakota women that the full-blood Lakotas looked down on the biracial women because of their cultural naiveté, and many still do.[17]

To complicate the issue, full-bloods often adopted attitudes similar to those of progressives. Ten years ago I conducted an interview with a ninety-eight-year-old Cherokee woman. When I asked if she spoke Cherokee and attended stomp dances—a logical question considering that she was a full-blood and descended from a prominent Cherokee leader—she answered, "Hell no, I'm no heathen." Native women share the common context of gender and the "common core" of struggle against colonialism (genocide, loss of lands, encroachments onto their lands by Euro-Americans and other Indians, intermarriage with tribal outsiders, and population loss from disease, warfare, and removal) and the consequent tribal cultural change and identity confusion. What appear to be similarities among women may actually be differences, however, because cultural disparities among tribes in areas such as religion, social systems, and economies caused Indigenous women to react to common experiences of externally induced adversity and change in dissimilar ways.

"Finding a Modern American Indigenous Female Identity" deals with one of the notable and enduring results of contact: the mixing of Native and non-Native blood and cultures, resulting in Natives with a variety of phenotypes and cultural adherences. Because one of the first steps to empowerment is becoming comfortable with one's identity, this essay focuses on the identity crises many Indigenous women face, in addition to the solutions that psychologists have offered for confusions about "one's place in the world."

What are the elements that make up a person's racial identity? These elements might include physical appearance, acceptance by the racial reference group, commonalties of culture and psychological identification with the group, percentage of biological heritage, and government and tribal restrictions. How do these elements contribute to the psychological and sociological makeup of Native women with bifurcated racial and cultural backgrounds? What are the expressions of Native identity? Did multi-heritage Native women mirror Everett Stonequist's model of "marginal" people—those of mixed heritage who live lives of frustration, unable to fit comfortably into any group—or did these women absorb the cultural traits of all their heritages, making them more like Malcolm McFee's proposed "150% Man?"[18] Are there categories in between?

For the most part, scholars have ignored the role that appearance played and still does play in Native women's lives. Appearance is the most visible aspect of one's race, and it determines how Native women defined themselves and how others defined and treated them. Their appearance, whether Caucasian, Indian, African, or mixed, either limited or broadened Native women's choices of ethnic identity and their ability to interact with non-Natives and other Natives. Appearance played a crucial role in determining status and ease of mingling within different cultural groups or societies. Consequently, many mixed-heritage white-and-Native women had numerous "worlds" open to them, while most full-blood Native women and those of mixed black and Indian heritage did not.

Essays in part 3, "Activists and Feminists," focus on ways some of these Native women have dealt with changes and their desire to find empowerment. Some women become evangelical and racist toward Natives of other tribes, members of their own tribe, and other people of color, just as many Euro-American oppressors have been to them. Others are not stringent about applying traditions to their lives and have fought for gender rights exclusively. Others are politically active and fight for tribal rights, while other women fight for both tribal and gender rights. Some women politick (and pray) for a resurgence of their tribal traditions and hope to apply them to everyday life, while others simply strive to survive.

"1970s Activist Anna Mae Pictou-Aquash" discusses identity, values, and inter- and intratribal politics among Native women in the 1970s with the American Indian Movement. Numerous women participated in activities of AIM and fought for tribal rights long before AIM was created. For the most part, however, women have not been discussed much when the topic is Wounded Knee or 1970s activism. Women such as Pat Bellanger, LaNada Boyer, Lorelei DeCora (then Lorelei Means), Millie Ketcheshawno, Harriet Pierce, Elaine Stately, Grace Thorpe, Faith Traversie, Madonna Thunderhawk (then Madonna Gilbert), Phyllis Young, Mary Jane Wilson, and Francis Wise spent as much time and energy as the men did fighting for tribal and Native rights, yet they appear as mere background figures in most literature on the Red Power Movement.

Women who participated in the volatile events of the 1970s in South Dakota may have had a common desire to eradicate problems facing Native peoples, but they had serious problems of their own: mixed-blood and identity confusions, reservation poverty, misogynist male AIM leaders, often a lack of cultural knowledge, and the AIM men's continuing threats to make the women remain quiet about events that transpired during that time period. These differences resulted in a variety of forms on activism among women, from passivity and doing what the males told them to do to taking a more active role and challenging the male leadership. Anna Mae Pictou-Aquash was one of the latter, and she received a bullet in the back of her head for her efforts.

Pictou-Aquash's life illustrates that "feminists" and "activists" are not the same things. She shows us that just because a Native woman is not formally educated does not mean she cannot be an effective advocate for Native rights. This essay is included because Pictou-Aquash and women like her epitomize the best of Native activism: a woman possessing solid tribal background, cultural awareness, and confidence in her identity. She was tolerant of others who attempted to discredit her with rumors and out of jealousy, and she held a deep commitment to fighting for Native rights no matter the cost. Discussion of Pictou-Aquash's life, in addition to the interview with Denise Maloney-Pictou and Deborah Maloney-Pictou, her daughters, is a springboard to discussion of events in the 1970s and some of the more volatile topics associated with Indigenous activism, such as sexism among Native men, how Native women rationalize their behavior, and how some Indian writers can use these topics to further their personal political agendas.

Because many authors write from a patriarchal or white feminist perspective, the value of Native women is vastly underrated. Despite overwhelming oppression at the hands of whites, Natives have persevered, but men have not been the only catalysts for survival, adaptation, and development. Women have been just as crucial to the economic, social, religious, and political survival of tribes. "Activism and Expression as Empowerment" is an overview of how some Native women have empowered themselves and have striven to empower their tribes. Women such as Wilma Mankiller, Ada Deer, and Winona LaDuke not only devote time and energy to what white researchers consider "female issues"—health care, education, and social work—but they also contend with economic development, environmental protection, treaty rights, and tribal sovereignty. Almost all prominent female Native leaders have stated that they gain confidence and strength to persevere from the knowledge that their female ancestors also were striving for many of the same goals. Strong women participate in their tribal ceremonies and serve as political leaders and as social and environmental activists. We read their forceful words in poetry and novels and watch documentaries and movies they write and produce.

Despite colonialism's oppressions and pressures on women's tribal cultural values, political system, and identities, hundreds if not thousands of Native women are actively making life more healthy, prosperous, and spiritual for their tribespeople. Some use traditional methods to obtain their goals, while others combine traditionalism with education they receive in white schools. Still other Native women are thoroughly acculturated to white society and have no concern for their tribe. Regardless of their cultural allegiances, Native women today are a far cry from the stereotypical images of the "princess" and "squaw drudge."

In *Fighting Words: Black Women and the Search for Justice*, Patricia Hill Collins writes, "if African-American women's experiences are more different than similar, then Black feminist thought does not exist."[19] Comparatively, because not all Native women are concerned with retaining cultural traditions, some are not even cognizant of their current tribal issues, and still others are traditionalists living on their reservations as distant from white society as possible, another necessary theme in this book is the heterogeneity among Native women. Because of vast differences in tribal cultures and personalities, in addition to identity issues (including "identity politics"), no one Indigenous woman can speak for all of us, and it is not possible for any one feminist theory or thought to summarize Native women. Native women do share historic oppression, but the cultural, racial, and economic variations among Native women render any sort of national coalition virtually impossible. As those of us who have sat on boards of American Indian centers, university "minority committees," and pan-Indian political organizations composed of members from different tribes can attest, our needs and wants may be similar, but they are not the same.

The final essay, "Feminists, Tribalists, or Activists?" discusses these terms and why many Native women call themselves one thing or the other. For example, many Native women vehemently shun feminism and will not associate with people who claim it. Other Native women, however, proudly call themselves feminists. Some women are concerned about tribal and cultural survival and advancement rather than male oppression or individual success in economic status, social circles, and academia, and they avoid feminists and their ideologies. Many of these Indigenous women argue that white women have enjoyed the power privileges that come with being white at the expense of women of color. Why, they might ask, should Native women align themselves with white feminists to denigrate men, when many white women denigrate Natives? Many of these Native women prefer the labels "tribalist" or "activist," terms that describe their struggles for racial equality and tribal rights. Imparting this bit of reality into an American Indian Women in History class composed mostly of white women usually results in looks of indignation. After all, many of these young women believe that all females are on the same side of the feminist fence.

I am speaking here as a formally educated, mixed-heritage, tribally enrolled Oklahoma Choctaw woman with serious concerns about tribal rights, nation-building, and how those of us in academe can help Natives serve those interests. I am also concerned about my Native colleagues. As one who has encountered racism and sexism in the academy, I hope that we can learn from each other about how we can better function as faculty, even though we often are viewed as having been hired only because of affirmative action. Ironically, much of what is included here about academia is of little interest to most Native women; they live their lives disassociated from academe, and discussions of feminism and ivory tower intrigues do not concern them. Yet, given the number of Natives now enrolled in higher education and of recently created Internet chat-rooms and Web sites that focus on Natives, and after observing, from my position as editor of the *American Indian Quarterly*, what people are writing, it appears that many scholars are genuinely interested in how to properly interpret Natives' behaviors, discussions, and writings.

I grew up in a household where my parents shared responsibilities equally, and within my house and in my extended family's homes there was never mention of women being inferior. In the communities and in all my family stories, women are strong and hold their families together. Their perseverance has affected me so strongly that I chronicled their lives (mixed with fiction) in my novel *Roads of My Relations: Stories*. I have also served on the board of directors of the American Indian Center of Dallas/Ft. Worth—home to almost forty thousand urban Natives—overseeing a drug and rehabilitation center, clinic, and bingo hall. I have been active in the repatriation controversy for fifteen years, was a member of the Texas Historical Commission and the Texas Indian Commission's Coalition for the Protection and Preservation of Sacred Cultural Items and Skeletal Remains, and was as angry with my formal tribal chief's womanizing—which forced his removal from office—as I am with Bill Clinton's. I write every day about issues that concern me, and I regularly speak to audiences who want to hear about issues that concern Native America. I feel strong emotional pulls in numerous directions: to my homeland and family that are the foundations of my identity and to my job, where I can accomplish much in the way of dispelling stereotypes and educating Native students so they can become effective catalysts who will ensure their tribes' survival. I am an activist.

This collection of essays came together after several colleagues suggested that I compile my works on Native women in one volume. I consistently receive requests to speak about Native women and to reprint my essays and speeches on Native females in anthologies or reproduce them in course packets. Therefore, I thought it might be time to take a look at what I have written over the past decade and combine my essays, book chapters, book commentaries, and presentations that focus on women into one volume. This collection does not contain the definitive work on anything. Instead, these are merely overviews of complex topics that, I hope, will continue the much-needed discussions.

### Terminology

Although it is preferable to refer to the Indigenous people of this country by their specific tribal names, for the sake of space I opt for "Indigenes" or "Natives" instead of "Native Americans," which signifies anyone born in the United States. I am well aware of the debates over these terms and am cognizant that many find "Indian" offensive;

however, my family and most friends and "Indians" I know say "Indians." "First Nations," "Indigenous Peoples," and other terms are fine for scholars, but most Indians, especially older ones, are puzzled at hearing them.[20] "Indigenous" most accurately describes the first peoples of this hemisphere. The term "Indian" occasionally appears in reference to established names.

# I. RESEARCH AND WRITING

# 1

## A Few Cautions on the Merging of Feminist Studies with Indigenous Women's Studies

At the millennium, more scholars than ever are writing about feminist theory. To borrow from Cheris Kramarae and Dale Spender, the field has exploded with theory, diverging opinions, and unanswered questions about women's marginalization.[1] At the same time, American Indian Studies has grown to the point that Standing Rock Sioux writer Vine Deloria Jr. writes, "I can see no useful purpose for any additional research or writing on Indians, other than as a form of entertainment."[2]

Literature about Indigenous women has increased dramatically during the past twenty years. Recent works reflect the progress ethnohistorians have made in recreating Native women's histories, and their publications illustrate sensitivity to their positions as interpreters of the lives, cultures, and histories of Others. While female scholars who study Indigenous women have made significant inroads into their histories, many interpretations remain incorrect and underdeveloped, providing only partial answers to complicated questions about Native women. The majority of writings are devoid of Native voices and are thereby only partial histories. In addition, most do not connect the past to the present, which is why we should be writing history in the first place.

While many works supply useful information for tribes who strive for empowerment and nation building, others have been written only for "entertainment" and to further the careers of the authors. Despite the increasing awareness among scholars that one must be sensitive to tribal secrets and that many writers are using Native voices in their works, one must ask what good all this historical, anthropological, and creative writing does. As Maori scholar Linda Tuhiwai Smith states in *Decolonizing Methodologies*, "taking apart the story, revealing underlying texts, and giving voice to things that are often known intuitively does not help people to improve their current conditions."[3]

Numerous feminist scholars express concern over the propensity of writers to ignore the heterogeneity among women, particularly among women of color.[4] Indigenous women are especially multi-faceted, and with few exceptions this fact is overlooked. Aspects that, for the most part, have not been addressed in historical works are the feelings and emotions of Native women, the relationships among them, and their observations of non-Natives. We have extrinsic knowledge of how women interacted with each other during events such as childbirth and healing and puberty ceremonies. We also know what was required of women in certain tribal roles. There are photographs showing us the clothes women wore and how they styled their hair during various time periods. The intriguing mystery is, what was behind their solemn gazes?

Women worked and socialized together throughout their lives, but we have not read much about their relationships with their family and friends. What did Northern Plains women discuss as they sat together during the long, cold months making clothes and doing bead and quill work? Were their conversations much different from what their modern descendants talk about during winter days while performing the same work? What did Southwestern women talk about as they spent hours together grinding corn and preparing food? Did they gossip, joke, and seek advice from each other as they do today?

Colonialism was a powerful force that affected women in countless ways. How did the women feel through time about intruders onto their lands, the devastation of their ways of life, and the cultural changes they underwent to survive? Did Native women discuss strategies of resistance to the onslaught of colonization, or did they conspire with men? Surely they pondered the intruders as intently as Euro-Americans speculated about them. Thoughts and personal dramas hold our attention and are what endear the women to us, especially if we encounter a semblance of ourselves in them. Historians might argue that depictions of personal conflicts, confusions, and expressions of happiness are best left to novelists, but I believe that without the inclusion of feelings and an understanding of motivations, histories of Native women—of all Natives—are boring, impersonal, and more importantly, merely speculative and not really history.

If writers want to find out what Native women think, they should ask them. If they want to know about past events and cultures, they should do the same thing. Unfortunately many scholars, historians in particular, have been loath to use Native oral accounts as source material. Almost every "resource guide" or "annotated bibliography" lists the requisite secondary source material, government documents, and tribal records, but few inform researchers about oral history collections, recorded interviews, or locations where personal narratives might be stored.[5]

Even fewer writers use literature and poetry as resources. Because many Native women writers possess empirical data that cannot find acceptance in historical or anthropological works, literature is one effective outlet for their stories. N. Scott Momaday has commented that "Language is the repository of . . . knowledge and experience."[6] Why, then, would the textualization of oral stories or of literature influenced by oral stories not have messages of import for readers? Works written by culturally aware Native women are derived from their consciousness, filled with experience and knowledge of tribal ritual. Chicana feminist Alvina Quintana explains that when women writers free their writings of patriarchal discourse, language becomes "a vehicle for the demystification through self-representation of that unity we call woman."[7] Indeed, it is through their writings that we can learn that Native women were and are powerful; they were and are as complex as their cultures are diverse. Their works are worth a look.

Though the integration of American Indigenous women's studies and feminist studies would seem a logical project for the new millennium, I would like to propose that efforts toward such an initiative be both cautious and deliberate. The introduction of the multifaceted lives and values of Natives into feminist discourse will necessarily and appropriately confuse the understanding of "women's" experiences. Indeed, while clarity about gender may be a compelling goal, it is often achieved at the expense of the visibility, agency, and identity of those represented. I therefore join my cautions here to the arguments put forth by other women of color who see both the need for appreciating the heterogeneity among women and the necessity for more sensitivity in studying and writing about individuals outside one's racial and cultural group. I believe feminists can learn from Natives, but care must be used in researching, interpreting, and formulating ideas about "Others."

At the year 2000, and 502 years after what Natives commonly refer to as the beginning of the "invasion," thousands of books and articles have written about Natives. With the exception of works of fiction, the vast majority of these works are written by whites who analyze their subjects using Eurocentric standards of interpretation and by omitting Natives' versions of their cultures and histories. Because whites are usually the ones speaking about women outside their group, as well as the ones gathering information, creating theories, and benefiting from all this writing, Natives' images are often at the mercy of author bias, power positions, and personal agendas of university scholars and authors of popular literature.

Scholars often rationalize their work by thinking that, because they are armed with written documentation and theories (formulated by thinkers who have never met an Indian), they can write from a Native perspective. It is dangerous and unethical to presume to know what motivates Native women without talking to them, but scholars do it all the time. Some refuse to speak with Natives, believing that informants who are not formally educated have no information worth garnering. Occasionally, shyness or respect keeps researchers away, as in the example of a former non-Native graduate student of mine who never completed her nicely conceptualized dissertation on the activist women at Wounded Knee (1973) because of my requirement that she conduct interviews with Native women present at the encounter. My personal standards—gut feelings, actually—are that I should not produce a manuscript about my tribe or another tribe unless it is useful to them, and I will not write about historic Native women unless the project benefits their descendants.

Feminist scholars who wish to write about Indigenous women must be aware of the various voices among them. For example, some writers suggest that traditionalist Native women who eschew all feminist ideals, rather than those who refer to themselves as feminists, are the authoritative voices on Indigenous issues (this conflict is discussed further in chapter 12).[8] Crow Creek Sioux novelist and editor Elizabeth Cook-Lynn offers a similar theme in her 1998 essay "American Indian Intellectualism and the New Indian Story," in which she argues that the writings produced by mixed-blood authors are rooted in the "dominance and patriarchy most noted in American society [rather] than [in] tribalness" and that successful writers such as Louise Erdrich, Paula Gunn Allen, and Wendy Rose (and males Sherman Alexie and Gerald Vizenor) exude "excesses of individualism," when she believes they should be advocating tribal unity.[9]

These stances include two of the important political issues among Natives within American Indigenous studies. The first is identity politics: women who are often taken to task for claiming to be feminists actually are strong advocates for tribal rights, and Cook-Lynn's argument ignores the reality that the majority of Natives today are mixed-bloods, often disassociated with their tribe's culture, perhaps, but still possessing Native identities. Within and outside the academy these voices debate, validate, and negate each other.

Second, these sentiments contribute to my answer to the issue of authoritative voice: there is not one among Native women, and no one feminist theory totalizes Native women's thought. Rather, there exists a spectrum of multi-heritage women in between "traditional" and "progressive," possessing a multitude of opinions about what it means to be a Native female. There is no one voice among Natives because there is no such thing as the culturally and racially monolithic Native woman. The label "Third World Women" is a large umbrella under which another umbrella, "Natives," may fit, but underneath that umbrella are each of the three hundred or so modern U.S. tribes and, still further under, each female member of those tribes. Thousands more umbrellas are needed to account for the tribal and individual sociocultural changes that occur over time. Knowledge of these complexities of value systems and personalities is crucial to understanding the rationales behind the Native voice the scholar listens to, in addition to knowing that it is not representative of all Natives.

Non-Natives must take care that the voice they hear actually is Native. Within the academy, numerous "wannabees" and "marginal" Natives with little connection to their tribes publish with the claim of writing from an "Indian perspective." The voices of Native women have also been undermined by the cultural and literary appropriations of fraudulent New Age "medicine women" who have convinced the public that theirs are the truthful works about Native religion and culture. For instance, the well-published charlatan Lynn Andrews distorts the reality of traditional Native male-female relationships and advises her followers that their quests to find their true "feminine" selves are hindered by male oppression.[10] Writers such as Wendy Rose and Andrea Smith discuss the potential damage done to constructive cross-cultural relationships between authentic Natives and non-Natives when these "plastic" medicine women and men (whose works have found their way onto required reading lists at universities) assert that they are the authoritative voices on Native spirituality.[11]

Assuming that the researcher has real Native informants in mind, she must be aware that many tribes have strict research guidelines that outsiders must follow when interviewing tribal members, as do universities with institutional review boards.[12] And good intentions do not always garner results. While some Natives are willing to share information with researchers, others are tentative and will discuss only bits and pieces of their lives and tribal goings-on. Traditional Native women—who might more accurately be called "tribalists" because they believe they are disadvantaged by the colonialist ideologies that disempower their race and contribute to dysfunctional tribal gender roles—have no interest in white feminist theory because they know from experience that white women have enjoyed the power privileges that come with being white at the expense of women of color. They are aware that white scholars usually want only information. Then they return to their university and use the data to build their careers, while the knowledgeable "objects of study" receive nothing in return.

There is much to do to give voice to Native women. Many books and articles about Native females desperately need reinterpretation. Native women's social, religious, political, and economic roles have been the focus of numerous articles, but few authors use Native women themselves as sources of information. Those who utilize only one or two informants believe that this is sufficient to write the "New Indian History." It is not.

Granted, the myriad lifestyles of Native women render them difficult to write about. Taking the less arduous route of writing descriptive, non-analytical history—which has been the traditional method for the majority of scholars who study Natives—will continue to have serious repercussions for Native history, for if we do not understand the complexity of Native females, we cannot hope to comprehend the whole of tribal existence.

If feminist scholars want to learn about themselves and others and to contribute to their discipline, they should approach Indigenous women only with a genuine, but respectful, curiosity about another way of life. Researchers may be politely turned away, but if they are allowed to enter the lives of Natives, they should be forewarned that interviewing Natives is very time-consuming, that interviewers must be sensitive to the privacy and self-respect of those women, and that their project must be important to the women whose voices they utilize. They must abandon any posturing about being an expert on what counts as important knowledge about Native women. If feminist scholars can engage in reciprocal, practical dialogue with their informants, then Native voices, too, will become a part of feminist discourse.

# 2

## Writing about Anna Mae Pictou-Aquash

The topic of writing about Anna Mae Pictou-Aquash opens the door for a variety of discussions, covering protection of sources, respecting the tribe and family of the subject, territoriality in activism and feminist studies, and the author's self-preservation. Writing the Anna Mae Pictou-Aquash essay (chapter 9) was a stressful exercise in addressing controversial issues that Natives know about but usually do not textualize for the world to read: the bad behavior of some Native men toward Native women, their lack of respect for tribal traditions, and the reality that many Native women condone their behavior. Some Natives might be disturbed by my bringing these realities to light, but my perspective is the same as that of many Native women who will not tolerate being victimized by Native men and other Native women. I have gone so far as to write about gender relations within the Red Power movement, but because discussions of ethnocentrism among tribes, personal knowledge of the behavior of some AIM men, and identity politics are complicated and painful to recount (and probably not very useful to anyone except voyeurs who like to read about such things), I decided to omit many of the original discussions in the Pictou-Aquash paper and the essay "Feminists, Tribalists, or Activists?" (chapter 12). Sweeping these topics under the rug, however, will not make them go away.

I was a senior in high school when Anna Mae was found murdered in South Dakota, and for twenty-five years thoughts of her have come and gone. When Theda Perdue invited me to write an essay on Anna Mae for her anthology *Sifters: Native Women's Lives*, I jumped at the opportunity, although I knew I could not do it without permission and assistance from her family. Long conversations with Anna Mae's cousin Robert A. Pictou-Branscombe and with her daughters reinforced my thinking that if I am going to write, then it needs to be about something worthwhile.

During the 1970s I, like many other young Natives, was caught

up in the excitement of what AIM appeared to offer. I taped poster
inserts from *Akwesasne Notes* over my bedroom walls and listened
to the awful music of the Indigenous band EXIT. My father followed
the events of the takeover of the BIA building in Washington DC, and
he was the first to show me a newspaper clipping about Anna Mae's
death in 1976. It was certainly easier for us to believe that the FBI
killed her than to consider the possibility that AIM did. After all,
Russell Means, Dennis Banks, and Clyde and Vernon Bellecourt were
our heroes. How could they possibly do anything like that or even
be parties to it? Twenty-five years passed, and during that time Anna
Mae was on my mind here and there, but because there was no new
information I never dwelled on her. I assumed that the FBI was at
fault and there was nothing any Native could do about it. Writing a
piece on Anna Mae several decades later has been an opportunity to
re-explore an old feeling and a person who interested me as a young
adult. And I knew that writing about her would entail more than just
a trip to the library and a study of back issues of *Akwesasne Notes*.

I spent time in South Dakota with friends at their homes and at
sun dances and visited Yellow Thunder Camp. I became aware that
the AIM guys were not what a lot of us thought they were. Everyone
is only human, of course, but not only did it become apparent that
these men were ignorant of their tribal histories and cultures, but
there also seemed to be something perverse in their behavior. Dennis
Banks had fifteen children by 1976, and perhaps only he knows how
many he has fathered since then. Clyde Bellecourt has a long string of
convictions related to drug use and dealing and a more recent arrest
for seriously abusing his wife. His brother Vernon supposedly gave
the order to have Anna Mae executed. Both brothers are reportedly
only one-sixty-fourth Indian blood. In 1986 Russell Means lied to me
about needing money for Yellow Thunder Camp when he actually
wanted it for his Nicaragua project. Prior to his death, a close friend
of mine sent me Means's "Porcupine diaries," which detailed more
than I cared to know about the comings and goings of Mr. G.M.A.S.
(Great Manipulator of Acquired Supporters, as my father nicknamed
Russell). And on and on. I was disappointed. Bubbles popped. But it
was not their fault. They were just being who they are. But because
of these men's popular images as activists, many Natives believe that
the weight the AIM men lend to Indian issues through their notoriety
in the media is more important than the way they treat women and
follow traditions of their cultures.

While many male Indians (and many white men, such as the writer
Ian Frazier, who wrote the dreadful *On the Rez*) idolize AIM leaders,
women like myself interpret their words and behavior through our

own value systems and experiences. I am fully aware of these men's contributions to the Red Power Movement and of how they have informed Americans of injustices against Natives. I know about their influences on Native America and their ability to make young Natives feel empowered, because they influenced me. However, outward appearances are not everything; hence my essay on Anna Mae.

A major issue in writing about Anna Mae is how one writes accurately about the topic while at the same time respecting her family. A number of Natives in universities are involved in creating research guidelines committees, or institutional review boards, but not everyone follows those guidelines. Writers not involved with academia usually do not consider how their subjects feel about being scrutinized and having their stories textualized. Anna Mae has numerous living family members. I could not, in good conscience, write about her life without talking to the family to see if it was acceptable to write about her. There are numerous articles and Web pages devoted to Anna Mae (or "Annie Mae," as some people call her; her family does not), and I did not want to add to the pile if the family preferred otherwise. It turned out to be fine with them, but the process then became complicated and stressful. I needed to write an essay that not only conformed to academic standards but also conformed to Anna Mae's family's standards. That is, they wanted to read the draft I planned to send to Theda Perdue. Anna Mae's family did not approve the first draft because I mentioned the names of some of Anna Mae's female adversaries, who the family claimed had a hand in her death. Anna Mae's family believed that mere mention of those women gave them undeserved attention. So, instead of referring to certain prominent AIM women, I had to make blanket statements about them. This also means that any larger study on Anna Mae is not possible, since an even-handed discussion of her life must also include consideration of the undesirable individuals who crossed her path and affected her life. A writer could proceed to write the story of Anna Mae's life, but the price would be ostracism and lack of input from her family.

This was a stressful project because it was dangerous. Anna Mae is a murder victim. Although the murderer and those closely involved with her death have not been formally charged, some have admitted their roles in the planning and execution of her death. It was clear that I had to be very careful in making certain that I didn't name the alleged guilty parties without also saying who did the accusing.

During the course of researching and writing the paper I met several times with members of her family who live thirty minutes away from me. There are numerous videotapes of Robert A. Pictou-Branscombe accusing the Bellecourts of instigating Anna Mae's death, and he fully expected them and other prominent AIM leaders to act on their anger toward him. When I was at his house, one individual always kept an eye on the hills by Bob's home, watching for intruders, and when we met for lunch or dinner, Bob sat facing the door. The family asked me to serve on the council for the ANNA Foundation, but I am not certain how safe it is to have my name on the Web site as being closely associated with the foundation. Clearly the assumption would be that I have crucial information about the case, even if I do not.

This would be a "proceed at your own risk" project. Luckily, Theda gave me a strict page limit that severely restricted the amount of information I could use.

The topic of activism—as well as other topics, such as identity—is highly territorial. Some scholars and activists believe that they should have the monopoly on writing about activism issues, AIM, or Red Power. They resent those who find access to hard-to-reach informers with information about Wounded Knee. I have been questioned about my "anonymous sources" and documents, with tones that imply they do not exist. These researchers defend misogynist AIM men in an attempt to affirm their personal identities as "Indian activists" even though some of them are not even Native. They use the term "feminism" as a political tool. They will argue that Native women who claim to be "feminists" are really "less Indian" than those who reject the term. Many hail Robert Warrior and Paul Chaat Smith's one-sided, male-oriented book, *Like a Hurricane: The Indian Movement from Alcatraz to Wounded Knee,* as the authoritative work on Native activism, despite the reality that the book mentions only a few women in passing (Anna Mae is mentioned once, and that is to tell us that she was married at Wounded Knee) and offers no analysis about AIM or the men's sexism. There is not even a comment about traditional gender roles among the tribes the men represented and why egalitarianism was thrown to the wind and self-serving behavior took its place. I purposely have not used *Like a Hurricane* in my essay because, with the exception of a few novel quotes, it tells me nothing that other books on AIM have not already said. This reality has not stopped the watchdogs from pouncing, chastising me for not using "the definitive book on Red Power."

When Anna Mae's family asked if I wanted to interview Anna Mae's daughters, I said yes because up to that point they had only talked with one newspaper for about ten minutes. After I completed the interview and it was copyedited for the *American Indian Quarterly,* I put it on my Web page and notified the manager of the Anna Mae pages, in case he wanted to link from his page to mine. This individual, however, was personally offended that I was approached by the family to do the interview while he has never been granted one. I received an aggressive e-mail from him stating that I was "showing off" and attempting to "one-up" him. Indeed, being an "activist" gives some people a sense of security and identity, and I have learned that writing about activist issues while not being a member of the "activist group" can be an exercise in developing thick skin. You will be questioned and criticized, and any of your own "activist activities" will be ignored.

Finally, I will say that topics such as this are best either left un-addressed or severely curtailed. Indigenous people often gravitate to topics that hold personal meaning for them or for their tribes, but one moral of this story is that just because a topic seems compelling and interesting does not mean one should write about it. After my Native students read the essay on Anna Mae they are indeed stunned to learn of her complex life and death, but it also inspires them to become active in their tribal affairs. Writing about Anna Mae Pictou-Aquash and other activist issues is certainly worthwhile, but how one manages the process is key.

**3**

## Review of Ian Frazier's *On the Rez*

In his 23 January 2000 *Los Angeles Times* review of Ian Frazier's new book, *On the Rez*, Sherman Alexie wrote that upon hearing the title of the book, "I laughed out loud." Alexie was referring to how Frazier, a white man and outsider, appropriated the familiar term "rez." When I saw Frazier's book profiled in the 24 January 2000 edition of *Time* magazine, I had the same reaction but not because of the title. Instead of providing readers with a photograph of the subject matter, such as an Oglala or beautiful scenery, *Time* chose to publish a close-up of the author, a non-Native who writes about Natives solidly from his perspective. Frazier and his new book were featured because of his reputation as a respected writer, and the book, of course, will sell thousands of copies. That Frazier is a gifted writer who likes Indians is not an issue. What he does with his enviable talent in this particular work is.

This is not a book about Oglalas. It is a book containing Frazier's ramblings about who he thinks they are. Frazier is very similar to Emily Benedict, the white journalist who wrote a short piece on the Navajo-Hopi land issue and then realized that "I was so interested in the people that I wanted to write more."[1] So she secured a book contract, swooped into a place she knew nothing about to gather information for her book *The Wind Won't Know Me*, then left the Southwest for good. Like Benedict, Frazier entered a place where he does not live and garnered information from a few confidants to whom he apparently gave money. Then he observed, exited to write his memoir, and now collects royalties.

This strategy has been used with great success by many white scholars for decades, but the difference between Frazier and most modern white scholars is that scholars know they had better thoroughly research their topics prior to blurting out what is on their mind. And, I hope, they undergo the processes dictated by university and tribal institutional review boards, entities that were created to

keep biased white perspectives about Natives—such as *On the Rez*—
off the shelves.

Frazier admits that "Of course I want to be like Indians. I've looked
up to them all my life" and that his "number one hero was the Oglala
leader Crazy Horse" (16). That leads Frazier to ask himself profound
questions such as, "Would Crazy Horse have spent this much to
remodel a kitchen?" And because he believes he is an expert on the
man, he advises us to refer to his book *Great Plains*. He tells us that
Russell Means's *Where White Men Fear to Tread* is "flawed," but he
does use Peter Matthiessen's *In the Spirit of Crazy Horse* and several
other mediocre books on AIM and Wounded Knee that rely on gossip
in addition to glorifying men's positions and ignoring women's. The
amount of source material Frazier fails to cite is stunning. Instead of
looking at notable academic works or even talking to Sioux scholars,
he turns to enlightened opinions about Indians by actors Elliot Gould
and David Carradine.

Some of Frazier's statements are so foolish that it is possible to have
a physical reaction while reading them. On page 17, for example, he
writes about AIM leaders, "I admired them. . . . AIM was very much a
'guy' organization." Another statement on the same page, about Clyde
Bellecourt, is even more stupid: "how much cooler can a middle-aged
father be?" Well, Ian, a lot. Frazier's ignorance of women's roles in the
AIM organization and of the misogyny of his heroes is inexcusable, and
his lack of sensitivity toward a certain Mi'kmaq family in particular
is staggering.

He incorrectly uses the singular instead of the plural when referring
to groups of people (the Navajo, the Cherokee, etc.); he is wrong
in comments such as "almost all Mississippi Choctaws still speak
Choctaw" (85); and he includes strange lists, such as a long list of his
"favorite Lakota words" (90) and an inappropriate list of clever Indian
names, because he believes that "one of the pleasures of reading about
Indians is in the names" (89–90). His incessant discussion of alcohol
misuse without any analysis about the roots of the problem grows
tiresome. He informs readers that Natives gave the world "corn and
tobacco, and potatoes" (13) but neglects to mention a thousand other
contributions. The only positive topic he brings up is the inspirational
life of the late basketball player SuAnne Big Crow, and even then it is
basically Frazier's interpretation of the young woman's life and death.
Surely she is not the only bright light in the South Dakota wasteland
he describes.

Then he makes the following spectacular statement on page 176: "I
reflected that the moment in history when white people and Native
Americans first discovered each other was so momentous and fateful

and even thrilling for each culture that some of us feel compelled to reenact it again and again." Millions of Indigenous people died after that "first discovery," from disease, genocide, warfare, and alcoholism, and there is not an Indian person in the country who would call the encounter "thrilling."

He is accurate in describing Germans' obsession with Natives, but he is wrong in thinking that Natives are just as wild about Germans. Just because Oglala boys at a powwow "looked at me with unblinking dark eyes" and asked, "Where are you from, Europe?" does not mean they were fascinated with him (177). Of course, I may be wrong. Their question could be a reversal of Frazier's insensitive statement on page 91: "Indeed, the Indians of America are so varied that I think you can find an appropriate tribe for almost anyone." Right. Just like choosing a pet dog. Perhaps the boys like to pick on that Euro-American breed called The Long-Haired Intrusive White Man.

One has to wonder who approved this for publication. It is simply a rhetorical question to ask if the editors at Farrar, Straus, and Giroux sent this out to Oglalas (or any other Natives) for their comments prior to making an editorial decision about publication. No reputable university press would have even solicited reviews, and if it had, reviewers' comments about the errors and insensitivity alone would have sent the submission to the recycle bin. To attempt to have a work published without having an understanding of one's subject matter is certainly unethical on the part of the author, but the publisher is also to blame for publishing it (and for the bleak cover that ignores the colorful and complex history and culture of the Sioux). The irony of all this is that many talented Native writers with vast knowledge about their tribes can hardly get their works published. (No, I am not talking about myself, so don't shout "sour grapes.") Apparently, marketable information about Natives has to come from a white person in order to sell to the mass market.

It is difficult to ascertain why this was published other than to make money. If Frazier is so enamored of Oglalas, why did he write such a damaging manuscript? Does he really believe he is helping the situation at Pine Ridge? *On the Rez* is certainly not written for Natives. We already know about the place, including details of the Wounded Knee takeover, what fry bread tastes like, and what takes place at a powwow. And we sure do not need to hear his bit of wisdom in regard to the Black Hills: "Perhaps now we could again consider the possibility of returning some or all of the stolen federal lands" (277). Thanks. We have never thought of that.

In his rebuttal to Alexie's review of his book, Frazier stated the same thing that white writers have argued for years. In regard to the issue of whether an outsider should write about Natives, Frazier wrote, "It's strange, because I thought of this as I was doing the book, but I never took it seriously." He then stated that "the outsider's perspective is extremely important in literature; the outsider is an important persona. . . . Alexie praised the writing, but the idea that I could do such a book without being an Indian seemed to be unacceptable."[2] Frazier is a fine writer who seems to mean well, but he does not know how to write about Indigenous people. His statement, however, is a logical one. Let me put into easy-to-comprehend terms what most Natives mean when they present an argument like Alexie's:

Most Americans know little, if anything, about Natives. To them, Natives are people of the past or drunks of the present who live in poverty and cry at the sight of litter. Some non-Natives believe they know a great deal about Natives because they have read the works of the New Age religious charlatan Lynn Andrews, the phony Native scholar Jamake Highwater, Native sell-out Hyemeyohsts Storm, and countless white writers who write solely from non-Native perspectives. Now they can also turn to non-Indian Ian Frazier to reinforce their beliefs that Indians really are drunks and that Pine Ridge is an "evil" place (253). They do not need to know details about tribal life or to hear stories from a Native's point of view. *On the Rez* is a book written completely from an outsider's perspective. Frazier's comments, read by informed Native and non-Native scholars, will reverberate like the words of James Clifton, an anthropologist who believes that outsiders know more about Indigenous people than Indigenous people know about themselves. There are many fine works about Natives produced by non-Natives. I do not agree with the concept of essentialism—that only Natives "know" about Natives—nor do I believe that only members of a tribe can write accurately about that tribe. Many non-Natives write perfectly acceptable works about Natives because they know and understand their subjects. Conversely, there are some poor works written by Natives.

Many of us have visited Pine Ridge, have friends there, and can relate scores of shocking stories about death, drinking, suicide, abuse, poverty, and the Indian Health Service, but it would never occur to us to write about such things. Why? Because it is not our business to talk about it. Residents of Pine Ridge know what is happening on their reservation, and they do not need outsiders to tell the world about it. If you have a strategy to perpetuate stereotypes of drunken Indians, then buy this book for your friends. Natives, however, will not spend the outrageous sum of twenty-five dollars to get a copy. I did so only because the company did not send a review copy to the *American Indian Quarterly.*

During a break at a sun dance at Ironwood some years ago, I had lunch with a Lakota friend (a schoolteacher) at her immaculate Pine Ridge home, which is full of books, flowers, and her beadwork and needlepoint. Her comment that "there are problems, but there also are people here that are the cream of the crop" is the opposite of what Frazier leads readers to believe about Pine Ridge. Indeed, people with alcohol-related problems live there, but while its residents may not be wealthy in the monetary sense, the reservation is also home to productive activists and thinkers and conscientious parents attempting to educate their children and to plan for the future. There are many residents who do not drink and never have, and many who do drink do so in moderation. During a discussion with another friend about *On the Rez*, she cried from frustration over what Frazier has done, and who can blame her? There is not much she can do about it. Regardless of the glowing reviews that whites who know nothing about Natives give this book, it is a damaging book, and many Natives will say so even though we know from experience how fans of this type of work will react.

This book serves a purpose other than just being a money-maker: hatemongers will use it as fuel for their fire ("See, Mabel, I told you they were no-good heathen drunks"), Indian-lovers can sob over how far their heroes have fallen, and white America will be reassured that the only noble Indians are those who lived in the past. This kind of book is very dangerous, and publishing houses need to take responsibility for what they release. A lot of Indigenous writers spend their careers trying to correct stereotypes and to convince other scholars and publishers to utilize Native voices and perspectives. A book like *On the Rez* can outsell all of our books put together, and it completely overshadows our efforts to properly educate Americans about American Indigenous history and culture.

Frazier has put together a manuscript that in large part features real names along with accounts of these individuals' unattractive physical attributes, personality deficiencies, and drunken escapades. I sympathize with the people who are victimized by Frazier's backhanded compliments (he "likes" and "admires" Indians, after all; that is why he lavished his attention on them). However, as a member of the Choctaw Nation of Oklahoma (a tribe too unworthy for him to notice), I say this in response to his comment that "the Oglala is my tribe" (92): thank goodness.

**4**

## Comments on Linda McCarriston's "Indian Girls"

While reading Linda McCarriston's poem "Indian Girls," I was struck by two things: one is the similarity between the theme of the poem and that of Ian Frazier's recent book, *On the Rez* (2001), and the other is that the poem clearly illustrates the reality that, despite good intentions, white authors who write about Natives often do more harm than good.[1]

Frazier is an adventure writer whose writing ability is well known (most notably from his work in *Outside* magazine). In *On the Rez*, he considers one of the problems that plagues many tribes—alcoholism—and then proceeds to give readers the impression that everyone on the "evil" Pine Ridge Reservation is an alcoholic who contributes to the poverty, pollution, and violence that swirl across the bleak landscape.

Like Frazier, the talented poet McCarriston likes Indians and is concerned about them and particularly about the abuse Native women suffer at the hands of Native men. Unfortunately, like Frazier, she gives the wrong impression of tribal life. As uninformed readers might interpret the poem, Native females in the cold, dark north are perpetual victims of abusive men, and their only recourse is to wallow in misery. Just as Frazier does not tell us about the myriad sober Sioux who strive to make life better for their tribe and family, McCarriston does not mention the strong women (and men) who do not tolerate physical and verbal abuse from each other. Both authors dwell on the negative aspects of tribal culture, which only reinforces non-Natives' stereotypes of drunk, misogynist Native men and easy, bar-hoppin' "girls" who cannot come up with any better solution to their problems.

The most volatile debates today in the realm of Indigenous Studies surface over questions of authoritative voice, who benefits from writing about Natives, and whether or not fiction and nonfiction writings about Natives should contribute to nation building, empowerment of tribal members, and continuity of traditional cultures. The number of Native scholars with terminal degrees is increasing in all academic fields, and we are more aggressive in asking these questions of ourselves and of white writers who use Natives as topics to further their careers. With good reason. Most writers who write about Native women, for example, do not understand females' powerful legacies within tribal traditions. Most tribes' cosmologies feature females as figures central to the survival of their tribes. Female deities provide their people with sustenance, fertility, and societal structure. Native women today look to their past for motivation, and they strive to empower themselves, to earn university degrees, and to refuse to become victims of what of my Native students term "that colonialism excuse"—that is, the argument that the invaders' political policies, Christian ideologies, and forced education contributed to the loss of men's traditional tribal roles and power, so the men take their frustrations out on their hapless female partners. Ultimately, some posit, men's abusive nature is beyond their control.

The problem with the colonialism-as-sole-instigator argument and with "Indian Girls" is that both accept men's violence and women's passivity. The poem does not address how women and men have dealt with the intrusion of Euro-American values into their traditions. By no means are all Indian men abusive, and in fact, they are as angry about violence as are the stricken women. The scenario of "Indian Girls" may be indeed be somebody's reality, but it certainly is not everyone's.

Publishers must be held accountable for the submissions they accept. As editor of the *American Indian Quarterly*, I would not have considered "Indian Girls" a viable candidate for publication. Despite McCarriston's credentials as a respected poet, this particular work does not benefit anyone besides the author. Native and non-Native scholars, writers, and publishers must consider how their works will be received by a public largely ignorant about Natives and by Natives who are hungry for role models, advice, and inspiration. This poem is, sadly, a large step backward.

# 5

## In the Trenches of Academia

For the woman writer, no matter what position she decides to take, she will sooner or later find herself driven into situations where she is made to feel she must choose from among three conflicting identities. Writer of color? Woman writer? A woman of color? Which comes first? Where does she place her loyalties? – Trinh T. Minh-La, *Woman, Native, Other*

What comes first, race, gender, or profession? – Sara Suleri, "Woman Skin Deep: Feminism and the Postcolonial Condition"

Our jobs as Indigenous women scholars are an integral part of our lives and identities. Success in the classroom and in the world of publishing contributes to our feelings of self-worth and confidence, but because we are Native female scholars we often face confusion in the workplace. Concerns about tribe, community, and family are major focus points in our lives. We also are interested in earning a degree, acquiring a job, publishing, and receiving tenure and promotion—all of which require approval from dissertation, search, and promotion and tenure committees that sometimes comprise individuals disinterested in minority issues. Tribes need us to utilize the data we amass to assist in political, economic, social, and educational spheres, but many universities do not support these activist interests. We are concerned about recruitment and retention of Indigenous students, and we are sensitive to how universities use images of Natives for self-promotion.

I am often asked by Natives with freshly earned Ph.D.s what they can expect after they find a position in academia. The answer is complex because issues of racism, sexism, identity, authoritative voice, and curricula consistently arise. Misconceptions about Natives in scholarly and popular literature, the media, and the entertainment industry compel many of us to spend much time correcting stereotypes and misinterpretations of tribal histories and cultures. We work with faculty and students who see no value in oral histories, American

Indigenous studies, and especially Indigenous women's history and culture. When we attempt to impart to students a more inclusive view of American history (including the roles Natives have played and still do play in American society), we are accused of being "politically correct." We refuse to be invisible members of the campus community. Therefore, the mere presence of our female, minority selves politically charges university committees, scholarly conferences, and classrooms.

James Axtell's *The Pleasures of Academe: A Celebration and Defense of Higher Education* is filled with wonderfully astute observations about working in academe. Regardless of readers' race or gender, they can understand Axtell's feelings about academia's shortcomings and pleasures. Yet, because he is a white man, he has not written about academe from the viewpoint of minorities. Most minority women scholars know that (1) the academic playing field is not always level when it comes to race and gender; (2) politics of identity and power are major factors in publishing, course approval, hiring, merit, and promotion decisions; (3) identity and power politics exist among Natives within the realm of American Indigenous studies; and (4) when we complain about racism in the curriculum and in promotion processes—no matter how legitimate the claim—we often are labeled the problem.

Native female scholars, therefore, are connected to and involved with a variety of social, political, economic, and religious events outside the university that may or may not be connected to what we try to do within the academy. Issues that matter to us pull our emotions and professional commitments in opposite directions. We continually look for ways to mesh our duties as scholars with our concerns about tribal interests and family. The lines between being female, Native, and scholar do indeed blur, and most of us are scholar-activists.

Indigenous women academics are complicated, so to Trinh T. Minh-La's list of conflicting identities I add a few more for us to consider: Native woman academic activist focused on tribal issues? Native woman academic who writes about topics unrelated to tribal reality? Native woman academic who writes about Natives but uses theory and methodologies approved by white scholars? Native women scholar facing stress and frustration for speaking out and not being accepted by those who subscribe to the status quo?

## Writing as Empowerment

The postindian warriors encounter their enemies with the same courage in literature as their ancestors once evinced on horses, and they create their stories with a new sense of survivance. – Gerald Vizenor, *Manifest Manners*

I detest writing. The process itself epitomizes the European concept of "legitimate" thinking; what is written had an importance that is denied the spoken. . . . It is one of the white world's ways of destroying the cultures of non-European peoples, the impositing of an abstraction over the spoken relationship of a people. – Russell Means, a former accountant-turned-AIM activist-turned actor (and author)

Despite Means's rhetoric about writing being a purposeful, destructive force against Natives, the reality is that in order for tribes to survive, tribal members must both know and understand the ways of Euro-Americans (including writing), in addition to knowing and understanding the traditions of their tribes. The irony is, of course, that more Native women are writing and publishing now. But who really listens to Native women? For that matter, who listens to Natives at all?[1] The black community has numerous voices to hear when issues of racism arise: Rev. Jesse Jackson, Louis Farrakhan, and Oprah, to name a few. Who are the strong voices of Native America when they are needed? Tribal leaders and activists, unless they have terminal degrees and can speak the language of the academy, are not taken seriously. The voices of traditionalists often mean nothing to mainstream society unless those speakers look like Natives (i.e., braids, dark coloring, jewelry, etc.) and discuss familiar issues such as pollution. These speakers also mean little to many university-trained academics who believe themselves more knowledgeable than Natives with little formal education. Ironically, despite the behaviors of AIM men, who have been less than stellar in their treatment of women (and, as many argue, limited in their knowledge of tribal traditions), they are still in demand as speakers mainly because of their nostalgia value. They provide fiery, entertaining rhetoric, and most people—including many Natives—are ignorant of what actually occurred during the heyday of the Red Power Movement.

Regarding the woman of color writer, Minh-La writes, "It has become almost impossible for her to take up her pen without at the same time questioning her relation to the material that defined her and her creative work."[2] Scholar-activists need to write about our concerns, and the most powerful way to express ourselves is through our writings. Writing is a way to empower us, to state that we are not victims and that we are attempting to find answers and to solve problems.

As writers we face numerous dilemmas, one of them being how we should celebrate the accomplishments of our Native and non-

Native ancestors while at the same time controlling our anger at what non-Natives have done to Natives. In the classroom, in our writings, and in mixed company (by race, culture, or gender), how do we maintain balance between aggravation and feelings of happiness and peace? These attitudes and the way we present our information make tremendous impressions on Native students—affecting their self-esteem and racial and cultural identities.

Frustrating tribal issues and blatant misrepresentations of Natives in the media, entertainment industry, and scholarly literature concern us enough that we continue to teach, write, and fight resistance to our endeavors. Following through with these efforts is no small task. Feeling obligated to correct false histories and to express discontent with misinformation can be stressful and dangerous. Anytime an Indigenous woman writes something political or personal, she becomes a target for speculation. And criticism.

We are aware that our personal perspectives are not the only truths and, while we do not ignore the canon of our fields, we must attempt to learn about ourselves and other modern and historical Natives by considering information from a variety of disciplines, in addition to the controversial methodology of talking to the "objects of study" and using our own voices. But we cannot always please everyone with what we write and how we go about writing. As Cheyenne poet Lance Henson explains about literature: "Most definitely it's a weapon. That's why writers' heads hit the chopping blocks first in any revolution."[3]

### Interdisciplinary Studies

When I applied for full professorship in the fall of 1998, despite having met all the requirements and, indeed, having outdone previous successful applicants in teaching, service, and publishing, my dossier was scrutinized far more carefully than those of white colleagues who had applied in the years before. Members of the promotion and tenure committees will never admit whether they felt disturbed about a Native woman applying for promotion to full professor (although they did deem me "arrogant" for including the required list of my accomplishments), but they did complain about my letters of recommendation. I had several from historians, of course, in addition to letters from a legal scholar, a sociologist, an anthropologist, and the chair of a women's studies program. "What do they know about the history field?" they asked. I should have included only letters from historians, they argued, because I am a historian, and only historians should assess my writings. Most of my books and essays are, however, interdisciplinary and deal with real-life, modern-day issues.

This example illustrates the difficulties many minority women face in regard to the methodologies they use. Instead of becoming culturally responsible, many scholars—often those in power positions—remain firmly ensconced in a colonial mindset, teaching their courses from a monocultural, ethnocentric perspective, while at the same time becoming intolerant of anyone who might have a different vision. As time marches on, scholars uncover and present us with more facts and figures, yet there remains an aversion to providing students with a complete view of the world and of the people who have, and still do, form our lives and cultures. The very nature of Native history and Indigenous studies as a whole requires that any study not be discipline specific. Issues of policy, self-determination, economic development, environmental protection, and social life are inexorably interconnected.

If we do what we should, which is to utilize every bit of personal, textual, and oral information we have to contribute to the literature about Natives, then Indigenous-based studies would be biased and, more often than not, not respected by traditional scholars who believe scholarship should remain unbiased, objective, and discipline-specific. And it is the traditional, older white scholars who have succeeded in their fields of study pertaining to Indigenes who decide what should be incorporated into the canon of our fields, who will win awards, and who possesses a rational voice.

**Finding Truth**

Truthful, honest, and complete storytelling should be the goal for all of us. Libraries are stocked with anti-Indian monographs created by authors who used selected data to "prove" that Natives were savage, uncivilized heathens who fought the poor whites at every opportunity. Throughout American history, white writers, politicians, and military men have authored biased works that describe Natives as being among the lowest forms of life. Examples include William Robertson's *History of America* (1777), in which Indians are described as "America's most uncivilized inhabitants"; Richard Irving Dodge's *Our Wild Indians* (1882) (the title says it all); Theodore Roosevelt's *Winning of the West* (1904), which describes Indians as filthy, lying, lecherous, and faithless; Frederick Jackson Turner's ideas about Indians as savage barriers to the spread of democracy and Protestantism, which have influenced hundreds of American historians to ignore atrocious wrongs done to tribal peoples; and the works of anthropologist James Clifton, which focus on his thesis that the only real Indians live in the past. On the other side of the fence are romantic books that glorify Natives. Dee Brown's *Bury My Heart at Wounded Knee* (1971) is an example of using selective data to make the point that Natives are basically victims of evil white people. New Age, non-Native writers such as Lynn Andrews assert that Natives can do no wrong and utilize aspects of tribes' religions and cultures to attract followers to their so-called traditional ceremonies. Laguna writer Paula Gunn Allen, in *The Sacred Hoop: Recovering the Feminine in American Indian Traditions* (1986), makes the political and unsubstantiated argument that because most tribes had strong, influential women in their societies, homosexuality among women was commonplace.[4]

As writings by flag-waving political and military writers and Natives with political agendas illustrate, we do not need to resort to embellishment and claims of academic freedom to tell history. Efforts to create empowerment at the expense of truth only generate more controversy and claims of identity politics. What we should consider is the ideology of the late Oklahoma historian Angie Debo: "Although it is fashionable just now to assert that no scholar can be objective, that he slants his findings according to his own bias, I do not admit this. When I start on a project I have no idea how it will turn out. I simply want to dig out the truth and record it. I am not pro-Indian, or pro-anything, unless it is pro-integrity. But sometimes I find all the truth on one side of the issue. I have the same obligation to correct abuses as any other citizen."[5]

## Theory

One way to find truth is through the proper use of theory. Unfortunately, many scholars use little restraint when utilizing the ideas of others. As Iain Chambers comments, "Here in the West, 'history,' with its desire for mastery and its drive to fully explain, has provided the perennial testimony to the rewriting of the world as European text."[6]

During a discussion with the director of a history graduate program that had recently graduated a few students who fancied themselves "Indian historians," I raised the question of how these graduates could call themselves "Indian historians" if they had not worked with specialists in the field of "Indian history." The answer came in one statement that illustrates the problem of academic elitism: "Unlike professors at other universities, I teach them to be theoretically informed!" Because many students in that program did not work with professors whose work focused on the topics in which the students now claimed to have expertise, I knew the director's comment meant that students should be allowed to graduate with knowledge of theories formulated by non-Natives, and then they could apply these ideas to every person, place, and thing they might come across. This departmental theorist believes that an understanding of the theories of elite scholars (many of whom have never met a Native) is adequate for anyone to understand, interpret, and categorize the life experiences and belief systems of people from other cultures.

In her provocative essay "The Race for Theory," Barbara Christian argues that "theory has become a commodity which helps determine whether we are hired or promoted in academic institutions—worse, whether we are heard at all."[7] In a surprising reversal of Christian's position, graduates with a lack of training in the basic facts of their discipline or even understanding of current debates about the politics of writing about Indigenes (which includes theory) are being hired as "authorities" because of their "postmodern theoretical knowledge." Perhaps this is the easy way out. As Gertrude Himmelfarb points out, "there is no doubt that the old history, the traditional history is hard."[8]

In a graduate seminar a few weeks after my exchange with the theorist, several students expressed concern with their graduate program's emphasis on theory. One white male commented that it appeared that theory "is taking over." A woman believed the obsession with theory overshadowed not only the facts but also the "exceptions to the rules." That is, the "rules" being the theories and the "exceptions" being real-life experiences and essential knowledge that outsiders and theorists do not have. These students were, simply put, feeling pressure to fit square pegs (their writing projects) into round holes (some theory, any theory). Some students searched for theory that suited their topics, while others found a topic (or rearranged it) to suit a theory.

Theories are ideas—everyone has them—and new ideas are formed all the time. Certainly it is crucial that scholars be theoretically informed, for, as Christopher Norris puts it, "one needs theory to avoid reading stupidly."[9] Theory helps us create paradigms for understanding confusing issues. Obviously, like facts, theories are part of the canon of our fields. We need to know others' ideas about the facts so we can have a point of departure for our studies and for formulating and refining our own ideas. A thorough evaluation of theory, combined with knowledge of solid data and correct interpretations about what Others have to say about themselves is good, useful scholarship. For my work on identity, I depend on theories developed by black, Asian, and Hispanic theorists. When I deal with Indian women, I also look at ideas formulated by black women, mainly, but also by Latina and Asian women feminists, in addition to poets and novelists. None of the theories I study, however, fully describe Natives or Native women.

But what good is theory if we do not have the facts? What good is theory if we do not really understand the people we study? What if the "famous postcolonial theory" does not really apply to anything? In other words, to what exactly are some of these people applying theory? And why should not the subjects of theory come up with their own ideas? We should not abandon theory, we simply must be more selective in applying it. And we must incorporate the ideas, opinions, and stories of Native peoples into our works. Of course, reflexive analysis in deciding what constitutes good theory is also subjective, which leads to its own set of difficulties.

A problem with dwelling on theory is that the ideas of a few are used repeatedly at the expense of the ideas of the not-so-elite, and the latter are usually the people being studied. One example is in the area of Indigenous literary criticism. Thirty years after the publication of N. Scott Momaday's *House Made of Dawn* (1968), submissions from literary critics (graduate students, mainly) that present their theoretical analysis of the book and are all basically the same continue to land on my desk at the *American Indian Quarterly*. The same can be said about analyses of Leslie Marmon Silko's *Ceremony*, James Welch's *Winter in the Blood*, and Louise Erdrich's *Love Medicine*. Because so many scholars seem to be under the impression that these authors alone make up of the canon of Native literature and that they speak for all Natives, I have put a halt to accepting submissions about their works, in addition to more of the same papers about the works of Michael Dorris, Thomas King, and Joy Harjo.

If an essay comes in about a certain writer, my policy is to send the submission out to reviewers deemed "experts" on that writer, of course, but I also send a copy to the subject who is being written about. Several times the subjects and the experts have clashed over how the subject's work is interpreted. For example, the second year I edited the *Quarterly*, I received a submission that focused on a work by one of the most prolific Native writers. I sent the essay out for review to four scholars who are deemed by their peers to be "experts" on this particular writer. I also sent a copy to the Native writer who was the subject of the paper. Three of the four reviewers—all non-Natives—were highly critical of the paper, stating that the author did not understand the Native writer's work, had no idea what the writer meant by certain terminologies, was incorrect in discussing theories about this writer, and so on. The fourth review was from a Native, who was much less critical of the essay. Interestingly, the Native writer whose work was the focus of the paper thought it outstanding and disagreed with the three reviewers who criticized it, writing simply that they did not understand the book being analyzed. Based on the latter recommendation, I published the essay.

Who, then, are the true authorities on the works of Native writers—literary critics and theorists or the writers themselves? Should we continue to voice our beliefs and write our narratives even though we are really being misunderstood? Or could it be that we Native writers do not understand the methodologies the scholarly world uses to evaluate our work? Should we stick to writing and not critiquing? I claim no expertise in literary criticism, but it does seem peculiar for writers to use purely non-Native theory to describe Natives.

Another pattern is clear, and it has discouraged some aspiring white writers who originally wanted to focus their careers on Native topics. In my work as editor of the *American Indian Quarterly,* I find that, more and more, there is a difference between what Native and non-Native reviewers say about a particular submission. Non-Native reviewers recommend rejecting papers mainly because basic facts are incorrect or a theory is misused. Native reviewers will recommend rejection for the same reasons but also because the writer has not included Native input, that is, the tribal version of an event. And they are right. We need less work about "common knowledge" issues and more that offer complete stories—archival data combined with theoretical considerations, discussion of gender roles, and Native perspectives. Unfortunately, professors who believe in the old school of thought—that oral histories are not viable because they are not textualized—still pervade the academy, and their students, non-Native and Native, follow in their footsteps.

## Our Voices

Patricia Hill Collins writes in *Black Feminist Thought: Knowledge, Consciousness and the Politics of Empowerment* that "Black feminist thought reflects the interests and standpoint of its creators."[10] This statement is similar to what we can say about Native women's thoughts. Native women—and there are many, many different world views, values, and traditions represented in those words—are the ones who can best describe what it means to be Indigenous women, because, like African American women, they are "those who live it"—not non-Native theorists.

It is presumptuous for non-Native scholars to assert that because of their "postmodern theoretical knowledge" they are sensitive to tribal matters and have somehow captured the "real story." Often, their works are compelling and serve as interesting points of departure for further discussion. But some recent works on Native women have been authored by so-called progressive white women ethnohistorians who use no Native voices. How, for example, can Nancy Shoemaker, a white author, in *Negotiators of Change: Historical Perspectives on Native American Women*, seriously claim that she writes her essay on an Iroquois woman who has been dead for 320 years "from the Indian perspective?"[11]

One of our duties as Native women scholars is to help pave the way for scholars to follow, so they may continue researching, writing, and advocating for Native rights. Personal narrative is necessary because how else will we know what Others think and need? Many scholars, however, resist a "memoir as methodology" manuscript because, as Sara Suleri tells us, these types of works can "serve as fodder for the continuation of another's epistemology." Indeed, using autobiographies, ethnographies, and memoirs can create more confusion. In order for readers to read these lived experiences, the works must first pass through the publication process, which includes an evaluation of the manuscript by reviewers trained in the academic sphere. Usually the author must change his or her language to make it more accessible to consumers (usually non-Natives), and the end result is a text that reflects Suleri's assertion that "realism locates its language within the postcolonial condition."[12] While we speak in one way to an academic audience (Gloria Bird and Joy Harjo have referred to it as "Reinventing the Enemy's Language"), we speak in another way to family, friends, and community, and the latter voice is not what usually finds its way into publication.[13]

Another problem with using memoir-as-methodology texts is that they can be misleading. Recent books and essays written by self-identified mixed-blood Native authors are often informative about scholarly and tribal issues, but the waters become muddy when they begin their vignettes about their vague tribal ties and imagined family histories. Writer Louise DeSalvo describes these created stories in *Writing as a Way of Healing: How Telling Our Stories Transforms Our Lives*: "We are the accumulation of the stories we tell ourselves about who we are. So changing our stories . . . can change our personal history, can change us. Through writing, we revisit our past and review and revise it."[14]

Readers must be aware that voices can be confusing. Tribes are made up of individuals with extraordinary differences in cultural adherence, geographical location, blood quantum, appearance, and reliable memory. Some tribes, such as those in the Southwest, tend to adhere more closely to tradition than others, but even then elders are concerned about the youngsters' lack of interest in traditions. Also, these stories and perspectives describe individual, not collective, tribal realities. Although our own words best describe our interpretations of our lives, all of the Native autobiographies put together cannot adequately address the question of what it means to be a member of our tribe. Even with all this empirical information at hand, scholars doing the studying will continue to interpret the information according to their perspectives. Facts do not speak for themselves, and there are as many different interpretations of, and theories about, what we have to say as there are people giving testimony. There certainly can be no theory that encompasses all these voices, except maybe that Indigenous women share what I call a "commonality of difference." Nevertheless, a variety of solidly-identified Native voices are needed to make certain that we are heard in fields that are dominated by non-Natives.

## Objectivity and Subjectivity

In the anthology *Writing Culture: The Poetics and Politics of Ethnography*, there is only one female writer. One of the male editors, anthropologist James Clifford, rationalized the dearth of women writers with his estimation that "Feminism had not contributed much to the theoretical analysis of ethnographies as texts. Where women had made textual innovations they had not done so on feminist grounds." To make his argument even more convoluted, he then wrote, "A few quite recent works had reflected in their form feminist claims about subjectivity, rationality, and female experience, but these same textual forms were shared by other, nonfeminist, experimental works."[15] So, to get this straight, if women attempt to be experimental they are not feminist enough, and if they are feminists they write with ignorance of textual theory. Female anthropologists will not get very far with Clifford, it appears, and needless to say, numerous scholars such as Ruth Behar, Judith Stacey, and Lila Abu-Lughod have taken him to task for his sexist thinking.[16]

Within the field of anthropology—and other fields, such as history—one school of thought holds that objectivity is associated with masculinity. Feminist writer Catherine MacKinnon cautions us about the obstacles we may face in balancing the male-female situation when she writes that "the male point of view has forced itself upon the world, and does force itself upon the world, as its way of knowing."[17] If objectivity is masculine, then is it not also subjective? *Newsweek* writer Anna Quindlen admits that, for journalists, "objectivity [is] a lofty goal, a great notion. . . . reporters are human."[18] So are scholars.

This theme of female/subjective versus male/objective writers can be rearranged to address how Native history and culture is written: the dominant, Euro-American/objective point of view, which is often actually subjective, versus Native/subjective points of view, which are often quite objective. This argument is interesting in that it is similar to current debates over authoritative voice. Non-Indian anthropologist James Clifton, for example, is cynical and derogatory toward Natives, and he says we cannot write about ourselves because we are too close to the topic. In other words, he as Outsider is appropriately objective, while Insiders are inappropriately subjective.[19]

Wahpatonwan Dakota historian Angela Cavender Wilson asserts in her essay "American Indian History or Non-Indian Perceptions of American Indian History?"(a piece that non-Natives have criticized for its subjectivity) that "To truly gain a grasp of American Indian history, the other historians—tribal and family historians—must be consulted about their own interpretations of and perspectives on history."[20] This is only fair. But here is a problem. If we do use all the information at our disposal, which includes Native and non-Native sources, should we then purposefully write our monographs with a subjective, female eye? Do we even want to read purely subjective works? What about facts and the opinions of other people? The new feminist history requests that history be rewritten according to the values and perspectives of feminist historians, thus remaking history for political purposes. What does that say about feminist scholars—and in this case, Native activists—who are supposed to find the truth? After all, truth and what we want politically are not always the same things. On the other hand, searching for truth is in itself a political act, and Native activists and feminist scholars believe this is their duty. Ironically, when they do coincide in our writings, we are often accused of exaggerating, using selective data to make a point, and falsifying conclusions.

## Empowerment through American Indian Studies

One way for Indigenous women scholars and students to find empowerment is through a properly organized and well-rationalized Indigenous studies program that features courses designed in large part by Indigenous scholars for the purpose of tribal nation-building and appreciation of tribal traditions and concerns. We also worry about Native students. Away from home and the security of family, young Natives look to their professors for guidance and knowledge. Because most of their professors are non-Natives with little firsthand knowledge of the realities of tribal life, the students have few role models to emulate. Young adulthood is an important life stage of identity formation; during these years students strive to become comfortable with themselves and to decide what career they should pursue. The college years are a time of confusion for most students of all races. Natives often face a curriculum more strenuous than they have been exposed to previously. In addition, they must deal with language barriers, insensitive professors, and lack of mentoring. Often their family encourages them to attend school but at the same time confuses them with remarks about "turning white" and "acting like they're better than everybody else."

Many Native students feel the effects of political and social oppression but believe they have to continue to tolerate repression. One function of Native faculty is to serve as role models. Native students can observe scholar-activists, and if they are guided by strong mentors students realize that they can become effective advocates for tribal rights. We are responsible for assisting Natives in learning about their cultures from the perspectives of Indigenes and not just educating them about the theories and suppositions of outsiders. Maori writer Linda Smith reminds us that "imperialism cannot be struggled over only at the level of text and literature."[21] It can be hoped, then, that after being informed, Native graduates will return to their tribal communities so they may utilize their education to help their tribes govern themselves without interference from the federal government. When Natives create their own destinies they also create self-esteem, confidence, emotional and financial security, and respect for others. By becoming informed, they also become empowered. In return, Native professors also grow inspired and empowered by educating Native students.

A point of departure for discussion about American Indian studies is the new Applied Indigenous Studies Department (AIS) established at Northern Arizona University in 1999. The major is designed for students to study tribal issues, including economic development, ecosystem science and management, policy analysis, lobbying, program management, enterprise management, and environmental resource practice, with certificates in the planning stages for museum studies, Native journalism, and recovering Indigenous knowledge.[22] Knowledge of history and culture is also crucial, and although Indigenous literature can offer much in the way of revealing Native authors' thoughts and concerns, I and other Native scholars are leery of including more than one course on Native literature. Students often mistake the purely aesthetic as the only way of learning about Native cultures, and many seem to believe that the fiction works produced by Native novelists and poets should supply them with all the answers to questions about tribal life, past and present.

This program makes sense for a university with over fourteen hundred Native students. Interestingly, 71 percent of those students are female. For once, these students find themselves the majority in the classrooms. They feel confident enough to speak their opinions, discuss sensitive tribal matters, and openly question long-standing stereotypes and ideologies about Natives. As the only female professor teaching in the program, I, too, feel a sense of freedom in relaying the realities of society without being labeled "politically correct" on the end-of-semester student evaluations. In their essays and classroom debates, students reveal that they are attempting to utilize traditional problem solving and strategies for tribal improvement. In a program such as AIS, the goal is that Indigenous students will have an opportunity to define what is important to their communities and to themselves. Students are encouraged to consider how their people lived traditionally and to keep in mind Natives' contributions and abilities.

In our AIS program, it is crucial to include discussions about the strength and power of Native women in tribal traditions. It is not a maneuver to subsume men; rather, students must be taught that colonialism and patriarchal thought affected—and still affect—Indigenous women. Native men, therefore, have also been negatively affected. Political policies, Christian ideologies, forced removal, physiological changes, psychological stress, and population and land loss from warfare and disease disrupted women's powerful economic, political, social, and religious positions within most tribes. Females are not honored as they once were. Violence against Native women has escalated, and many suffer from psychological stress and identity crises.

Although Native women did not serve as tribal "leaders" per se, they did control tribal activities by dictating the recipients of crops, declaring leaders, and serving as mothers, advisors, medicine women, midwives, and manufacturers of skins, hides, clothing, and implements. Females also figured prominently in tribal religious stories. Many modern Native women leaders point to their tribal religions and traditions as inspiration and justification for their authoritative positions. Today, more Native women participate in tribal politics than ever before. They argue that taking leadership roles is a way of regaining the prestige and power their ancestors once held, in addition to assuming equal responsibility for the welfare of their tribes.

In courses within AIS, it is important to point out to students that the past does affect the present and that knowing tribal traditions, which includes egalitarianism between males and females, can help modern Natives cope with the complex—and impersonal—world by offering them foundations to form their identities and to create strategies for dealing with adversity. Native scholars must question methodologies, theories, and suppositions about their people and assert what they need. They should learn to integrate tribal and academic ways of knowing. It is up to professors to foster an environment that allows that line of thinking. Indigenous professors and students should heed feminist scholar Adrienne Rich's advice to participants in women's studies programs, that they should "claim an education" rather than passively receive one.[23]

By being a part of an AIS program, Native women faculty help develop a curricula of importance and consequence. Teaching about gender relations in traditional societies not only helps pull together cultural ideologies for Native students but also means that women's studies programs can cross-list the courses, an important step in educating feminist scholars about the realities of Native women's lives, past and present.

## Empowerment Policies

Many tribes are inundated with scholars wanting to study them, and universities have an obligation to make certain their faculty and students are sensitive when researching and writing about cultures other than their own. The word is out about Natives being dissatisfied with how they are portrayed in literature, yet many scholars and writers continue to write about Natives without considering that their subjects may not want to be the focus of scholarly works.

Today, a major controversy within academia focuses on the methods and manners surrounding in the way "Others" are written about by authors outside of that culture or gender. Often those researchers will hide behind the ideology of "academic freedom," as if the term is an encompassing justification for doing research of any kind. While "academic freedom" is supposed to also protect Natives' writings, it often shields those scholars who write about sensitive, "taboo" tribal issues. For example, do Pueblo women actually need a book that focuses on Pueblo female sexuality authored by a Mexican American male (i.e., Ramon A. Guiterrez's *When Jesus Came the Corn Mothers Went Away: Marriage, Sexuality and Power in New Mexico, 1500–1846*)? Do Hopis really need *The Bedbugs' Night Dance and Other Hopi Sexual Tales*, by the German male Ekkehart Malotki, who wrote the book against the protests of the Hopi tribe and is considered persona non grata on the reservation?[24]

American Natives are not the only Indigenous groups that have been exploited, over-analyzed, and used as the focus of many a white scholar's career. A common complaint throughout the world's Indigenous communities is that colonizers have barged into these communities and written what they pleased about the people and cultures with no regard for what the subjects have to say about it. As thousands of historical and anthropological monographs show us, non-Natives persist in stereotyping and incorrectly theorizing about people they often know little about.

Native women have been portrayed as everything from ugly squaws to beautiful princesses to New Age gurus. Many scholars argue that the Native-woman-as-princess is a compliment, but this distortion of reality is quite damaging. For example, a survey in a journalism course taken by one of my Navajo students several years ago revealed that that the majority of non-Natives responding to the question "What is your perception of Indian women?" have distorted images of Native females. Some thought they had "pretty hair and eyes" and were "baby makers." The student was mortified when she walked into her classes and for the next few years felt that that was how everyone perceived her. Of course, this is how most Native women are portrayed in movies and on television, so she should not have been so surprised.

Because most institutions do have institutional review boards (IRBs) and some work closely with local tribes, Native women scholars can demand to be placed on review committees. We can also demand that scholars who write about Natives take responsibility for what they write and that they be held accountable for producing inappropriate work. We as Native scholars can create dialogue about what should not be studied, and we are in positions to help set standards.

As Indigenous female scholars we have a responsibility to review inappropriate works and discuss why they are problematic. We also must attempt to educate publishers about what is unacceptable and to work toward guidelines that educate authors and disallow inappropriate writings. Our goal is a tough one. Authors write about topics that interest them, of course, but sometimes they put forth writings that are harmful, even if that is not their intent. IRBs and tribal guidelines were created to sift out undesirable works, but many writers still fly under the IRB radar because they feel they do not have to be accountable for what they write. Novelists and popular writers often escape IRB scrutiny because their publishing houses do not require them to pursue the review process. In the past few years, I have reviewed manuscripts on Native women that should never have passed the editors' desks for external review. As editor of a journal, I have read numerous papers that make me question who the authors' major professors are and what is taught in their classes.

Taking charge of volatile issues can be risky, especially for females. In 1992 the president of NAU appointed a group of five faculty members to create research guidelines for scholars who write about Hopis. At that time, a controversy had arisen over a manuscript that Malotki wrote on the religious aspects of the Hopi Salt Trail.[25] To protest the impending publication of that manuscript, I broke my book contract with the publishing house that was, by coincidence, on the verge of publishing the offensive manuscript. I was at once called "a hysterical female" by an editor (who also said, "I will not have little red people telling me what I can and cannot publish"). It is doubtful that I would have been called "hysterical" had I been a male. Further, after the news leaked out, I came to work one morning to find a large phallic symbol drawn on my door.

Issues of ethics also enter the classroom. Native students often are intimidated by an imposing Affirmative Review complaint process, so they instead complain to me and other Native professors on a regular basis about what happens in their classes. They are distressed about professors calling them "red men" and telling them that their cultures had no "civilization" until whites brought it to them, that Native students cannot write term papers or book review topics about Natives, even though other students can write about whatever they wish, or that oral histories are not really histories because they aren't textualized, thus ignoring the reality that the written word can also be embellished, selective, and misinformed.

Indigenous students are bothered by what they perceive as the arrogance of teachers who will not accept alternative viewpoints or will not stand corrected. In my classes, we discuss the controversy over whether the ancestors of Natives crossed the Siberian Land Bridge or were created on this continent, as the majority of tribal creation stories tell us. Many students argue, rather vehemently, that they learned in anthropology classes that Natives migrated here, so that must be the correct theory. But the absolute truth is not the point. Rather, the issue should be, why cannot the accounts of Native peoples be respected? What is to lose by knowing and pondering multiple versions of a story or issue without making accusations of superstition and ignorance?

A question for Indigenous scholars to ponder is, should we be so concerned with writing to please the scholarly world and those who are situated in academic power positions but who only imagine that they have the education to tell the world what counts as important knowledge about Indigenous women? Most Natives want to live and express themselves without being endlessly analyzed and theorized about. I have reached the conclusion that I simply must spend my energy being useful. To be sure, we must jump through hoops to finish theses and dissertations and to achieve tenure and promotions, but we also must be true to ourselves and write what we believe is balanced, useful scholarship.

I find this aspect of my job—being fearless in teaching, learning, and writing—quite comparable to my winter activity, skijoring, the sport of being pulled on skis by dogs. Not a lot of us do it. We leave the shoot at 25–30 m.p.h., and if we fall, we fall very hard and on occasion get hurt seriously. Those of us who participate have a motto: No Fear, No Brakes. Skijoring is comparable to the thrill of performing well as a scholar and being recognized for it, to the joy of informing students and having them say they appreciate it, but it is also similar to what I term "mind pain," which I have encountered since I started my journey as a historian in 1984. From enduring questions about why I was hired to being called "politically correct" and the "department token," in addition to facing a lack of support from colleagues, the pain is irritating, deep, and long-lasting. It leaves permanent scars. Yet, at the same time, as with skijoring, I have no intention of stopping just because I might get hurt. It is not a case of being a glutton for punishment; as I have told friends in regard to academic issues of late, I am simply getting used to it. Writing about these issues is like flying across hard-packed snow with icy spots. I take a chance revealing concerns and realities, but I do it anyway, knowing that Advil, friends' support, and remembrance of the legacy of strength of millions of Indigenous women who have already lived and died work very well.

# 2. COLONIALISM AND NATIVE WOMEN

# 6

## Colonialism and Disempowerment

We, collectively, find that we are often in the role of the prey, to a predator society, whether for sexual discrimination, exploitation, sterilization, absence of control over our bodies, or being the subjects of repressive laws and legislation in which we have no voice. This occurs on an individual level, but equally, and more significantly on a societal level. It is also critical to point out at this time, that most matrilineal societies, societies in which governance and decision making are largely controlled by women, have been obliterated from the face of the Earth by colonialism, and subsequently industrialism. The only matrilineal societies which exist in the world today are those of Indigenous nations. We are the remaining matrilineal societies, yet we also face obliteration. – Winona LaDuke, environmental and political activist

Colonialism, a powerful force, continues to affect Indigenous females in countless ways. Women faced the intruders who invaded their lands and watched the devastation of their ways of life. Their populations decreased from smallpox, measles, whooping cough, alcoholism, and numerous other diseases, in addition to warfare and fertility decline. Their lifeways eroded; bison and fur-bearing mammals were over-hunted almost to extinction, and many tribes were removed from their traditional lands and forced to migrate. Tribes were not allowed to perform religious dances. All Natives became dependent upon material items from the Old World, and although metal implements and firearms made their lives easier in some ways, Natives had to compete with other Natives in order to keep in good stead with the Euro-American suppliers of those items. Indigenous women suffered sexual violence and abuse at the hands of Euro-Americans, and those men created stereotypes and false images of Natives for their own gain. Although today most diseases are under control and health care is available, many Native women face poverty, racism, cultural confusion, and psychological problems, often as a result of being of mixed heritage.

Traditional gender roles eroded from the impact of patriarchal thought, and those ideologies still affect Native women's positions within their tribes and the respect given to them by men. As former Cherokee chief Wilma Mankiller observes, "Our tribe and others which were matriarchal have become assimilated and have adopted the cultural value of the larger society, and, in so doing, we've adopted sexism. We're going forward and backward at the same time. As we see a dilution of the original values, we see more sexism. . . . The thinking that people come to in a patriarchal society is crazy."[1]

Most tribes were egalitarian, that is, Native women did have religious, political, and economic power—not more than the men, but at least equal to men's. Women's and men's roles may have been different, but neither was less important than the other. Females toiled hard at their various "jobs," but they received recognition and compensation, often in the form of controlling the economic output; in addition, they were secure knowing they would always have food, shelter, and support from their extended families and clans.

Prior to contact, men and women performed tasks specific to gender. Perhaps men hunted while women farmed, or men performed heavy labor while women cared for the children. Although the duties were different, none was inferior to the others. All work was necessary, and the tribe needed the hands of both men and women. The influence of Europeans' social beliefs, however, changed the way Natives interpreted the world, themselves, and gender roles.

Many traditional tribal religions include a female divine spirit, a cosmology that positioned Native women in prominent and respected positions. Among Navajos, for example, the term "mother" symbolizes the earth, sheep, and corn—the three major elements of Navajo subsistence—and along with Apaches (the Navajos and Apaches were originally one group), the earth mother is also known as "Changing Woman," a self-renewing entity who symbolizes hope. In spring she is young; she bears her harvest in the summer, grows old in the fall, dies in the winter, and is reborn the next season. White Mountain Apache girls participate in the four-day Sunrise Dance the summer after their first menstrual cycle in order to prepare for their adult life. During the dance, the spiritual presence of Changing Woman endows the girls with strength and health. Navajo girls perform a similar puberty ritual (*kinaalda*) that was given to the tribe by the Holy People, one of whom is Changing Woman.[2]

Cherokee women believe they came from Corn Mother or Selu. For the Tewa Pueblos, the first mothers were known as Blue Corn Woman and White Corn Maiden. The Shawnees' creator is known to them as "our grandmother." Cheyennes believe their food is supplied by a female who takes the shape of an elder. Iroquois came into the world from mud on the back of Grandmother Turtle. Some Apache tribes are descendants of Child of the Water, who was kept safe by his mother, White Painted Woman. For the Sioux, White Buffalo Calf Woman gave them the gift of the pipe and thus the gift of truth. The Okanagan Nation of British Columbia have a legend that states the earth was once a woman. And so on.[3]

Generally speaking, matrilineal clans within societies determined one's political alignment; furthermore, one received his or her social and political rights from clan membership. Because a person's clan was determined by his or her mother, women possessed much political and social power, in addition to a guaranteed network of female relatives who lent support and companionship.[4]

Some scholars have taken this woman-centered society to mean that homosexuality among women in tribes was commonplace. Paul Gunn Allen posits in *The Sacred Hoop* that "Some distinguishing features of a woman-centered social system include free and easy sexuality and wide latitude in personal style. This latitude means that a diversity of people, including gay males and lesbians, are not denied and are in fact likely to be accorded honor." She goes on to write that women spent "long periods together in their homes and lodges while the men stayed in men's houses or in the woods or were out on hunting or fishing expeditions. . . . In such circumstances, lesbianism and homosexuality were probably commonplace."[5] While Allen's statements may be true for some Native groups, there is too little research on the sexuality of the hundreds of tribal groups to make such sweeping assertions. Personally speaking (and that is what Allen is doing), I have never heard anyone knowledgeable about my tribe's (Oklahoma Choctaw) traditional gender relations speak of such commonplace homosexuality, and neither my husband (Comanche) nor anyone in his family has heard of such things among his tribespeople, either. My Navajo, Apache, and Hopi students (many of whom hail from traditional families), in addition to my Mohawk, Salish-Kootenai, Sioux, Cherokee, and Assinaboine friends and colleagues—both heterosexual and homosexual—also find the notion unsettling. Often, discussions about homosexuality (such as this one) reveal that there is a connection between the authors' personal lives and the topic they write about, rendering the issue interesting but subjective.

Like women in other Iroquois tribes, Mohawk women traditionally had prominent places within their group. Katsi Cook, a Mohawk activist, describes traditional Mohawk women as "having relationships, not roles, within the universe and within society. Within these relationships, there were responsibilities that were met as mothers, grandmothers, aunties, and daughters. From the bodies of women flow the relationship of the generations both to society and to the natural world. In this way is the earth, our mother, the old people said. In this way, we as women, are earth." She is also quick to say that despite this female power pervading the tribe, men and women have equal powers: "The men have their council fire and the women have their council fire. This is a reflection of the balance and harmony between the genders."[6]

In traditional matrilineal societies, the husband left his home to live with his wife close to her extended family. Children belonged to their mother's clan and traced their lineage through their mother's line. Girls received education from their mother and aunts. Boys learned to hunt from their mother's brothers. After divorce, the children could stay with their mother, and women retained family property. Females held responsibility for agricultural activities, while men either hunted or also worked the fields. Elder women among the Iroquois Confederacy (a government created by six northeastern tribes—Onondaga, Oneida, Mohawk, Seneca, Cayuga, and Tuscarora), known as Clan Mothers or Matrons, chose the tribal leaders that in turn represented the tribe on the Grand Council. The Clan Mothers also controlled and divided the agricultural goods, declared and halted war, oversaw burials, and affirmed the agreements between the Iroquois Confederacy and the European powers. Among some tribes, such as the Delaware, Cocopah, Quinault, Yurok, Copper Eskimo, and Southeast Salish, both men and women served as religious leaders.[7]

Some tribes did have females who served in authoritative roles, although they did not wield exclusive authoritative powers like European leaders did. During the colonial period, a Narragansett woman chief named Magnus was executed after their defeat, and a "Massachusetts Queen" headed the Massachusetts Confederacy throughout much of the 1600s. Other tribes such as the Cherokee, Cheyenne, Esophus, Natchez, Nisenan, Osage, Sakonnet, Sinkaietk, Tsimshian, Wampanoag, and Winnebago (Ho Chunk) all reportedly had females as social and/or political leaders at some point.[8]

In some societies, such as many Plains tribes, men were the providers and fighters, and families were centered around men's activity, thereby isolating women from their extended families. Men were the only voices heard in council, and men controlled all aspects of war. Women dealt with domestic duties, but because women were dependent on men for sustenance, Plains men often stood as authority figures. The Plains tribes' cosmology, however, features female figures in their religions (such as the White Buffalo Calf Woman who brings to the Lakotas the Calf Pipe, which, along with the Seven Sacred Rites, comes to their aid in times of hardship), and it is argued that many of these tribes were egalitarian. Ojibwes, Arapahos, Gros Ventres, Winnebagos (Ho Chunks), and Menominees are traditionally male-centered, yet women had considerable freedom socially. Some were medicine women. Female Piegans, Cheyennes, Crows, Kootenais, Modocs, Ojibwes, and Apaches reportedly fought in battle, often beside their husbands or in their place if they died. Other tribes, such as the Nachez and Yuchi, were divided into matrilineal clans, but their organization appears to have been patriarchal.[9]

How much prestige and power women actually held will never be known. Most observations of Indian women in traditional societies were written by Euro-American men, who judged them by the same standards that they judged women of their own societies. Many non-Natives misunderstood tribal kinship systems, gender roles, and tribal spiritual and social values. Their observations also reflected their biases and, perhaps, their desire to manipulate reality to accommodate their expectation that Native women were held in lesser regard in their tribal societies because women were subservient to men in European societies. As Paula Gunn Allen has stated, this lack of proper documentation, including ignoring women's prominent roles altogether, "reinforces patriarchal socialization among all Americans."[10]

For example, almost all the historical and cultural studies of the Choctaws examine only the male tribal members. Choctaw women are rarely mentioned, not even the wives of prominent tribal leaders. When discussed, their roles as Choctaws are described by non-Native men who evaluate women's roles by their own European, male-oriented standards. Some early commentaries portray Choctaw women as useful tribal members because they prepare food or bear children, but they are also characterized as subservient drudges with no economic, political, or social influence on the tribe.

These viewpoints are incorrect. In the pre-contact period Choctaws were successful agriculturists; the women tilled soil, sowed seed, and harvested crops. Men hunted deer and turkeys and fished the numerous Mississippi and Alabama waterways, while women dressed and prepared the game. In addition, women made clothes, reared children, and held positions of religious importance. Descent was matrilineal, and women retained control over tribal property.

Today, because of movies and television that distort tribal reality, the general public seems to be aware only of prominent Native men. For example, by the mid- to late 1800s (a popular time period for television and movie Westerns), the East was settled and whites continued to move west in search of wealth, land, social prominence, fame, and adventure. Many tribes were surrounded by whites, and they reacted to the encroachments onto their lands in a variety of ways: warfare, negotiation, surrender, migration. The Natives normally portrayed are men who either tried to fight against Americans (e.g., Crazy Horse, Geronimo, Quanah Parker, Manuelito, Captain Jack, Wild Cat, Osceola), tried to lead their people to safe havens (Chief Joseph, Dull Knife), attempted to live peacefully according to treaty terms (Black Kettle), or tried revitalization dances (Big Foot). The Native women the public remains aware of are Sacajawea and Pocahontas.

Other Native women, however, showed intellect and determination in dealing with whites, but little is heard about them except in scholarly literature, which until recently often misinterpreted their actions. Quite often, women such as Paiute Sarah Winnemucca and the LaFlesche sisters of the Omaha tribe had to "dress the part," that is, look like a Native to get attention. These women had to be well versed in the ways of white society before they gained Americans' respect and certainly before whites bothered to listen to them. Sarah Winnemucca (c. 1844–91) dressed as an "Indian Princess" to lecture to white Americans about the injustices against her tribe, including their removal from Nevada to Oregon and Washington. She also founded a school for Indians with her own funds and donations.[11]

The daughter of a Mohawk chief and an English woman, Emily Pauline Johnson (1861–1913), also known as Tekahionwake, was thoroughly bicultural and a prominent figure in Canadian and Native historical literature. She was strongly influenced by Shakespeare, Byron, and theatrical performance, and after attending Central Collegiate School, Johnson began writing poetry. Her first collection, *The White Wampum* (1895), was published by Bodley Head Press in London, and her second set of poems was published in 1903 by a Toronto publishing house. She continued to write stories that featured strong Native women as the protagonists, and she toured throughout Canada as the "Mohawk Princess," enacting her stories through theatrical performances. Some of her later works were *The Legends of Vancouver* (1911), *The Moccasin Maker* (1913), and *The Shagganappi* (1913).[12]

The LaFlesche sisters, Rosalie Farley LaFlesche (1861–1900), Susan Picotte LaFlesche (1865–1915), Marguerite LaFlesche Picotte Diddock (1862–1945), and Suzette Tibbles LaFlesche (1854–1903), were the daughters of Omaha leader Joseph LaFlesche (also known as Insta Maza, or Iron Eye), a mixed-heritage French-Ponca who served as chief of the tribe from 1853 to 1866. Their mother, Mary Gale (Hinnuagsnun, or One Woman), was mixed white and Omaha. Susan, Marguerite, and Suzette were educated in white schools such as the Elizabeth Institute for Young Ladies in New Jersey and the Hampton Normal and Agricultural Institute in Virginia. Susan was the first

Native woman to receive her medical degree (the second was Belle Cobb, a Cherokee woman discussed in chapter 7), graduating in 1889 from the Woman's Medical College in Philadelphia. Iron Eye was a proponent of assimilation and pushed to have tribal children educated. Susan continued her father's quest to have Omahas adopt white ways. Although she was not well versed in the culture of the Omahas, she nevertheless dressed in traditional Omaha clothing while traveling the country to speak to non-Natives about tribal issues and treaty rights. Suzette also served her people by lecturing extensively to white audiences about broken treaties, tribal cultural deterioration, and the loss of tribal lands. Interestingly, she also believed in assimilation. Rosalie, on the other hand, pushed for self-government and self-sufficiency. Marguerite believed in education as a means of making the tribe self-sufficient.[13]

The mixed-heritage Christal Quintasket, more commonly known as Mourning Dove (1888–1936), was born in Idaho to a Okanogan father and a Colville mother. Mourning Dove received education in a few government Indian schools. After a 1914 meeting with *American Anthropologist* editor Lucullus V. McWhorter, who became her friend, advisor, and collaborator, she published, most notably, *Co-Ge-We-A, the Half-Blood: A Depiction of the Great Montana Cattle Range* (1927) and *Coyote Stories* (1933). Mourning Dove is known for her desire to preserve her cultural heritages and to retain tribal "secrets" while at the same time creating powerful fiction steeped in reality.[14]

Since contact with Europeans, Native religions have been termed "uncivilized," "barbaric," and "pagan." Foreigners certainly did not understand tribal cultures, much less respect the position women held within their tribal structures. European colonists were influenced by Renaissance ideologies, notably the concept of the "Great Chain of Being," that everything in the universe should be in order (i.e., that God is at the top of the hierarchy, with Hell and chaos at the bottom, or, in politics, the king is at the top and peasants are at the bottom). Natives needed to be placed within the order, and generally they were seen as inferior and therefore positioned at a low rung on the ladder of civilization. As non-Christians (who were lumped into one cultural category instead of being seen as diverse, complex groups), Natives were then dealt with in several ways: they were "civilized" via Christianity, education, farming, allotment, and termination; because many Euro-Americans believed Natives to be hopelessly "uncivilized," they pushed for policies of destruction and justified brutality by rationalizing it as "God's will" that tribes become extinct so American civilization could spread across the continent; and tribes were moved and/or confined to reservations out of the way of "progress."[15] Among those who preferred to try and "civilize the savages" were Euro-American missionaries, who pressured Natives to convert to Christianity, which, among other things, included them accepting the concept of the male God and thus reinforcing the superiority of males.[16] Females were (and in many Christian traditions still are) expected to submit to the authority and will of men.

Some Natives complied and attempted to acculturate to the ways of white society. Others, however, staunchly resisted and continued with their own beliefs and rituals. Missionaries brought with them the policy of discipline to be used against transgressors, and in the Spanish Southwest, Pueblo medicine men were flogged, burned, or hung for leading religious ceremonies, resulting in the Pueblo Revolt of 1680.[17] Despite non-Natives' lack of appreciation of tribal religious beliefs and their attempts to eradicate them, Natives have continued to practice their beliefs and ceremonies. Although many Natives resisted the lure of converting to Christianity, others were intrigued with the missionaries' promises. Natives had witnessed the destruction of their tribes and loved ones, the loss of their homelands, and the results of alcoholism. Why, they wondered, should they not adopt the ways of the conquerors and, they hoped, avoid these problems? Maybe Christianity was a way to cope with the destruction of their peoples by disease and white intruders. Some Natives were attracted to the ritual of the Catholic church, especially because the beads, incense, and ceremony reminded them of their tribal rituals. Others, like many Pueblos, knew that a strategy for survival was to at least claim they wanted to convert. Regardless of who converted and why, missionaries did manage to instill foreign values into tribes, affecting even those who wanted nothing to do with what Christians had to offer.

Natives on the verge of utter despair because of loss of land, culture, and loved ones turned to the numerous revitalization movements led by prophets such as Wangomen, Handsome Lake, Tenskwatawah, Kenekuk, and Smoholla in hopes that the prophets' promises were true and God would restore the land and peoples as they had existed prior to contact.[18] In 1883 Secretary of the Interior Henry M. Teller introduced the series of laws known as the Indian Religious Crimes Code, which were intended to disallow any Native ceremonies, including dancing, feasts, and giveaways in addition to any "heathenish" practices performed by spiritual leaders, with transgressors punished by imprisonment. Although the laws were not lifted until 1933, Natives continued to hold ceremonial dances, including the "pagan" Sun and Ghost Dances.[19]

Tribes still practice old dances and ceremonies, although they have been forced to alter portions of the rituals. For example, because of the threat of AIDS, at some sun dances, instead of using a communal knife or eagle talon, dancers are required to bring their own scalpels, and dancers are not pierced as deeply as they were traditionally because tearing a large muscle like the pectoral would prevent them from attending work.[20] In the Native American Church, the dwindling supply of peyote causes some ceremonial leaders not to use as much or to be more selective in who gets to use it. There are other examples, of course, but the point is that while the ceremonies may be altered, the symbolism usually remains.

After contact, missionaries seemed to be almost everywhere. Because they had ingratiated themselves into many tribes, tribespeople began to seek the counsel of the missionaries instead of their traditional tribal religious leaders, many of whom were women. By the 1830s, for example, many Cherokees were Christians and began ignoring their *adaehis* (medicine people) when in need of medical attention. Tribal women and men in prominent religious positions quickly became less respected.[21]

Some men among Plains tribes and tribes on the Plateau had more than one wife. With the introduction of European material goods, men could range longer distances to hunt and raid. They killed more animals than before and, because hides had to be tanned and the animals dressed, having more than one spouse alleviated the work burden and helped create more prestige for the male. As they did with other tribes, missionaries objected to the practice of polygamy and pressured Plateau tribes, for example, to change the family social units by encouraging tribespeople to build small homes that could accommodate only the basic nuclear family instead of the traditional longhouse that sheltered extended families.[22]

Because of religious influences and intermarriage with whites, kinship systems among tribes were disrupted. Generally speaking, the status of women diminished as male power increased. For example, by 1808 many white men had intermarried with Cherokee women, and many Cherokees had adopted Christianity. In an effective attempt to undermine the female-dominated clan system, a Council of Headmen declared that the patriarchal family was the norm, not the traditional matriarchal model in which children belonged to their mother's clan and property belonged to the woman. A police force was organized to enforce a new law that stated children were heirs not only to their father's property but to the widow's share as well. Two years later, the council abolished the female-ruled "blood vengeance" and replaced it with the tribal courts. Additionally, a woman who married a white man immediately lost all rights to her land. By the 1830s a dramatic increase in wife abuse was reported. Among Cherokees and Creeks, at least, overuse of alcohol caused men to behave irrationally, which disrupted the male-female balance of respect. Despite laws that declared men the property owners, they still lost their tribal lands to outsiders, and they took their frustrations out on their wives, leading to tribal-wide chaos.[23]

This change from an egalitarian tradition brought numerous problems for Native women. Once men took over as heads of family, women moved to their husband's residence and often lost their relatives' immediate support. A woman's security in all facets of tribal life was diminished. She became less important economically, and when she and her husband divorced the woman lost all her assets. Men were instated as heads of their families, and children inherited their father's estate.

Among Iroquois tribes, in which women's roles were similar to those of women in the Cherokee tribe, trade with whites increased, which temporarily raised women's status because of their ability to create the desired trade items. Women continued to control the output of corn at least until the early 1800s, when Canadian and American powers attempted to persuade Indian men to farm, thus displacing the women in the fields. Women lost political power after white Europeans convinced Indian men not to listen to females' advice, a move that shifted women into less pivotal positions. By the early nineteenth century the matron-appointed leader system among the Iroquois tribes was gone, replaced with a system of elected representatives—and only men's votes counted.

Unlike women from many of the southern tribes, some Iroquois women did not loose all power within the various tribal spheres; rather, their roles were altered, still allowing them a measure of equality within the tribe. In her 1991 essay "Rise or Fall of Iroquois Women," Nancy Shoemaker concludes that Seneca women traditionally had great influence within the tribe, offering their choices of men for political leadership roles, serving as advisors to the political headmen, and controlling much of the economic production and distribution. Unlike in other tribes that attempted to completely subsume women within the tribes, after contact the Seneca men "defended women's rights as part of the larger effort for community survival."[24]

Like the Cherokees, the Senecas adopted a written constitution. But at least the Senecas allowed the Clan Mothers the right to vote on land issues. Unlike the Cherokees, who disenfranchised women, Seneca women retained their rights in property and divorce settlements. One's tribal membership is still determined through matrilineal heritage (by virtue of one's mother being a tribal member). Shoemaker cautions, however, that just because Seneca women appeared to have numerous powers within the tribe does not mean they were "better off" than white women in regard to women's rights. The high marriage and illegitimacy rates "could support contrary arguments of women's social dependence or independence."[25]

Women of some tribes, like the Muscogees, initially gained status from marrying white men. Women like Mary Musgrove Matthews Bosomworth (also known as Coosaponokeesa) aided their white husbands' efforts to become successful businessmen or traders by serving as interpreters, culture "coaches," and co-partners in business and thus gained financial status and retained security for themselves.[26]

By the 1830s enough time had passed and enough hardships had been endured by white Americans for them to believe that democracy and the American form of government were successful. Because the country was predominately Protestant, many Americans believed that the combination of Protestantism and democracy would serve as the best hope for the world. In addition, the idea of "Manifest Destiny," that Americans were God's chosen people, swept not just through the political system but also through the country. Many Americans believed they could—and should—attempt to absorb the entire land area from coast to coast, although some thought America should expand from pole to pole. This belief in Manifest Destiny was a feeling of superiority, and Indians felt the brunt of Americans' pride and determination.

These ideas about Natives being inferior were especially popular in the early 1800s, when the "scientific" idea of "inherent racial inferiority" gained support. Charles Caldwell, a physician, in *Thoughts on the Original Unity of the Human Race* (1830), presented his theory that there were four distinct human species: Caucasian, African, Indian, and Mongolian. Each possessed differing abilities and intellects, with the Caucasian species being superior to the others. He also attributed any successes among Natives to their intermarriage with Caucasians. Nine years later, Samuel George Morton published *Crania Americana*, a highly influential work that discussed his belief that differences between the races resulted from biology, not environment. Further, Morton asserted that separate creations had taken place for each race in different parts of the world, basing his theory that the Caucasian race was superior on extensive crania studies that included measuring the amount of mustard seeds that could fit into a variety of skulls: the one that held the most had the most room for brains and therefore intelligence. Between 1844 and 1857 Southern surgeon Josiah C. Nott wrote profusely, if not rationally, about the superiority of the Caucasian race. He also was convinced that any achievements made by the Southeastern tribes were solely because of their intermingling with whites.[27]

Not all Natives were aware of these social and "scientific" ideologies, but some, like Cherokees who were educated by teachers from New England schools such as Yale, were. Many Natives, therefore, believed that one way to survive was to imitate their oppressors.

The influence of "scientists" in addition to the ideologies and policies of missionaries created factionalism within tribes, between those who cling to tradition and those who see change as the route to survival, either tribal, familial, or personal. Intratribal factionalism might also be termed "culturalism," a form of oppression that dovetails with racism. Natives in tribal power positions, political, economic, or social, often use expressions of culturalism against those who do not subscribe to their views. "Colorism," the intragroup stratification often associated with blacks, is also an ideology prevalent among tribes. As Potawatomie scholar Terry Wilson discusses in his essay "Blood Quantum: Native American Mixed Bloods," people who identify themselves as Native but do not look phenotypically Native are seen with suspicion, especially by Natives with darker skin.[28]

Among Lakotas, those who do not live on the reservation or do not speak the language do not enjoy the "cultural entirety of being Lakota."[29] A historic example is writer and activist Gertrude Simmons Bonnin (1876–1938), also known as Zitkala-Ša, a Yankton Sioux. Bonnin acquired an education at Earlham College in Indiana and the New England Conservatory of Music in Boston, taught at Carlisle, published stories in prestigious publications such as *Atlantic Monthly* and *Harper's*, and became involved with the American Indian Defense Association, the Indian Rights Association, and the National Congress of American Indians. Despite her strong concerns for her people's welfare and constant travel to educate white America about Natives' problems, she did not live among her tribe, failed to retain strong kinship ties, and therefore lost status among her people.[30]

"Class" is one way to differentiate among Natives, but class does not always refer to money issues. Among Indian people it can also refer to levels of cultural knowledge and blood quantum. Marxist feminists are partially correct in asserting that economics account for Natives women's inferior status. And so are socialist feminists' assertions that a low economic position combined with gender also explains some Native women's status. However, while Native women may be oppressed because of their lesser economic status, capitalism and gender are not the only forces of oppression against them.

Native women were gender oppressed (most notably after contact with Euro-Americans) and, like other women of color, they also are subjugated because of their race.[31] Native women, however, because of their varied economic situations, social values, appearances, and gender roles, are oppressed by men and women—both non-Natives and, interestingly enough, other Natives (see chapter 7 for examples among the Cherokees).

Among tribes around the border of the United States and Canada, the demand for beaver pelts especially emphasized the men's roles and lessened women's status. Women also were seen as commodities, valued for their abilities to hunt, trap, skin, and survive in harsh weather and to assist in bringing positive relations between cultures. Jennifer S. H. Brown and Sylvia Van Kirk have shown that northern Native women were adept at trapping, skinning, and curing hides, yet kinship systems unraveled.[32] Like Muscogee women in the Southeast, who played an important role in the deerskin trade and spent long hours at work away from their clan lands, females in the north became dependent on men for material goods essential for survival.

Van Kirk discusses how Cree, Ojibwe, and Chipewyan women contributed to the success of fur trade rivals the Hudson's Bay Company and the North West Company.[33] Natives recognized the marriage of their women to European men as social and economic alliances: traders were given rights to the women, and Natives received rights to the fur trade posts. The trader benefited from the union because his wife was usually adept at canoeing and trapping in addition to knowing how to cook, sew, and make shoes. Despite the women's contributions to their husbands' success, by the early 1800s when the fur-bearing mammals were almost depleted, Native women were not so much in demand as wives. Some white men remained faithful to their Indian wives, and many European men continued to marry Native women into the middle of the century, but many other Native women were abandoned and abused when white women arrived in North America. The mixed-blood female offspring were often sent to boarding schools to learn the ways of white society, resulting in further loss of tribal members and cultural knowledge.

To the south, white men who married into the Cherokee tribe usually demanded that their families adhere to the man's values, which included a market economy dominated by property-owning males. Women of Plains tribes fared the worst. They were basically slaves for a market to which they had no access. Men controlled almost every aspect of tribal life, and women themselves became commodities in the exchanges between their fathers and their new husbands.

The Navajo tribe is traditionally egalitarian, with sheep and wool a focal point of its economy. Both men and women cared for sheep, and along with the matrilocal residence pattern, matrilineal structure of lineage, and prominent female figure in Navajo religious beliefs, women were economically and socially secure. With the imposition of federal mandates to curtail overgrazing of lands by sheep in the 1930s, the amount of wool produced was reduced, thereby reducing women's work as rug weavers. Additionally, demand for rugs lessened because consumers bought cheaper imitations. Women did not ordinarily engage in wage work, while men already worked in construction, mines, and fields and on railroads. Wage work for men increased, wages for women decreased, and men then became the primary earners. Women, especially unmarried and older females, fell victim to financial insecurity, and men often emerged as the authoritative figures in the household because they controlled finances.[34]

Native women have lost more than just social status and political prestige. Florida Seminole and Santo Domingo women who marry white men are disallowed from living on the reservation; however, if a Native man marries a white women, he and his family are permitted to live on the reservation.[35] The Santa Clara Pueblos have a similar law. In 1978 the Supreme Court ruled that it would allow the Santa Clara Tribe to decide on the tribe's rule that states that if a tribal woman marries outside the tribe, the children of that union are not considered full tribal members (they cannot vote or inherit their rights to communal lands); however, if a tribal man marries outside the tribe, the children could be full tribal members.[36] The Indian act in Canada, which stipulated that Native women lose Indian status upon marrying non-Indian men even though the reverse is not true for Native men and Indian status is given to non-Indian women who marry Native men, was not overturned until 1981, in *Sandra Lovelace v. Canada.*[37]

Legal scholar and feminist Catharine A. MacKinnon considers this case and Santa Clara tribal ideology in her essay "Whose Culture? A Case Note on *Martinez v. Santa Clara Pueblo*" and asks the provocative question "Is male supremacy sacred because it has become a tribal tradition?"[38] Roxanne Swentzell, a Santa Clara Pueblo artist, has remarked about her tribe that "Most of the people here at Santa Clara don't have anything to do with the land, with the place, anymore. They go off to work from eight to five just like everybody else and they want their new car and their TV and their VCR. What they really want is to be middle-class white Americans."[39] If she is accurate, then one might consider that the tribe has indeed adopted patriarchal thought.

Men of God, along with the federal government, also established schools throughout Indian country in an attempt to "save souls" and to teach Natives to become civilized. The problems created for Natives by these schools have been well documented. Since the 1600s non-Natives have attempted to educate Indigenes in the ways of Euro-American society. Missionary and secular schools, which aimed to "kill the Indian in order to save the man," were brutal to Native children. In the mid-1880s Native youths were forced to leave their homes and live in boarding schools far from their families. Taught by white teachers and missionaries who assumed they knew what was best for Native children even though they knew nothing about tribal cultures, Native children were forced to wear white clothing, cut their hair, and give up their religious paraphernalia. Students were not allowed to speak their native languages and, as one boarding school alumni comments in the movie *In the White Man's Image*, "My language was beaten out of me." Students were repeatedly told that because they were Natives, they were inferior. The result was depression, confusion, and loss of culture. Some students committed suicide; others died of loneliness. The irony is that after they were educated they were not accepted into white society, and many could not fit into their tribe's society again either.[40]

By 1900 the government maintained at least twenty thousand students in 148 boarding schools and 225 day schools, which were located closer to tribes. The Meriam Report, issued in 1928, revealed that children at the boarding schools faced health problems, poor living conditions, inadequate diets, and extreme punishments, in addition to untrained teachers and impractical curricula that did not pertain to students' needs.[41] Importantly, the Natives whom reformers had hoped to make over in the white man's image clung tenaciously to their identities and cultures. With the passage of the Indian Reorganization Act in 1934, the government focused on tribal self-determination rather than acculturation, and community schools were established in order to help Natives help themselves. This ideology was reversed in the 1950s with the establishment of the government's policy of terminating the tribes' relationships with the federal government. Bureau of Indian Affairs schools under the government's control again adopted the policy of assimilation. Although in the 1960s the tide turned again in favor of Indian self-determination and Natives started to become more active in education affairs, not all schools are adequate today.[42]

Problems at Indian schools are not limited to the past. Numerous schools have inadequate texts and teachers, deteriorating buildings, poorly managed lands, and a legacy of student molestation. In 1984 the Phoenix Indian School in Arizona, for example, was found to use Mace, straightjackets, and shackles as disciplinary tools.[43]

Modern Indigenous mothers still must carefully review their children's textbooks for stereotypical images of Natives, and they also must be diligent about their children's classrooms. Too often kindergarten teachers will decorate their classrooms with alphabet letters that include images of an animal or object whose name begins with that letter. Even "enlightened" teachers will use the image of an Indian to go with the letter *I* and will use animals dressed in feathers, war paint, and leather to depict other letters. Prior to Thanksgiving, parents must be alert to the probability that teachers will have their students dress as Pilgrims and Indians, a misleading image that gives the impression Indians and colonists always "lived in harmony."[44]

## Abuse and Violence

Various studies have revealed that during the 1970s between 25 and 50 percent of Indigenous women between the ages of fifteen and forty-four were sterilized. These women were not told they were signing consent forms, the surgeon did not wait the requisite seventy-two hours after the woman signed the consent forms before performing the procedure, or the women were not informed what sterilization meant or about the risks of the procedure. Some gave their consent when heavily sedated during another surgical procedure, and some signed forms they did not understand because they did not speak English or because the forms used medical jargon that was difficult for them to read.[45] As a result of being sterilized, many women suffered depression, guilt, and shame and turned to substance abuse. Many divorced or encountered marital problems, and some became overly fearful of losing the children they did have.

Violence against Native women is not committed only by non-Natives. Across the country Native women complain of misogynist behavior by Native men that includes verbal and physical abuse. In her 1992 book, *Death and Violence on the Reservation*, Ronet Bachman wrote that, of 92 women questioned at two women's shelters on two different reservations, 79 percent had been sexually abused by their husbands or boyfriends, 75 percent said that abuser was under the influence of drugs or alcohol at the time the abuse occurred, and 35 percent had received physical injuries from the assault.[46] In another study conducted in 1992, 3,421 abused Navajo women were interviewed, and 52.5 percent cited at least one incidence of domestic abuse by a male.[47] There are only two shelters on the Navajo reservation, the Tohdenasshai Shelter Home in Kayenta and the Native

American Family Violence Prevention Project in Shiprock; three "safe houses" exist in three other cities. The reservation has also built two facilities in Chinle to deal with youth problems, but neither is open because of intratribal disputes. According to one study, in New Mexico there is a higher rate of domestic violence–related homicide among Native women than in any other group in the state, and the violence is usually instigated by Native men under the influence of drugs or alcohol.[48]

Perhaps it is frustration and confusion over the loss of traditional gender roles and the adoption of white society's values that has contributed to spousal abuse and tension between the sexes among Natives today. For example, bison was a main source of food for many of the Plains tribes and tribes peripheral to the Plains. With the near extermination of the buffalo during the late 1800s came the disintegration of many tribes' cultures, including the distortion of gender roles. Males, who were the hunters, no longer had bison to hunt and, according to many Natives, their frustration has led to alcoholism, spousal abuse, and "woman hating."

On the Navajo reservation, where violence and gang activity have increased in recent years, it is believed that factors such as the breakup of multigenerational families, the loss of elders and the elders' inability to communicate with youngsters, the "code of silence" among family members that keeps guilty parties from being punished, fewer ties to the land now that many Navajos move to cities to seek employment, and the feeling among young Navajos that their education is of no use on the reservation, contribute to apathy, depression, and boredom.[49]

As Lakota Mary Crow Dog (now Brave Bird) observed about the bad behavior on her reservation: "There is nothing for the young people when they grow up. There is a lot of alcohol. There is a lot of drugs, a lot of young people dying. Like some of those gang members, I talk with them. If you can find unity, you know, even with their own leadership, if you form unity, you can make a strong movement within yourself. Because they are all, you know, fighting over drugs, over women, or whatever. . . . There is nothing in the tribe."[50] Other factors that spur spousal abuse and violence against fellow tribal members include personality disorders and insecurities, unemployment (which is rampant among reservation Natives), lack of formal education and knowledge of tribal culture, drinking, drug abuse, and childhood sexual abuse.

One major cause of the abuse of others (and of the self, for that matter) is what many black scholars refer to as "self-hatred," although other scholars argue that there is no such thing.[51] Nevertheless, as with blacks, numerous Natives point out how many Natives lash out at each other because of insecurity and the desire to have what others possess. Lee Maracle, for example, a member of the Stoh:lo Nation, writes in *I Am Woman: A Native Perspective on Sociology and Feminism*, "I am so weary of men who, guilt ridden by their own treachery, attack me and accuse me of the very things they are bogged down with." She also writes, in her poem "On Native Resistance":

> In the Third World, Natives resist oppression.
> In America, the Natives resist each other.
> Our loyalty consists of our own self-
> and mutual contempt.[52]

Jimmie Durham, a self-identified Cherokee, writes in "Those Dead Guys for a Hundred Years," "We hate ourselves and each other . . . and now there we all are, out there trying to impress the white folks with one thing or the other. . . . Our regular folks are usually drunk or bad-mouthing their neighbors."[53]

Maracle and Durham state what many Natives think but do not say out loud: Native people do verbally and physically abuse each other—at home, in the academy, and in literature. A common joke among people of color is the "crab joke," in which an enterprising crab manages to make it to the top of the fisherman's bucket. Just as she is about to escape (read: succeed), the other crabs grab her legs and pull her back into the bucket. The metaphor is that when a Native person (or black or Chicana or member of other groups who have adopted this story) succeeds, the other crabs become angry and jealous and try everything they can to keep her from doing so. Natives usually laugh at the joke because they understand the concept.[54] As a Native woman commented to me several years ago, "The most supportive people for me in the university have been Indian women. But at the same time, other Indian women have been the most vicious because of their jealousy and insecurity. Nobody can destroy a person like an Indian woman."[55]

In a competitive society (a reflection of centuries ago when tribes competed for the favors and material goods of the colonial powers), Native men and women often find themselves striving for the same job. In academia, they often are in positions where they evaluate each other's performance, and often they do so with unjustifiable negativity. How, for example, should we deal with the bright, young (and well-published) Native female professor who recently said to me in private that "I can't trust anybody," because she knows from painful experience that trusted male or female Native allies are hard to come by? Other women of color feel the same pain. Gloria Anzaldúa, in

*Borderlands/La Frontera: The New Mestiza,* writes about how those who have been "pounced on" may also have pounced on others, and she asserts that all of us need to be accountable for our behaviors, responsibilities, and privileging.[56]

## Stereotypes and Images of Indian Women

Changes in tribal roles, violence, and psychological conflicts are not the only problems Native women faced in the past or in the present. Although all Natives suffer from stereotypes, Native women were and are especially romanticized and abused.

Upon arriving in the New World, the newcomers began speculating on the flora, fauna, and peoples they encountered. They also were entranced with what they perceived as a bountiful land filled with interesting peoples (whom they believed to be inferior). As opposed to portraits of European women, who were shown fully clothed and demure, paintings of the New World included depictions of Native women as symbols of savage sexuality in the wilderness: topless and voluptuous, often carrying a spear, adorned with feathers and tobacco leaves, and surrounded by animals.[57]

Europeans were fascinated with Native women's lack of clothing, and this cultural difference caused misunderstandings about sexuality. Native women were viewed as decadent and sexual—dark-skinned whores—while the lighter-skinned, clothed European women were the more "pure," respectable females. Native women were seen as sexual beings free for the taking, and indeed, sexual violence against Native women was common after invasion.

Christianity played a large role in ideas about skin color. Christians' religious beliefs included ideas about dark skin being associated with evil and dark souls, so the Jewish Christ has been depicted in paintings as light-skinned, with blue eyes. In the pre–Civil War South, slavery proponents justified the enslavement of African Americans by arguing that dark skin was God's punishment for blacks. Indeed, white skin has been desirable among individuals of many cultures around the world during many time periods. In Europe during the Middle Ages and Renaissance, artists depicted their subjects with pale complexions. Women and men powdered their faces and hair and whitened their skin with lemon juice, mercury, and later, arsenic in order to achieve a well-to-do pallid look, and Elizabeth of England painted blue veins on her forehead.[58]

Mormons assert that American Indigenes are descended from Lehi, an individual who allegedly departed Jerusalem in 600 B.C. and came to the Americas and whose children divided into two warring groups here in the New World: the light-skinned Nephites and the evil, dark-skinned Lamanites. The Book of Mormon states that Lamanites are the ancestors of modern Natives and that once those Lamanites convert to Mormonism they will somehow change into "white and delightsome" peoples, a claim that has proven a powerful incentive for Natives to join the church.[59] This story also was the rationale for taking Native children from their homes and placing them with Mormon families to be raised as Mormons.

Native women are not the only victims of the "white is right" belief. The award-winning Caribbean poet and novelist Edwidge Danticat states that during her adolescence she was admonished by her uncle to stay out of the sun. "The sun will spoil you," he told her, out of concern not for her health but for her social status.[60] All females are bombarded with images of white beauty everywhere they go— at grocery checkout stands, on television, and in magazines. Many feel that looking white means acceptance by the dominant society, so they submit to dyeing their hair, perming their straight hair into tight ringlets or straightening their "too curly" hair, and wearing the latest clothing styles. In 1990, 20 percent of patients seeking cosmetic surgery were people of color (Jews and blacks altering their noses, Asian women lifting the epicanthic fold, blacks submitting to skin lightening and lip shaving, for example), whereas in 1980 it was less than 2 percent (whether this increase is because of increased ability to pay for such surgeries is unknown).[61] Although there has been a slight increase in the number of ethnic models on fashion magazine covers, the vast majority of cosmetic, shampoo, and clothing commercials in magazines and television and on billboards feature Caucasian women as the ideal. The "ethnic" Barbie dolls may have varying skin tones and wardrobes, but they also have Caucasian features.[62] The recent animated movie *Pocahontas* (1995) set yet another standard difficult for Native women to adhere to: the Native woman as bombshell. Obviously, Native women do not dress like Disney's Pocahontas, nor are the vast majority of Native women built like the animated version (she was, in fact the composite of several models).

A multi-million-dollar enterprise known as "Indian Maiden Art" (marketed on the Web auction site E-Bay, for one place) usually depicts wildly beautiful women with "impossible hair" (that is, hair that is long, luxurious, and full of unnatural body), with feathers, in various stages of undress (wearing fur and hides, mainly), and with an animal as her object of focus (wolves, mainly, but sometimes owls, which are viewed as omens of bad luck and death to some tribes). The women's features, however, are always Caucasian. In a course I teach on American Indian women, I show slides of paintings of Indian

Maiden Art, and students always comment that the subjects look like white women with brown skin and heavy eye make-up.[63]

Some Native women strategize in order to obtain lighter skin coloring, presumably to distance themselves from blacks or from their own African American blood. At a powwow outside of Lawton, Oklahoma, about ten years ago an elderly Muscogee woman asked me to retrieve her umbrella from her truck's cab, saying, "Get me my umbrella, Hon, otherwise I'll be lookin' like a nigger by supper." Worrying about the same thing over a hundred years ago, students at the Cherokee Female Seminary were never without their parasols and wide-brimmed hats (see chapter 7).

On the other hand, many multi-heritage Indians may be comparatively dark in color but nevertheless lay in the sun to darken their skin in order to be accepted by their own people. Despite her Native appearance (to most non-Natives, at least), Mary Brave Bird recalled that in her youth she "waited for the summer, for the prairie sun, the Badlands sun, to tan me and make me into a real skin."[64]

Some Native females have felt justifiably confused about what they do look like to other people. When Leslie Marmon Silko was a girl, tourists visiting Laguna wanted pictures of her friends and not of her, because she did not look Native enough. Ironically, years later she was detained at the U.S.-Mexico border because in the eyes of the border patrol she appeared dark like some Mexicans.[65]

As the next two chapters discuss, pressures that Natives and non-Natives put on Native women as to what they should look like, how they must behave, and who they should associate with cause emotional distress and identity confusion. Appearance is only one of their concerns.

# 7

## Culturalism and Racism at the
## Cherokee Female Seminary

> The elevation of the Cherokee people also depends upon the females, and
> perhaps, particularly upon those who are just springing into active life,
> and who enjoy the privileges of this Institution. How necessary is it that
> each one of us should strive to rightly improve and discipline our minds
> while at school, and to be governed by principle and not by impulse, so
> that when we are called to other stations and our field of effort widens,
> our influence may have an elevating and ennobling effect upon all with
> whom we come in contact. – Qua-Tay, seminarian, 1855

The Cherokee Female Seminary was a nondenominational boarding
school established by the Cherokee Nation at Park Hill, Indian Territory, to provide high-quality education for the young women of its
tribe. The curriculum was based on that of Mount Holyoke Seminary
in South Hadley, Massachusetts, and it offered no courses focusing
on Cherokee culture. The seminary opened in 1851, but in 1887 it
was destroyed by fire. Two years later, a larger, three-story seminary building was erected on the outskirts of the Cherokee Nation's
capital, Tahlequah. By 1909, when the building was converted into
Northeastern State Normal School by the new state of Oklahoma,
approximately three thousand Cherokee girls had attended the seminary. A male seminary was built at the same time, three miles from
the female seminary; it educated Cherokee youth until it burned in
1910.[1]

While the female seminary was indeed a positive influence in the
lives of many of its pupils, there is much evidence to suggest that
the social atmosphere at the seminary contributed to the rift between
Cherokee girls from progressive, mixed-blood families and those from
more traditional, uneducated backgrounds. Although many of the
girls hailed from traditional families, the seminary did nothing to
preserve or reinforce Cherokee customs among its students. Retention of ancestral Cherokee values was not the school's purpose. It was

1. The second Cherokee Female Seminary building (circa 1902) was closer to
Tahlequah, with a better water supply. It measured 246 by 96 feet, with an
eastern wing measuring 70 by 100 feet, and it cost seventy-eight thousand
dollars to build. Courtesy of University Archives, John Vaughan Library,
Northeastern State University, Tahlequah, Oklahoma.

created so that females of the tribe would learn to imitate whites and
become "True Women."

Many acculturated, mixed-blood Cherokees believed themselves
to be more "enlightened" than the less affluent, uneducated, and
darker-skinned Cherokees. Ironically, the latter believed themselves
to "more" Cherokee and therefore in a higher "cultural class" than
the former. The more acculturated Cherokees did not always have
much money, but in their eyes their lighter skin and greater formal
education put them in a higher cultural class. Because they were
strongly pious, they believed that God favored them. As students,
they spent a good deal of time arguing the merits of the white world
and decrying the negative aspects of Cherokee culture.

Women such as Belle Cobb, Rachel Caroline Eaton, and Nannie
Katherine Daniels went on to graduate from universities (Cobb earned
her medical degree in 1892, the second Native woman to do so), but
they did not use their extensive education to help their tribe. Only
one seminary graduate, Jennie Ross Fields, was an advocate for Native
rights. These women offer a sharp contrast to modern women such
as Wilma Mankiller, who served as chief of the Cherokees. While

these young women utilized their femininity in their attempts to convince others of their cultural superiority, they also deferred to men. Although they had pride in being Cherokee, they did not aspire to retain traditional Cherokee values that included equality between genders. They did want to remain Cherokees, but they strove to be "white Cherokees."

Progressive and traditional tribal members each considered themselves to be more Cherokee than the other. The progressives believed that, because of their enlightening educational and religious experiences, their intermarriage with whites, and their successful reestablishment in Indian Territory after their removal from the East, they were the new and improved Cherokees. The traditionalists, on the other hand, viewed the mixed-bloods not as Cherokees but as non-Indian "sell outs" or, at best, "white Cherokees." Interestingly, just like many mixed-bloods today, the Cherokee women who looked Caucasian found that their appearance, in combination with their educational backgrounds, gave them an advantage. They were able to slip back and forth between the white and Cherokee cultures—or at least the Cherokee culture they were used to—depending on their needs.

The establishment of the Cherokee seminaries created a tremendous amount of pride among many Cherokees, but not all tribespeople liked the idea of the expensive schools. Most of the pride came from those who believed they should compete with whites on white terms. Because the schools espoused Victorian women's roles (holding women inferior to men), the success of the seminaries is measured by non-traditional Cherokee standards, not from a traditional, egalitarian Cherokee standpoint.

The Cherokee National Council was controlled by progressive, educated, mixed-blood tribesmen, many of whom subscribed to the value system of the upper-class antebellum South. Their decisions regarding the seminary were supported by most of the mixed-bloods of the tribe, white men and their Cherokee spouses (for the most part mixed-bloods), and to a lesser extent, by the progressive full-bloods. The prime interest of these progressive tribal members was indeed education, but they were also interested in the proper "refinement" of their daughters, to enable them to serve as knowledgeable, but dutiful, wives in the Cherokee Nation. Another reason for the seminary was the acculturation of the poor full-blood girls, but apparently this idea did not come about until 1871, after the council was pressured by disgruntled tribesmen to establish a "primary department" to provide free education to full-blood children who could not afford the five-dollar-per-semester tuition.[2]

The social aspects of the seminary are intriguing. Regardless of social, economic, and ancestral backgrounds, all the girls (with the exception of a few white pupils and girls of other tribes) identified themselves as Cherokees. Because of these socioeconomic differences, within the seminary walls a definite class system evolved, creating tension much like that which existed throughout the Cherokee Nation between the mixed-bloods and the full-bloods, between the traditionalists and the progressives, and between those tribal members who were proslavery and those who were not.[3]

During the seminary's early years (1851–56) there was no tuition fee, but money undoubtedly determined who entered the seminary. In the 1850s, according to the laws of the Cherokee Nation, the only prerequisite for admittance was an acceptable score on the entrance examination (except during the summer sessions, when all students paid), combined, perhaps, with a first-come, first-serve priority. But daughters of politically prominent and affluent families (Adairs, Bushyheads, Hickses, McNairs, Rosses, and Thompsons, to name a few) were always enrolled.[4] These girls were from acculturated, educated households, had already attended good public schools, and had no difficulty passing the written examination. Most full-bloods who wanted to enroll did not have an educational background that would enable them to pass the test. The schools they attended in the distant reaches of the Cherokee Nation were not as well equipped as those closer to the capital, Tahlequah, nor were there enough Cherokee-speaking teachers to help them learn English.

In 1856 the seminary closed because of financial difficulties. After it reopened in 1872, the enrollment situation changed somewhat, but money still gave students an advantage. Some students who failed courses semester after semester were repeatedly granted readmittance as long as they could pay the tuition.[5] Indicative of the lenient standards for tuition-payers is this excerpt from a student's letter to her sister in 1889: "I seat myself this evening to right you a few lines to let you know that I am well at the present and hope this to find you the same I was glad to hear frome you this evening I haven't got but 2 letters frome home and one frome you and I have writen 6 letters since I have been here and this is the 7 I aint rooming with no body yet here is the picture of the jail house."[6]

Although the majority of the students came from families that could manage to pay the tuition, truly wealthy students were in the minority.[7] In fact, daughters of the wealthier families were sent to schools outside the Cherokee Nation and never attended the female seminary.[8] Each year, dozens of primary students went to the school free of charge. The class system at the seminary, then, was based on family income from 1851 to 1856, but from 1872 until 1910 it apparently was based more on race (Cherokee and white blood quantums), appearance (Indian or Caucasian), and degree of acculturation.

Acculturated teachers and students took tremendous pride in their education and appearance. Mixed-blood students frequently scorned those girls who had less white blood and darker skin. A few progressive full-bloods also belittled those who had limited understanding of white ways. It was the general consensus among the mixed-blood students that the full-blood girls were "a little but backward" and well aware of their inferior status.[9]

Many factors contributed to the feelings of inferiority and alienation experienced by the full-bloods and "unenlightened" mixed-bloods at the school. Since most full-bloods and some poor mixed-bloods worked for their room and board, they were assigned to the third floor with the primary students. Because they were often behind academically, many were placed in classes with the younger girls. They were left behind on social excursions, because only those in the high school grades were allowed to attend events in Tahlequah and the male seminarians' ballgames. Unlike the pupils whose parents sent them spending money, the poorer students were unable to afford party clothes, nor could they buy after-dinner snacks from the local vendors—also a social occasion.

The attitudes of some of the teachers also led to resentment among many of the full-bloods. The National Council employed many qualified mixed-blood instructors, but there were no traditional Cherokee teachers. Despite the instructors' sympathies for the traditional girls, they rarely understood the problems the full-bloods faced. In 1908, for example, mixed-blood seminary superintendent Albert Sydney Wyly (an 1890 graduate of the male seminary) expressed his impatience with the full-blood girls by referring to the mixed-bloods as "whiter" and therefore "more intellectual." He criticized the full-bloods for their "pathetic attachment to home" and remarked patronizingly that at least they "possess a great deal of artistic ability."[10]

Another example of insensitivity is cited by teacher Dora Wilson Hearon, who in 1895 noted that she and her aunt, Principal Ann Florence Wilson, took the third-floor inspection duty because the other teachers were repelled by the students' head lice.[11] In 1907, prior to the school's first rehearsal of the annual Shakespeare production (*A Midsummer Night's Dream*), a mixed-blood senior responded to the administration's concerned query "Full-blood girls to do Shakespeare? Impossible!" by saying, "You don't know [teachers] Miss Allen and Miss Minta Foreman!" implying that these instructors were indeed miracle workers.[12]

2. The fourteen members of the Cherokee Female Seminary class of 1905.
Courtesy of University Archives, John Vaughan Library, Northeastern State
University, Tahlequah, Oklahoma.

The teachers also relentlessly reinforced the importance of learning
and retaining the values of white society. At the same time, they
repressed Cherokee values, thereby causing confusion among the
more traditional students. One instructor, Kate O'Donald Ringland,
later recalled that in regard to seminary philosophy, "anything 'white'
was ideal"; an alumna remembers learning in primary grades that the
"white way was the only acceptable way."[13] DeWitt Clinton Duncan
spoke for his fellow National Council members in a lengthy diatribe
in the *Cherokee Advocate* (the Cherokee Nation newspaper) when
he asked, "Can the mental wants of an Indian youth be satisfied . . .
by resources less fruitful than that which caters to the Anglo-Saxon
mind? The Cherokee language, at the present advanced period of
their [Cherokees'] civilization, cannot meet the exigencies of our
people."[14] With the National Council advocating white education, the
traditionalists were continually pressured to adopt a different culture
if they wanted to attend the seminary.

Not all seminary full-bloods felt ostracized. At least 165 full-bloods
enrolled in the seminary (about 11 percent of the 1,500 students
whose blood quantums can be ascertained), and they stayed an average
of four semesters, two semesters longer than the average for mixed-
bloods (but five semesters less than the average for graduates).[15] This

was probably because girls of one family attended school together, which helped to alleviate homesickness. Some were even adopted into the "big happy seminary family," a phrase used by a mixed-blood (one-thirty-second Cherokee blood) to refer to the upper echelons of the student hierarchy.[16] Because of interruptions such as the Civil War, the destruction of the school by fire, smallpox epidemics, and alternate educational opportunities, not one student, not even a graduate (many of whom enrolled for more than ten semesters), remained in the seminary from first grade through graduation.[17]

Full-bloods who enrolled in the common schools usually learned to speak and read Cherokee, but many were not particularly happy about it and wanted the type of education offered at the seminary. A student at the Cave Springs common school who desired to attend the seminary explained that the common schools could not compete with the female seminary because "we can only interpret Sequoyah's alphabet."[18] After the 1870s many of the neighborhood common schools taught in the Cherokee language for the benefit of the full-bloods; therefore, high school–age children who could not afford the seminary tuition were limited in their educational choices.

Some full-bloods who wanted a seminary education were willing to work for their tuition, but only a limited number of workers were allowed each semester. Some of the more acculturated full-blood girls at the seminary were from families that could afford the tuition. Thus these students were able to live with the mixed-bloods on the second floor and enjoyed an elevated status. Many of them did not speak Cherokee, nor did they have any interest in traditional Cherokee customs. As seminary alumna Charlotte Mayes Sanders recalls, the "full bloods went to Tahlequah to become like the white folk."[19] Indeed, many of their families had already succeeded, and the children came to the seminary armed with the knowledge of white society that was necessary to function among their acculturated peers.

Especially in the early years, citizens of the Cherokee Nation charged that elitism and prejudice against the full-bloods existed at the seminary. But in 1854, progressive full-blood student Na-Li eloquently defended her seminary by stating, in *The Cherokee Rose Buds* (the newspaper of the seminary in the 1850s), "it is sometimes said that our Seminaries were made only for the rich and those who were not full Cherokee; but it is a mistake. . . . Our Chief and directors would like very much that they [full Cherokees] should come and enjoy these same privileges as those that are here present." Na-Li, however, had been adopted by a mission at an early age, had had a thorough primary education, and had easily passed the admittance examination. In further defense of her heritage and skin color, Na-Li asserted that although her parents were "full Cherokees . . . belonging to the common class," she felt it "no disgrace to be a full Cherokee. My complexion does not prevent me from acquiring knowledge and being useful hereafter. . . . [I will] endeavor to be useful, although I sometimes think that I cannot be."[20] It appears that the more Cherokee blood a girl had, or the more Native she looked, the more she felt she had to prove herself as a scholar and as a useful member of a society that (she believed) valued only those women who were white in appearance and in attitude.

Na-Li probably was not entirely incorrect in her interpretation of the values of the mixed-bloods. Even progressive mixed-blood girls who were dark-skinned faced prejudice. Florence Waters (five-sixteenths Cherokee) was told by a lighter-skinned classmate that she could not participate in the elocution class production of *The Peri* because "[a]ngels are fair-haired and you are too dark for an angel."[21] When the full-blood girls did go to Tahlequah, and especially when they went outside the Cherokee Nation, they had more difficulty adapting to society's "whiteness." In 1899, the preponderance of mixed-blood Cherokees in Tahlequah was illustrated by *Twin Territories* writer Ora Eddleman, who expressed dismay over the wealthy Cherokees and the "blond Cherokee women.[22]

The seminarians were indeed defensive about their hair and skin coloring. In an 1855 issue of the school newspaper, *A Wreath of Cherokee Rose Buds*, girls complained in an editorial about the Townsend, Massachusetts, female seminary's paper, the *Lesbian Wreath*, which referred to the Cherokee girls as their "dusky sisters."[23] A popular practice of the Cherokee seminary's paper was to tell anecdotes and stories in which appearance, particularly blue eyes, featured prominently. For example, one story tells of the consequences that young "Kate M." faced after plagiarizing a poem for literature class. "Fun and abundance," student Lusette writes, "peeped from her blue eyes . . . and the crimson blush stole upon her cheeks." In the same issue, author Inez writes about what her schoolmates might be doing in four years. One student is described as a "fair, gay, blue-eyed girl," and another is a "fairylike creature with auburn hair." Still another story, by student Icy, entitled "Two Companions," pairs Hope ("the very personification of loveliness") with a "tiny, blue-eyed child" named Faith.[24] Evidently, to many seminary students, blue eyes were the epitome of enlightenment and civilization.

Unquestionably ethnocentric, the seminarians were convinced of their superiority over individuals of other tribes. After a group of Osage men visited the seminary in 1855, student Irene wrote a romantic essay not unlike those of white authors of the day about the "lofty, symmetrical forms, and proud, free step, of these sons of nature just from their wild hunting ground." She found their war dance amusing ("those tall, dusky forms stomping and stooping around . . . making a wailing sound"). In comparing her tribe and theirs, she pointed out that the Osages listened attentively to the seminarians singing "Over There" because, she figured, at least the "wild and untutored Savage has an ear for music as well as the cultivated and refined."[25]

Other essays in *Wreath of Cherokee Rose Buds* include anecdotes about "hostile Indians" attacking peaceful Cherokees in the "wild and unknown regions" on the way to the California goldfields and about "barbarous Camanches [*sic*]," living in their "wild wilderness." A student named Cherokee describes a Seneca Dog Dance in which the drum "made a very disagreeable noise. . . . What there was in such music to excite the Senecas' belles is more than I can imagine." Although she judged the dancers to be graceful, she believed they "ought to have been at something better."[26] Many of the girls came from slaveholding families, yet the issue of slavery was not mentioned in any issues of *Wreath of Cherokee Rose Buds* nor in any of the female students' or teachers' memoirs. (A male seminarian later referred to a black man as a "nigger.") Separation of the Cherokee and black races was a fact, however, and the children of black freedmen could only attend the "Negro High School."[27]

Yet, at the same time that the "upper class" Cherokees believed themselves to be elevated above the unenlightened members of their tribe and above other tribes as a whole, these same girls and teachers felt inferior to whites, despite the fact that many of them had more "white blood" than Cherokee.[28] They took every opportunity to flaunt their white ancestry. Female seminary superintendent and male seminary graduate Spencer Seago Stephens, for example, proclaimed in 1889 that "it is the white blood that has made us what we are. . . . [I]f missionaries wish to lift up Indian tribes . . . let them encourage intermarriage with whites." Unsure whether the Cherokees could obtain a high level of civilization by themselves, he asserted that "intermarriage will accomplish the purpose quickly."[29]

Commentary from Cherokee citizens who shared Stephens's belief in the productive influence of association with whites appeared in the *Cherokee Advocate.* Writer "Cherokee" observed that "the gloom that pervades the red man's mind is fast disappearing: instead of darkness and doubt, his countenance is being lit up with intelligence." To indicate that the traditionalists of the tribe were perhaps heathenish compared to their progressive peers, he further asserted that "those

3. Female seminarians on the school's front porch, 1897. Courtesy of University Archives, John Vaughan Library, Northeastern State University, Tahlequah, Oklahoma.

who cling with death-like tenacity to our old rites and ceremonies do not consider that a moral change is taking place in the [Cherokee] world."[30]

The attitude that the Cherokees needed a moral change was also illustrated in the *Sequoyah Memorial*, the newspaper of the Cherokee Male Seminary. One student wrote that "the bow and arrow have been laid aside" and that until the Cherokees reached the "summit of civilization and refinement," they could never be happy and contented.[31] Female seminary student Estelle stated, "O! that all, especially among the Cherokees could but learn the vast importance of a good education. This and this only will place us on equality with other enlightened and cultivated nations."[32]

Students were profoundly influenced by the comments of their chiefs. In 1877, at the annual May picnic celebrating the opening of the seminaries, acculturation advocate William Potter Ross expressed his fears that his tribe would be outdone by other tribes in Indian Territory: "While our neighboring Tribes and Nations are pressing forward in the pursuit of knowledge, let not the Cherokee . . . be second in the race." The last thing his tribe needed, he warned the seminarians, was "lazy and useless men" and "slouchy and slipshod women."[33] To make it clear that the Cherokees still had not reached that summit of equality with whites by 1884, Chief Dennis Bushyhead earnestly spoke of the importance of praying at the same altar with "our whiter and stronger brothers [giving] our common

4. Female and male seminary dance club members performing in blackface, 1896. This skit was titled "De Dabatin' Club." Courtesy of University Archives, John Vaughan Library, Northeastern State University, Tahlequah, Oklahoma.

thanks to God . . . [that they] will show magnanimity and justice to their weaker brethren."[34]

Students also took pleasure in comparing the old Cherokee ways with the new and improved lifestyles of the tribe to show that many tribal members had progressed past savagery and were on their way to equality with whites. In an 1854 issue of the *Cherokee Rose Buds*, student Edith championed the virtues of nineteenth-century white society and boasted of the progress the Cherokees had made: "Instead of the rudely constructed wigwams of our forefathers which stood there [in the Park Hill area] not more than half-a-century ago, elegant white buildings are seen. Everything around denotes taste, refinement, and progress of civilization among our people."[35]

The prolific Na-Li collaborated with another student in 1855 to illustrate their uneducated ancestors' backwardness and, more importantly, to emphasize the vast improvements the tribe had made. In scene one of the essay "Two Scenes in Indian Land," Na-Li describes a "wild and desolate" estate of a Cherokee family, composed of "whooping, swarthy-looking boys" and plaited-haired women, all of whom "bear a striking resemblance to their rude and uncivilized hut." She concludes that the poor imbeciles "pass the days of their wild, passive, uninteresting life without any intellectual pleasure or enjoyment," except, she adds, to attend the Green Corn Dance, a "kind of religious festival."[36]

Scene two, by author Fanny, paints a completely different picture of Cherokee life. In her commentary, even the environment around the family's home has magically blossomed from the influence of the missionaries. "Civilization and nature are here united," she expounds. "Flowers, music, and even better, the Holy Word of God is here to study, showing that religion has shed its pure light over all." The Indian lad, "in place of his bow and arrow, is now taught to use the pen and wield the powers of eloquence." The girl, "instead of keeping time with the rattling of the terrapin shells [around her ankles], now keeps time with the chalk as her fingers fly nimbly over the blackboard." Fanny then professes her hope that "we may advance, never faltering until all the clouds of ignorance and superstition, and wickedness flee from before the rays of the Suns of Knowledge and Righteousness."[37] In these tales, then, there was the possibility that the "wild Cherokee Indian" could be changed and become a new person. The seminarians were not shy in vocalizing their hope that their unsophisticated peers would do the same.

The seminarians hoped to accomplish their goal of enlightening other Cherokees about the merits of white civilization by having their newspapers distributed throughout the Cherokee Nation. Even if they could not understand the English language, Cherokees could read the students' commentaries because the papers were printed in both English and Cherokee. Students spread the word personally when the seminary opened for "public inspection" several times a year. Students also frequently paraded into Tahlequah to mingle with Cherokee citizens in the shops and churches, and they regularly attended Sons of Temperance meetings. Every May during graduation ceremonies, the Cherokee Female Seminary hosted an elaborate anniversary celebration to commemorate the opening of the school; hundreds of Cherokees (and members of other tribes) attended and witnessed the product of seminary training.

The female seminarians had no problem in using their femininity as a lever to attract attention. As far as they were concerned: "What more admirable than the noble form, erect in God-like majesty, or the more perfect gracefulness of woman? The blushing smiles that play upon the rosy cheek, the silken hair falling luxuriantly over the shoulders, the sparkling eye;—these are all lovely and call forth many a word of praise."[38]

Colonialism had a distinct impact upon women's roles, as I discuss in chapter 6, and the Cherokees were indeed affected. Traditional

Cherokee women's roles became less important as white men began to influence the Cherokees' social and religious values. Although many Cherokee women were expected to adopt Victorian social skills, that did not mean they all accepted their subservient roles. The seminary girls discussed marriage among themselves and in the newspaper once posed the question "The State of Matrimony: Is It a Free State or a Slave State?"[39] They did not, however, answer the question, perhaps out of fear that they would insult the male administrators. Little is known about what happed to most of the seminarians after they left the school, but I have ascertained that some of the seminarians dropped out of school, married, and stayed housewives their entire lives. Others married and worked outside the home, while a handful did not marry at all and concentrated on careers.[40]

Although the Cherokee seminarians often came across as smug and self-righteous, other newspaper passages reflect the students' feelings of inferiority to whites. The same issue of *Cherokee Rose Buds* that discusses the "elegance and civilization" of the Cherokee Nation also compares the tribe unfavorably with the eastern United States by stating that the new bride of Chief John Ross, Mary Stapler, admirably left her more civilized surroundings in Philadelphia in order to "dwell with him in his wild prairie home."[41] Another editorial, commenting on the completed 1855 spring term, declares, "We present you again with a collection of Rosebuds, gathered from our Seminary garden. If, on examining them, you chance to find a withered or dwarfish bud, please pass it by. . . . We hope for lenient judgment, when our efforts are compared with those of our white sisters." In the same issue, "Exchanges" acknowledges the newspapers received from other girls' schools in New England but notes that the Cherokee seminarians did not send copies of *Rose Buds* in return, because "we feel ourselves entirely too feeble to make any adequate recompense. . . . We are simply Cherokee school girls."[42]

In light of the reverence that progressive tribal members felt for the Cherokee Female Seminary and considering the reason for its establishment, it is little wonder that the 212 girls who graduated from the seminary and, to a lesser extent, those who did not graduate but used their seminary education to obtain degrees from other institutions were considered the créme de la créme of the Cherokee Nation.[43] That narrow-minded attitude ignores the more than 2,770 girls who did not attend the female seminary or graduate from any other school.[44] Granted, many girls left the seminary before they had completed their first semester, and some left after only one week. But their early departures do not necessarily indicate an inability to handle the workload or the social atmosphere of the school.

Some dropouts had problems with the course of study, but not all of them had been unable to master the difficult subjects. According to the student grade lists from 1876 to 1903, most were able to cope with the Mount Holyoke–style curriculum.[45] Prior to their enrollment in the female seminary, many of the pupils had attended the Cherokee common schools, the Cherokee Orphan Asylum, or one of the missionary schools or other high schools outside the Cherokee Nation and had reasonably good educational backgrounds.[46] In addition, many mixed-blood parents hired private tutors if their daughters had difficulty with their studies or if the common school teachers were incompetent.

The graduates, of course, made high grades (80s to 90s) throughout their careers at the seminary. Most of those who graduated were from comparatively affluent families, which enabled them to visit their homes more often than poorer students from remote areas.[47] Many of the graduates attended the school at the same time as their relatives, which helped to alleviate homesickness.[48] And, like successful students today, the girls who performed best received encouragement from their parents. Of the parents whose records could be examined, graduates' fathers had a 98 percent literacy rate and their mothers 100 percent, compared to the 82 percent and 86 percent literacy rates of the non-graduates' fathers and mothers, respectively. Most of the full-bloods' parents could not write in English, and just 69 percent of their fathers and 55 percent of their mothers could read.[49] Only two of the graduates were full-bloods, and they had been adopted by white and mixed-blood parents and were educated in mission schools prior to seminary enrollment.[50]

Most of those who dropped out after one semester still made medium to high grades (70s to 90s). These dropouts usually left because of personal or family illness, an impending marriage, or homesickness. Other factors, such as the seminary's closure in 1856, the destructive fire in 1887, the departure of Principal Wilson in 1901, and the creation of Northeastern State Normal School in 1909, caused students to enroll in other schools. In 1893, several girls voluntarily went home because of the crowded living conditions. In 1902, because of the increased prosperity of the nation's farmers and the need for a "large force" to harvest crops, many students returned to the farm to do "home work."[51] A large number of these dropouts (except those who married immediately) enrolled in and graduated from other institutions.

Dropouts who had made low grades (50 or below) were in the minority. These students often left soon after enrolling (within the first day or month). Most were traditional full-bloods or mixed-bloods of one-half to three-quarters Cherokee, who had attended distant Cherokee-speaking common schools and were not prepared for the difficult curriculum or the oppressive white atmosphere of the school.

Indeed, while some Cherokees did want to send their children to the school but could not afford to, some full-bloods opposed the seminaries and did not send their children to them even if they had the money. Prejudice against traditional Cherokees was the parents' main argument against the seminaries, but they also had doubts about the practicality of the schools' curricula. The seminaries met the expectations of the National Council, the teachers, and most of the Cherokee Nation's citizens, but some Cherokees protested that the academic curricula were not applicable to the needs of the students.

This attitude was expressed in a letter to the *Cherokee Advocate* in 1881, signed "Bood Guy." The writer stated, "What our youngsters ought to be . . . are farmers and stock raisers." He doubted that the students heard "the words 'farm' or 'farming' during the entire three or four years' course of instruction." Preferring practical training over academic courses, the writer asked, "What sense or good is there in preparing our youth for their [white] business?" He concluded that both seminaries were merely "pieces of imitation, with the high schools of the United States for models," and therefore served no practical purpose in a nation composed mainly of farmers. The education that the students received, he believed, "ought to conform to, and fit them for, what they expect to become."[52] In 1880, out of a population of approximately 25,438 Cherokees, 3,550 were farmers, 135 were mechanics, and 82 were teachers.[53]

The debate over educational priorities had begun as early as 1823, when Chief John Ross and Second Principal Chief Charles Hicks disagreed over the type of "national academy" the tribe should establish. Ross advocated the traditional, New England–style school, while Hicks championed what he believed was the most practical education for tribal members, a vocational school.[54] The council disregarded Hicks's suggestion, and thirty-three years later Indian Agent W. A. Duncan reported that the seminaries still "were only producing intellectuals. . . . [but] not everyone can become a professional . . . [or] live here without manual labor."[55] Because of pressure from tribal members who wanted vocational training to be available, the National Council gave the Board of Education permission to declare the boarding schools "industrial or manual labor boarding schools."[56]

Within the next few years, Principal Chiefs Dennis Bushyhead and Joel B. Mayes took a strong interest in the accomplishments of the seminaries. Bushyhead acknowledged the "gratifying results" of the seminaries' curricula, but in 1881 he advocated using more of the tax revenue for a mandatory "system of manual labor" for the primary-grade students (who were usually from poor, farming families) that would be "optionary" for upper grades. In the 1890s Chief Mayes tried to persuade the National Council to purchase Fort Gibson for use as an industrial school, but the council was not receptive to the idea, presumably because most of the councilmen's children attended the seminaries and had no intention of becoming farmers or laborers.[57]

The Department of the Interior's annual report for 1899 stated that instead of "being taught the domestic arts [girls] are given . . . Latin and mathematics while branches of domestic economy are neglected. The dignity of work receives no attention at their hands."[58] The seminary administrators yielded to the pressure, and by 1905 the school's "domestic science" department included lessons in cooking, cleaning (dusting and making their beds; a laundress washed their clothes), and sewing (usually to mend torn clothes; only a few girls became skilled seamstresses) and a modest agricultural program that featured botany, gardening, and flower arrangement.[59]

Many alumnae did become agriculturalists, but others had a profound interest in the whites' more lucrative businesses. Because many of their parents and siblings owned and operated stores in Tahlequah or other parts of the Cherokee Nation, the girls already had developed the confidence to pursue careers in the business world and were not afraid to interact with whites. In addition, many of the more progressive girls came from families that had hired help to perform domestic chores.

The girls who graduated were, as a whole, the most acculturated and affluent students at the seminary. After graduation they became educators, businesswomen, physicians, stock-raisers, and prominent social workers, among other professions. They also followed their mothers' examples and "married well." Of the 212 graduates, at least 189 eventually married. Most of them married white men or men who had a smaller amount of Cherokee blood than they had. In a few cases, the husbands had a greater degree of Indian blood, but in every such instance, they were either physicians, politicians, or members of prominent (usually wealthy) Cherokee families. Clearly, the more white blood the woman had, the more apt she was to marry a non-Cherokee, a tribal member with high social status, or a man who at least had the same degree of white blood that she possessed. Indicative of the latter were the 15 women who married graduates of the male seminary.[60]

Another interesting aspect is the value placed upon blood quantum as a source of identity. Many of the girls who went to the seminary had brothers and sisters who did not attend. In a comparison of the quantums of entire families, it is apparent that the women who married white men, or men with a lesser degree of Cherokee blood than they had, had tended during tribal enrollment to claim a lesser degree of Cherokee blood than their siblings, perhaps in an attempt to appear "whiter," while at the same time retaining their Cherokee identity. Many of these women's descendants today claim a Dawes Roll error and argue that their ancestors were much more Cherokee than they said they were. It appears that there is a modern movement among many Americans to find or inflate their Cherokee roots, a distinct contrast to many of the seminarians, who were more interested in their non-Indian backgrounds.[61]

Despite the differences of opinion between the traditional and the progressive Cherokees over education, and despite the school's class system, the Cherokee Female Seminary survived as a tribal institution for over five decades.[62] The hundreds of Cherokee girls who passed through its halls were profoundly influenced both positively and negatively by their experiences at the school.

The girls' seminary experiences helped to strengthen their identities as Cherokees, although there were differences in opinion as to what a Cherokee really was. At least 30 percent of the students were of one-sixteenth degree or less Cherokee blood, yet they still considered themselves to be Cherokees.[63] Many girls never even heard the Cherokee language. One student admitted years later, "I did not realize what my Indian heritage meant to me when I attended the Cherokee Female Seminary."[64] All she heard was the word *Cherokee*, and she assumed that all tribal members lived like the seminarians. But the full-bloods who were fluent in their native language and participated in tribal ceremonies also saw themselves as Cherokees, and their tenure at what they regarded as an oppressive school only strengthened their ties to their traditional families.

Despite its shortcomings, the Cherokee Female Seminary and its counterpart, the male seminary, were unquestionably the catalysts for the prosperity of many Cherokee women, men, and their families. That is why, for over a century, alumnae and their descendents have gathered together on the grounds of Northeastern State University to celebrate the seminaries and all that the schools meant to them. To those Cherokees, the old Cherokee Female Seminary building that now stands on the campus of Northeastern State University in Tahlequah remains a symbol of adaptation and progress in a changing, and often inhospitable, world. They were grateful to receive skills that enabled them to survive in white society. To others, the acculturation policies of the schools, intertribal racism, the social class system, and emphasis on Christianity disrupted their lives, and the schools remain symbols of that inhospitable world.

5. Members of the class of 1903, left to right: Leola "Lee" Ward Newton, Grace Wallace Richards, Caroline "Carrie" Freeman Baird, and Laura Effie Duckworth Boatright. All four were one-thirty-second Cherokee blood. Courtesy of University Archives, John Vaughan Library, Northeastern State University, Tahlequah, Oklahoma.

Not all tribal members subscribed to the school's philosophy, but a large portion of them did. Although there undoubtedly was prejudice against the traditional girls and these students were often devastated by their seminary experiences, full-bloods were at least exposed to the ways of white society, and the mixed-blood girls had the opportunity to interact for a short time with less acculturated tribal members.

The Cherokee Female Seminary is remembered for what it stood for: acculturation, assimilation, enlightenment, or survival, depending on the needs and values of the alumnae. The school was not meant for every female Cherokee; the seminary's atmosphere and attitude were white, and the progressive Cherokees were attempting to acculturate their peers. While the school contributed to a detrimental class system, it offered a strong educational background to those who went on to colleges and universities and was invaluable to the acculturated girls' success in business and in social circles within and outside of the Cherokee Nation.

Some modern Cherokees decry the establishment of the school and especially the attitudes of the progressives who placed themselves in a higher social and moral category than those less educated and less racially white. One Cherokee, a Keetoowah and former tribal registrar, commented that "the closing of the female seminary was the best thing that ever happened."[65]

Despite its shortcomings, the Cherokee Female Seminary was unquestionably the catalyst for the prosperity of many Cherokee women and their families and that is why, for over a century, alumnae and their descendents have gathered together on the grounds of Northeastern State University to celebrate the seminaries and all that the schools meant to them. To many Cherokees, the old Cherokee Female Seminary building that now stands on the campus of Northeastern State University in Tahlequah remains a symbol of adaptation and progress in a changing, and often inhospitable, world. To others, it remains a symbol of that inhospitable world.

# 8

## Finding a Modern American
## Indigenous Female Identity

We can't know where we're going without knowing where we've been.
And right now, the "where we've been" is a fantasy. It's very detrimental
to us. How can we be mentally healthy when we don't have a clue of
where we came from? It's all fantasy. And I can't really blame our people.
Everybody's always so busy saying, "The white man did this to us," "The
white man did that to us," but we are living in the here and now. And we
need to look at what can we do now to be healthy. – Joyzelle Gingway
Godfrey, Teton/Yankton Dakota/Ottawa professor of Lakota Studies at
Lower Brule Reservation Community College

Some of the greatest stressors that Indigenous women face have to
do with their appearances and with not knowing their tribe's history
and culture and, therefore, their identities as Natives. Identity conflicts among Native females are critical and ongoing psychological
problems, especially for multi-heritage women.

Shortly after tribes' contact with Euro-Americans, a generation of
mixed-race Indians emerged. Some of these individuals still appeared
phenotypically Native and retained their cultural values. Others may
have adopted the ways of their non-Native parent (almost always
their father, initially) but appeared to be Native. Continued intermarriage with Euro-Americans and other mixed-bloods resulted in
multi-heritage women whose appearances and cultural adherences
were and are often indistinct.

Even if she is racially "full-blood," a Native woman still may
face cultural confusion and have several identities (individual, oc-
cupational, religious, social, etc.) that correspond to her allegiances
(family, tribe, community, state, country), and her identity constantly
develops in response to her social, political, and economic environments. Some mixed-heritage Native women believe that meshing
Native and non-Native social and cultural values is key to tribal and
personal survival and happiness. Other Natives with bifurcated back-

grounds are often confused about the culture to which they should adhere.

The journey to "self-discovery" can be particularly arduous for Native women who desire to understand their traditions so they can utilize that knowledge personally and politically to improve their tribes. As Paula Gunn Allen comments, a lack of understanding about who your mother is, that is, "your position and its attendant traditions, history, and place in the scheme of things, is failure to remember your significance, your reality, your right relationship to earth and society . . . is the same thing as being lost—isolated, abandoned, self-estranged and alienated from your own life."[1] Indeed, tribespeople express frustration that knowledge of their clans has disappeared; some who espouse a Native identity do not know to which clan they belong, and not even their grandparents can inform them. Lack of a positive identity or even a concrete identity can result in a variety of emotional and psychological problems for Natives, such as spousal and child abuse, turning to drugs and alcohol for anxiety relief, and ultimately, a lack of respect for tribal traditions that destroys cultures.

Allen also describes how knowledge of one's traditions can keep conflict to a minimum: "The Native American view, which highly values maintenance of traditional customs, values, and perspectives, might result in slower societal change and in quite a bit less social upheaval, but it has the advantage of providing a solid sense of identity and lowered levels of psychological and interpersonal conflict."[2]

Numerous Natives feel conflicted, as Allen describes, but fortunately some reach the point that Wilma Mankiller has found:

Feeling firmly rooted in my own sense of tribalism and my own culture keeps me strong and able to share with women no matter what their racial, cultural, or economic background. Because I feel very Cherokee and have a strong sense of self and history, I'm more able to interact with other tribes and women of other races. Now, at my home at Mankiller Flats, surrounded by my books, my art, my grandchildren, and the natural world, I realize that my journey has indeed brought me to the place where I was destined to be. As I sit by a winter fire or walk to the spring where my family has gone for generations or rest on the porch where the walkingsticks like to come to munch on redbud leaves, I often think about my past and the history of my people.[3]

As this essay discusses, it often takes Native women a lifetime of emotional wrestling to reach the same comfort level as Mankiller.

Most research on identity development focuses on African Americans (usually referred to as "black" in the literature), Asian Americans, Mexican Americans, or "biracial" peoples in general.[4] One of the most thoughtful efforts is the "life stages" paradigm for African Americans proposed by William Cross and extended by Thomas Parham, who used the term "cycles of Nigrescence" (meaning "the process of becoming Black").[5] Cross posits that as blacks respond to a variety of social events, pressures, and expectations they progress through a set of definable stages that lead to identity resolution. Indeed, blacks and American Indigenes are different peoples, and American Indigenes may be too complex to categorize according to identity formation and resolution. Because blacks and American Indigenes have a similar history of racial oppression, however, and it appears that for these groups, like Asian Americans, "oppression has a major impact on the identity formation of the oppressed," Cross and Parham's model is useful for discussing Native identity.[6]

If we substitute Natives for blacks and figure in social, economic, and political influences, in addition to considering female tribal roles and stereotypes, then it is possible to use the Nigrescence outline to consider logically—albeit briefly—the various elements that influence the identity choices of females who claim to be racially and/or ethnically Native. For comprehensive psychological studies of Native identity choice and development, it is, of course, advantageous to more comprehensively investigate the development of ethnic identity as studied by developmental psychologists.[7]

One assumption of this discussion is that Natives, like blacks, live in a white world. Historically they have, and presently still are, dealing with racism, stereotypes, and oppression. It is also necessary to expound upon sociologist Maria P. P. Root's assessment of biracial peoples, that "it is the marginal status imposed by society rather than the objective mixed race of biracial individuals which poses a severe stress to positive identity development."[8] First, when Root uses the term "society," she is referring to white society, but it is apparent that the standards, expectations, and prejudices of tribal societies have the same power to affect a Native's identity formation. Second, the self-image of Native people not of mixed races (usually referred to as "full-bloods") also is affected by white and Native societies' influences.

### Life Stages

As applied to blacks, those in Cross's first stage, *pre-encounter*, know they are black, but they give little thought to race issues. Some see their blackness as an imposition on their lives. Because of exposure to racial stereotypes and miseducation about their race, they may perceive blackness as negative, and some individuals may adopt a white "worldview"—that is, using white/mainstream standards to judge one's self and everyone else. An individual may devalue black culture (everything from their skin color and hair texture to African art and religion) and glorify white/mainstream culture.[9]

It is during the first part of Cross's second stage, *encounter*, that individuals experience a shocking event that jolts them into considering that the frame of reference for forming their identity is inadequate. Cross uses the examples of a black person being denied access to an exclusive non-black neighborhood because of her skin color, the death of Martin Luther King Jr., or time spent in prison—like Malcolm X— as catalysts for exploring the Black Power movement and listening to different opinions on life. The second part of the encounter stage is when the person decides to develop her black identity.[10]

The third stage, *immersion-emersion*, is marked by an intense interest in all that is black. Everything pertaining to "blackness" (hairstyles, clothing, mannerisms, speech) is enthusiastically incorporated into that person's life. She attends activist meetings, studies black history, and denigrates white and "less black" people, sometimes aggressively. Feelings of insecurity about her identity remain high, and she often will criticize anyone who resembles unattractive aspects of her old self.[11]

The fourth stage, *internalization*, is reached when the person attains a sense of inner security and self-confidence about her black identity. Defensiveness, stress, and anti-white behavior regress in favor of "ideological flexibility, psychological openness, and self-confidence." The person is at peace with herself and is able to express feelings of dissatisfaction about racism and inequality through constructive, nonviolent means.[12]

### The Cross Model and Indians

When I first read the Cross model it was easy to insert the names of Native acquaintances into the model and to see myself scattered throughout. As Cross explains, however, the stages are not always clear-cut and simplistic for blacks. Nor are they for Natives. Some individuals might remain at one level or hover between two or more stages simultaneously; some may arrive at one stage and then move back to a previous stage. Some Natives never feel the need to change or develop their identities at all, and they fit into the internalization stage all their lives. Cross's model presents an adequate outline to begin discussion of identity development for Native women, but numerous factors must be taken into consideration and most spur confusion.

First, tribes are not alike. They have different languages, religions, histories, and methods of dealing with non-Natives. Full-blood members also retain a notable degree of physiological distinctiveness. Even within a single tribe there may be subgroups of persons with value systems much different from others within the tribe. Some tribes with divergent groups retain a sense of solidarity without possessing cultural integrity. One example is the three thousand female Cherokee students I used as a cross-section of Cherokee society for my book *Cultivating the Rosebuds: The Education of Women at the Cherokee Female Seminary, 1851–1909.* I distinguished at least four distinct historic and modern cultural subgroups, from traditional (adhering almost completely to tradition and possessing large degrees of Native blood) to progressive (knowing almost nothing about their tribal culture and possessing mainly non-Native racial heritage); yet all proudly identified themselves as Cherokees.

Second, many tribes incorporate members with minimal biological heritage and no knowledge of tribal culture, giving the impression to some that all one needs in order to be Native is to prove that one has a distant Native ancestor. Some tribal members only pronounce themselves as "Indian" (or their preferred label) in certain circumstances, such as in the workplace, at tribal events, or within the family unit.

Third, many members of tribes phenotypically appear to be something other than Native. Fourth, many people with little or no knowledge of Natives want to identify and be identified as Native. Fifth, the historical time period of the person's life must be taken into account. In the year 2001, Natives are considerably more outspoken, populous, and accepted by non-Natives than they have been historically. Their physiologies, images among non-Natives, and individual and tribal socioeconomic situations are different, as are their "worldviews."[13] Sixth, even within a group, the personal needs, physiology, and environmental influences of each individual are different. Seventh, mixed-heritage people often must contend with psychological and social issues of more than one group, making them more complex than those people of one racial and cultural background.[14]

Finally, unlike modern whites (and blacks who are unaware of their African tribe[s]), who do not have the same history to point to, Native women traditionally played a primary role in their tribe's creation stories and, therefore, in the tribes' religious traditions. Historically, Native women also played important political and economic roles that ensured tribal survival. Modern Native women have strong role models and powerful sources of religious strength to draw on, often more so than males. Provided that a Native female has access to information about these social and political roles, she has some basis for formulating her identity.

Cross designed his model with the idea that blacks will become more so after progressing through the stages. In regard to Natives, I posit that (1) some Native women go through stages on their way to becoming like whites; (2) some white, black, and Hispanic individuals and mixed-heritage people of minimal Native heritage who desire to become Native also progress through stages in their quest for a Native identity; and (3) multi-heritage females, especially those who do not have knowledge of cultural mores and traditional female roles of the group they aspire to become a member of and/or do not physically resemble other members of that group, will have more difficulty in establishing a comfortable identity.[15]

## Indian Life Stages

### *Stage 1. Pre-encounter*
Cross writes that black individuals at the pre-encounter stage may identify with white culture or focus on aspects other than blackness (such as their job), denying their blackness in favor of being accepted as "just a human being."[16] Some Natives in the pre-encounter stage are well aware of themselves as Natives, yet they know little about their tribal history and culture, much less anything about other Natives or about the political, economic, and social state of tribes in general. They do not necessarily identify with whites, although some do. Others see themselves as racially and culturally Native, but they also believe themselves to be inferior to whites and at fault for their economic, social, and/or political conditions. Of course, many Natives have no feelings of inferiority. They are fulfilled, satisfied with their place in the world, and never seek an identity change.

The home environment and cultural orientation of their parents are where children first learn values and begin to form their identities.[17] As Pawnee/Otoe-Missouria writer Anna Lee Walters expresses it, "Family is very important—we are always conscious of family relationships. Family make us what we are. They give us our cultural and tribal identity."[18] It is during adolescence that children's developmental process becomes more complex, and they strive to create an identity while at the same time attempting to conform to the norms of peer groups.[19] Neighbors' ethnicities and attitudes, radio, movies, and literature also affect children's worldview. Studies of television's effects on children reveal that what children watch "becomes their reality."[20] The parents may be full-blood or mixed-blood, or one may be white and one Native—full or mixed—and they possess a variety of values that affect their children, as in one of the following modern scenarios:

1. The parents may possess only a white worldview and be Natives

by merit of blood, not by cultural connection. These individuals may be of minimal Native blood and know they are Native because of "family legend" (often without proof of tribal membership) or because their ancestors are indeed listed on tribal rolls. Throughout their childhood, the children often hear that they are Native, but they are not taught any details about tribal life. Because of their possible connection to Natives they often romanticize Native culture as monolithic and inherently good (one with nature, etc.), but they know nothing of tribal politics, health statistics, poverty levels, or other realities of daily tribal life. The children are essentially white in every way, including in appearance. If they do pursue their Indianness, it is usually during adulthood.[21]

2. The parents may be white with no knowledge of Natives while the children are adopted Natives. Even if the parents teach the children about Natives it is often a superficial attempt, and the children desire to find out about their heritage as they grow older. The children are taught to live as whites, but they will know at an early age that they look different from their parents and neighbors.

3. The parents may possess an understanding of their tribal culture and of the white world because they are forced to interact in mainstream society. For example, during the relocation period (1950s) some Natives moved to large cities and found themselves isolated from other Natives. They either learned about white society, remained frustrated in a foreign environment, or moved back home.[22]

Wilma Mankiller, former chief of the Western Cherokee Nation, for example, was initially confused in the foreign city environment:

It seemed the only option available to us, so we went into the [relocation] program. We moved from a rural, isolated and insulated community to an urban, ghetto area. It was frightening and a difficult period of adjustment for us. We were put into a hotel. Our first experience of urban life was watching an elevator open up and swallow people. They'd disappear into a wall, and God knows where they'd go. . . . It was culture we didn't know anything about: roller skates, bicycles, and telephones.[23]

The noises of the city, especially at night, were bewildering. We had left behind the sounds of roosters, dogs, coyotes, bobcats, owls, crickets, and other animals moving through the woods. We knew the sounds of nature. Now we heard traffic and other noises that were foreign.[24]

In regard to the relocation program, Mankiller believes that "It simply doesn't work . . . with people who are interested in retaining their own sense of identity and culture."[25]

More currently, in Flagstaff, Arizona, because of the Navajo-Hopi land issue numerous Navajos have moved from their reservation homes to urban areas next to non-Natives. Although they attempt to retain traditions, they must learn about and interact with white society to survive. These individuals may be surprised at the level of racism toward Natives, but because of their traditional family values and extended family on the reservation most remain confident about their Native identity. Many of the children become acquainted with the values of non-Native society while attending white schools and playing with white children. Some grow judgmental against their tribespeople and question the value of their tribal culture.

Others maybe come confused by what they learn in boarding schools. For example, Edna Manitowab, an Ojibwa, grew up on a small Canadian reserve; she was aware of her tribal culture through family and friends and was satisfied with her identity until she was sent to a Catholic "residential school" at age six:

Living on the reserve I had naturally thought that all people were the same and spoke the same language. I did not know that I was an "Indian" and that there were a lot of important people in the world that were "white." I stayed there for four years and I don't think that I ever stopped being scared and lonely. I was scared of being caught speaking Indian, scared because I didn't understand the English of the teachers and could not follow the lessons. . . . I remember when I went home the first summer I would insist on speaking English at home, although I know that my parents didn't understand it. I don't know exactly why I did it, but I have often felt guilty about it afterwards. Maybe it was that some of the values of the boarding school had rubbed off on me, and I felt superior to them because I spoke English and they didn't. I also think that I was still mad at them for having me sent away, and this was a kind of revenge. I never again felt close to my parents. I have often wondered what would have happened if they had refused to send me to school and taught me at home instead. I might have known them in an entirely different way, feeling more affectionate towards them and understanding them better.[26]

4. The parents possess both white and Indian blood, or one parent may be Native and the other non-Native, and they want the children to know about both cultures. The children may attend white schools and participate in tribal activities after school and on weekends, and they have access to their extended family. They may have a confusing childhood, especially if the child appears phenotypically Native, has one white parent, and lives in a predominantly white community.

For example, a nontraditional Navajo woman who is married to a white man and lives in Flagstaff recounts that their mixed-heritage son used to tell people he was Italian, and because he attended a primarily white school told his parents that he wished he was white. Another Navajo woman married to a white man (who lived on the reservation until recently), however, comments in regard to their children's concerns over their appearances and mixed lineage, "It hasn't been any kind of problem." The mother of the former "separated from the reservation to find a better life" and urged her daughter to do the same, while the latter's family strongly supported her living on the reservation.[27]

Children can also become confused if they have a white mother and a Native father but the mother succumbs to the "white mother martyr syndrome" and tells her children that they are Native, not of mixed-heritage, even though the children can clearly see the truth. The children not only become resentful of not being allowed to be a part of their mother's heritage, but they can also come to believe that they are not good enough to be part white.[28]

Root also surmises that many multi-heritage people will encounter discrimination within their family from the group with higher social status.[29] The group of higher status, however, is not always white. Mary Brave Bird, for example, recounts how she felt growing up: "I have white blood in me. Often I have wished to be able to purge it out of me. One day I told my mother, 'I'm gonna grow up to be an Indian!' She did not like it. She was upset because she was a Catholic and was having me brought up in her faith. . . . I was then white outside and red inside, just the opposite of an apple."[30]

If a portion of the multi-heritage child's family is composed of a socially dominant racial group, then the child may perceive that race as the superior one, especially if racist remarks and jokes are made about the other racial group. For example, multi-heritage children with a white mother and Native father who are never allowed to visit their father's family may begin to believe that their white blood is superior to Native blood. Conversely, if the children were to spend that time with their father's Native relatives, they might hear enough negative comments about whites to believe that their white blood is inferior. This scenario could also be true of full-blood, multi-cultural Native children whose parents are representatives of two (or more) different tribes. Another cause for confusion is when the extended family refuses to accept an interracial marriage and will not visit a son or daughter who married outside the group. Children are, however, less likely to become upset and confused by their mixed ancestry if both parents and the extended families have pride in themselves and their cultures and if both have equal social status within the family unit.[31]

5. The parents may be bicultural. They often live in urban communities, sometimes a long distance from their tribal communities. They live like whites during the week, when they work and socialize with non-Natives, and they resemble Natives on weekends or other times when they attend powwows, sun dances, tribal activities, or

other Native social and familial functions. They are comfortable with the bicultural lifestyle. The children have extended family members they can turn to for information about their heritage. This family will look phenotypically like Natives, some of mixed heritage.[32]

Numerous Native women I worked with while serving on the board of directors of the American Indian Center of Dallas in the mid-1980s were businesswomen, educators, or housewives and on the weekends participated in ceremonies of various kinds, brainstormed about tribal or center business, or attended the principal "Native activity" in Texas: powwows. With the exception of two full-bloods, we all were of mixed heritage with extended family living in Oklahoma.

6. One or both parents may be racially Native, repress Native values in the home, and refuse to impart tribal knowledge to their children. Some parents may try to de-emphasize Native culture either because they think that white culture is superior to Native cultures or because they believe that by learning only the ways of white society their children can succeed socially and economically.

A Native's rejection of Native culture does not necessarily mean "self-hatred" (discussed in chap. 6). As Cross discusses, despite the reality that we live in a complex, pluralistic society, most white children usually "see the world in monoracial terms" and perceive no need to learn how to interact with other racial and cultural groups.[33] Because of their oppression or need to compete in the white world, many black children are taught to be biculturally competent. Similarly, many Native parents who appear to reject Native culture do not want their children to become white. They want them to have equal access to the socioeconomic privileges that whites have.

7. Children with parents who possess a Native worldview exclusively are likely to live on a reservation or in an area inhabited by other Natives with traditional values. The family is mainly exposed to other Natives and their tribal cultures. The children are similar to those in example 2 in that they may become alarmed at the racism they encounter if they leave the home environment. Wilma Mankiller recalls the strange way she was treated while attending boarding school at Daly City, California, when she was in grade school: "I was uncomfortable. I felt stigmatized. I continually found myself alienated from the other students, who mostly treated me as though I had come from outer space. I was insecure, and the least little remark or glance would leave me mortified."[34]

Some of the children may be similar to those who discover desirable aspects of white culture and begin to question the value of their traditional tribal culture. The same can be said of some Native children who enroll in university away from their home environment, in addition to those who were forced to attend federal boarding schools in the 1800s. These children may have "gone along" with school policy but retained their identity, adopted some white ways and afterward were rejected by their family and tribe, or adopted white ways and were rejected by both societies. Some became distraught and committed suicide.

8. The biological and cultural Native family may live on the reservation or in an urban area in poverty. One or both parents and some extended family may be uneducated alcoholics in poor physical and mental health. This family identifies as Native, but they see little hope for advancement, so they do not try.

Some children on reservations have resorted to joining gangs in hopes of finding a "family" that will accept and support them, even if the gang does not focus on tribal values. "This is the way we grew up," says one young Navajo member of the Insane Cobra Nation gang. "We didn't grow up with traditional values and all that. If we did, then maybe we would be different people. But I am not in control of how we grew up and what we were born into." He also says that now that he has a taste of what that violent lifestyle is like, he is ready to receive an education so he can return to his community and teach his children the tribal traditions.[35]

9. The family members look phenotypically black and possess Native blood. Even if they desire to pursue a Native identity their appearances alert others to the reality that they are part black. Depending on the attitudes of the neighborhood and nearby tribes, the people who look black will most likely be viewed as black.

In late 1998, a member of the Navajo tribe took issue with that year's Miss Navajo, who was part black. The writer stated in the newspaper *Indian Country Today* that "Language, weaving, beading, and being able to dance is all culturally correct, but nonetheless, it is still learned behavior. . . . when the Navajo people select a person to represent their nation as Miss Navajo, that person must possess the appearance and physical characteristics of the Navajo. Miss Cody's appearance and physical characteristics are black, and thus are representative of another race of people."[36] For this Navajo, cultural adherence is not necessarily a prerequisite for tribal admission, nor does he believe that black "blood," or at least the appearance of black blood, can be integrated into his tribe.

10. Historically, Natives were comfortable with their identities and tribal settings. Upon contact with Euro-Americans, Natives necessarily reacted in a variety of ways: they became convinced that their tribal culture was inferior and attempted to adopt the ways of the newcomers (going to school, dressing like whites, becoming Chris-

tians, etc.); they attempted to adopt the ways of the newcomers but also attempted to keep their Native identity; they realized their tribal life was crumbling and searched to recover traditions through revitalization movements instigated by tribal prophets; and they fought and either died or were removed to reservations.

There are other examples, of course, but regardless of the home arrangement the individual will in large measure adopt the values and identities that are prevalent in the household. According to Parham, it is during late adolescence/early adulthood that children begin to locate their place in the social environment. Natives, like blacks, realize that they are at once "a part of, yet apart from" American society.[37] Not every Native, however, becomes aware of this.

Individuals who are mixed Native and white, are Caucasian in appearance, and were not taught any aspects of Native culture may experience no or only minimal negative feelings about being Native because they do not perceive themselves as Native and neither does anyone else. They can "pass" as white and can "stay white" if they so choose. C. Matthew Snipp's analysis of the 1980 census reveals that the majority of persons who claimed Indian *ancestry* did not claim to be of the Indian *race* and are termed "Americans of Indian descent." Most of these individuals are no different from other whites except that they have a Native ancestor in their family tree. Snipp proposes that socioeconomic factors account for the choices evidenced in the census. Many people, such as New Agers and writers, become Native only when it is economically profitable and socially desirable to be a Native.[38]

In addition to their home values, children are influenced by teachers, television, radio, books, sports mascots, and the reactions of people on the street. Seemingly positive comments directed toward mixed-heritage children may cause them to realize that they are different. For example, at around the age of three children become aware of skin, hair, and eye color.[39] Children also becomes aware that their "ethnic" name sounds unlike other children's names. Harold R. Isaacs notes that "names are essentially group names too. Family surnames carry with them all the associations of the language and tradition from which they come. . . . the uttering of the name itself can and does serve as an instant signal for behavior based on group affiliation, producing its almost automatic response, open or closed, welcoming or rebuffing, including or excluding. . . . It is in effect the functional equivalent of skin-bleaching or hair-straightening by blacks or double-lid operations by Japanese women. The purpose is to be more 'like' those more favored, to a gain a more comfortable anonymity by sharing, at least in name, the identity of the dominant group."[40]

Root posits that it is when children encounter negative experiences at an older age that their identity conflicts—including aspects such as names—will arise.[41] Ruth G. McRoy and Edith Freeman write that if adolescents cannot resolve their mixed-heritage backgrounds by receiving support from family and peers so that their identity is acceptable to them and others, then they will not complete this developmental stage and will likely engage in neurotic behavior.[42]

### Stage 2. Encounter

Cross explains that after a black individual encounters a negative or positive event she may be jolted into reevaluating her place in the world.[43] In regard to Natives, a person may hear a moving speech about Indigenous history and culture that makes her want to know more about her tribal history. This is an encounter because the person had previously heard only a negative version of her history and is enthused enough by the new version to embark upon a quest to discover the truth. Individuals who have an "Indian encounter" have three basic goals and may focus on any or all aspects of identity (appearance, cultural traditions, kinship, etc.) in aiming for these goals.

### Goal 1. Becoming an Indian

Appearance may be one of the first catalysts for exploring identity possibilities. If a Native child is adopted by white parents, the child wonders at an early age why she appears different from the parents. If the parents attempt to keep the child from exploring her Native heritage the child will become curious as to why the parents feel Indianness is "bad" when other people may say the opposite. The adopted child's jolt may be a discovery of her tribe. Some white parents may attempt to educate the adopted child about her Native heritage, but if they know nothing about Natives they may take her to general events such as powwows and movies dealing with Natives and read her books with Native characters. The lack of depth in any of these activities usually proves to be unsatisfactory to the child. The parents may attempt to involve their adopted child in specific tribal functions, but usually this does not happen as most white parents keep their Native children away from their true origins out of fear that they may be taken away from them. In a few instances the white adoptive parents and their adoptive Native child have good relations with the child's Native families, thus providing the child with an outlet for obtaining information.

For a lot of adopted Native children, however, their lack of kin relations and knowledge of tribal culture remind them that they are marginally Native and their distinctive Native appearance disallows them from becoming white. Although they are Natives by race, they remain culturally unsatisfied. Unfortunately, they illustrate Michael R. Green's thesis on loss of culture: "Deculturalization can lead to severe psychological disorientation, such as dissolution of the self, a sense of meaninglessness, aimlessness, and depression. This creates a painful situation, which the individual then may attempt to escape by the use of alcohol or drugs or by selfstupefication through plea-sures."[44]

Some children who were raised in households that did not impart values of Native culture but are linked to a tribe because of blood might hear positive facts about Natives at school and become increas-ingly interested in meeting their extended family. Often such people will explore archives to find relatives listed on tribal rolls and will enroll themselves if they have not been enrolled already.

White adults who have "always been interested in Indians" and become disillusioned with other white people are jolted when they hear a Native speak because they identify with put-upon peoples. Or perhaps they feel guilt for what has been done to Indians. They may especially admire radicals who garner attention through their flamboyant actions and rhetoric. These people adopt a "mixed-blood" Native identity because that claim is usually easier to defend than a full-blood one (although many will claim a full-blood Native grand-mother).

After attending a "sweat lodge ceremony" conducted by white people, a white person may discover that it can be profitable to impart the teachings of Native religions to others, so she will embark on a journey "on the red road" to gather information. The "white shaman" will retain her knowledge of white ways, especially marketing and accounting. After assessing the preponderance of ethnic fraud in the United States, I propose that the majority of wannabees have assessed the economic possibilities of becoming a member of the group and have formulated a new identity for monetary reasons. Therefore, a person claiming Indianness may be perceived as trying to fit in to get a job, to gain prestige, to write a book with an "authoritative voice," or to gain notoriety and fame as a "medicine person." Some wannabees, however, do not necessarily desire money, they desire the attention they will receive as a Native that perhaps they do not receive as a non-Native. Still others can be seen in archives across the country attempting to locate a Native ancestor on tribal rolls so that they can receive whatever moneys they believe Natives have coming to them each month.[45]

Natives are not seen with the same prejudices in all parts of the country. Among affluent suburbanites in some cities a person who looks white but claims to be part Native may garner the response, "That's so neat." Being "part Indian" but not really looking it affords a form of status among some Caucasian groups. Receiving kudos for one's racial claims can jolt the individual to garner more attention.

Herbert Gans describes a leisure-time form of ethnicity that some engage in as "symbolic identification" with their ethnic heritage when they are reminded of it. For example, some people claim to be Irish only on St. Patrick's Day, while others may "become Indian" when Natives are in the news and are the topic of public conversation. They become "ethnic" only when they want to.[46]

*Goal 2. Becoming More Indian/Rediscovering Indianness*
Some Native women may never have been aware of their history or culture. Some Natives move away from their tribal area, while others join a non-Native religious group or marry a non-Native or a Native person with little interest in Native culture and then loose their connection to their tribal cultures. They speak English exclusively and do not attend tribal ceremonies. Still others may retain a strong connection to their tribe but, in their estimation, not strong enough. Mary Brave Bird (Lakota), who grew up with her grandparents on the Rosebud Reservation in South Dakota, was surrounded by Lakota culture, but her grandmother was Catholic and "tried to raise us whites, because she thought that was the only way for us to get ahead and lead a satisfying life, but when it came to basics she was all Sioux, in spite of the pictures of Holy Mary and the Sacred Heart on the wall. Grandma had been to mission school and that had influenced her to abandon much of our traditional ways. She gave me love and a good home, but if I wanted to be an Indian I had to go elsewhere to learn how to become one."[47]

Numerous events may jar Natives who have lost touch with their heritage into becoming a Native or "rediscovering their Indianness." A Native person who heard negative comments about Indians all her life from television, radio, and teachers—while the family did nothing to correct the misinformation—may hear from an informed teacher that Natives have a rich and positive history and culture. These people become alert to the possibility that the negative view of themselves and their cultures is unfounded. Other Indians may attend a traditional marriage, puberty, or healing ceremony and be moved enough by the event to learn more about their religion and culture.

Cree musician Buffy Ste. Marie has discussed her "white-dipped" childhood: "In my case, a white-dipped childhood gave me enough suffocation to show me the difference between breath and death, between Indian sharing values and white gobbledy greed. Day after day, my white-dipped childhood stuck me with little needles, painful little needles piercing me in places where I should have known joy— my heart, my eyes, my womanplace, my sleep—giving me little doses of hate regularly, frequently, silently."[48]

A Native student in an anthropology class may hear the professor refer to Natives as "our" Indians. The student may visit an archive filled with skeletal remains and sacred cultural objects and become insulted, outraged, or even scared, and upon realizing that the professor is referring to her ancestors as "objects of study," the student may be stirred into political activism. Some Native students in the mid-1900s, such as those who attended the boarding school in the town called Spanish, in Ontario (who are described in Basil H. Johnston's *Indian School Days*), heard enough negative comments about their culture and religion that they responded by rebelling, thereby retaining their identity and self-respect.

A prison sentence might give the Native person the time and impetus to learn about other tribes and cultures with similar histories of oppression. The inmate may decide that an organized movement to improve conditions for oppressed peoples is in order and become determined to learn about her tribe and to fight for her people, as many of the original members of the American Indian Movement did.[49]

Native females who were cognizant of their Native heritage and wanted to know more about it or who were unaware of issues facing Native peoples often encountered activists who then inspired them to search for information about their culture and to become involved in the Red Power Movement (see chap. 9). For example, Dagmar Thorpe, the granddaughter of athlete Jim Thorpe and the daughter of activist Grace Thorpe, believes the takeover at Alcatraz was her "jolt": "My life as it is now began with the Alcatraz Island occupation in 1969. That was a real turning point for me. Until then I had pretty much lived in white suburbia. Although my grandfather is well known as a Native person, I was not exposed to Native thinking or ways of life until I was in my late teens."[50]

Wilma Mankiller recounts in her autobiography that she always felt connected to her Cherokee tribe, yet,

Whenever I do pause to reflect, I find that many of my hopes and aspirations were formed during those wonderfully sad and crazy years of the 1960s in San Francisco. Everything that was happening in the world at that time—Vietnam, peace demonstrations, the civil rights movement, and the seeds of the native-rights movement—had a lasting influence on me. Then something happened that gave me the focus I was searching for. It all started in November of 1969, when a group of Native Americans representing more than twenty tribes seized a deserted island in the midst of San Francisco's glittering bay. . . . They did this to remind the whites that the land was *ours* before it was *theirs*. . . . The name of the island is Alcatraz. It changed me forever.[51]

*Goal 3. Becoming Less Indian*
Not all Natives desire to find a Native identity. Some Natives have searched and still do search for an identity that is more white-oriented. Just as some non-Natives attempt to legitimatize their claims to Indianness by marrying a Native or some multi-racial Natives try to become more Native by marrying a Native darker in color and with cultural knowledge, some Natives may attempt to become less Native by marrying a white person or a Native with lighter coloring. Examples of the latter are graduates of the Cherokee Female Seminary who married either white men or Cherokee men with smaller amounts of Cherokee blood than they had (see chap. 7).

Not all women who marry outside their group wish to become non-Natives. One example is found in the *Arizona Daily Sun*'s special series "The Edge of the Rez," which focused on Native-white relations in the "bordertown" of Flagstaff. One Navajo woman who married a white man commented that "It's been really convenient for me. I did things that I would probably never have done if I were married to a Navajo. I followed him to school, pushed me to get my degrees. And I know for a lot of my friends I have who married Navajos, that hasn't been possible. I am a traditional Navajo. Navajo is my first language. I went to mission school and all that, and was baptized as a Catholic—but that was just when you were in school. But being Navajo is really my tradition. I tell my children, I tell students, you live by the values of your tradition." Another Navajo woman, the only one of ten siblings to marry an Anglo, said, "My mother and father raised me traditional. My mother doesn't speak any English and my father just a little. But when I was 20, I became a Christian. That helped my parents. They knew I had left the traditional way, so they weren't surprised when I married him."[52]

Frantz Fanon's remark about men of color and white women, that "I wish to be acknowledged not as black but as white. . . . who but a white woman can do this for me? By loving me she proves that I am worthy of white love. I am loved like a white man," could be a truism for some Native women who marry whites.[53] In his 1994 essay "From Dezba to 'John': The Changing Role of Navajo Women in Southeastern Utah," Robert McPherson describes an encounter with a Navajo woman who might be admitting just that: "Marrying into your tribe is like falling back down or a step down instead of going up. . . . It seems like things would never change for you in life. Marrying an Anglo, that would be a really a neat change, I think."[54]

### Identity Resolutions during the Encounter Stage

Root's series of identity "resolutions" for "biracial" peoples may be appropriate to include here because it is during Cross's encounter stage that the person considers what identities she can and cannot choose to pursue.[55] Acceptance of these resolutions depends on the social, political, economic, and environmental situations the person encounters. Therefore, the person may change resolutions more than once in a lifetime or may settle on two resolutions at once.

*Solution 1. Acceptance of the Identity Society Assigns*
Root posits that multi-heritage people who are part white, who do not appear to be Caucasian, and who are reared in "racially oppressive parts" of the United States will have little choice about their racial identity.[56] If a person looks black or Native she will be seen as black or Native regardless of whether she wants to identify as white. Root's supposition can also be taken to mean that those Native women who appear white or black may not be accepted as a Native among Native societies. The person does not have to live in "racially oppressive areas."

A problem with this resolution is that the person may feel comfortable with her chosen identity in one area of the country and may be perceived by others in another area as belonging to a different racial group. For example, a multi-heritage woman whose racial reference group is an Oklahoma tribe may be accepted as a Native in the Plains states. In the Southwest however, where Pueblos, Navajos, and other tribes have members with substantial blood quantums and distinctive Native appearances, that same woman may be viewed as "barely Indian" or as a non-Native. In fact, numerous members of tribes from outside the Southwest either attending or working at Northern Arizona University complain that "Navajos think if you're not Navajo then you're not an Indian."

Natives who are enrolled in tribes but look white often identify themselves as Caucasians in order to avoid racism. LaVera Rose explains in her thesis that many biracial Lakota women try to hide their Native racial heritage when they move to non-Native society because they perceive that non-Natives view all Natives as inferior to Euro-Americans.[57] Some black or mixed-heritage Indian-black individuals identify as Natives in an attempt to escape racism against blacks. As Brewton Berry describes the mind-set of many Nanticokes, Chickahominys, and Lumbees, "Most of them would doubtless prefer to be whites. But, since that goal is beyond their reach, they will settle for Native. It is better to be red than black—even an off-shade of red."[58]

*Solution 2. Identification with Two or More*
*Racial or Cultural Groups*
Root asserts this to be a positive resolution only if the person is able to retain her personality across groups and feels welcomed in both groups. This resolution may only be possible in parts of the United States where interracial marriages and mixed-blood children are tolerated.[59] The challenge for multi-heritage Natives wishing to "live in both worlds" is to construct strategies for coping with social resistance to their membership in both groups. A problem for many is that if they look Caucasian, black, or Asian or have little knowledge of tribal culture then they may not be accepted by the tribal community that they wish to be part of. This is especially true if they have inadequate background to enroll in "their tribe" and no kinship ties. Conversely, multi-heritage Native women who look phenotypically Native may not be considered as equals by whites.

Some multi-heritage individuals identify as simultaneously Native and non-Native, are accepted by all sides of their family and tribe, and, because of strong familial connections to all parts of their heritage, feel secure in themselves. These people resemble Malcolm McFee's proposed "150 Percent Man" in that they are able to absorb and use both "new" and "old" ways.[60] Few, however, are able to meet the "membership" demands required by both groups. Instead, they are recognized as "multi-heritage" and not purely of one group or the other. A critical issue for Native females who live in both worlds is to find ways to meet the demands in one environment without losing the other identity.

Numerous Natives acknowledge the stress of "living in two worlds." Florence Jones, the last Wintu doctor, has spoken of her tortured childhood after she returned from government school in San Francisco: "What happened to me, I came home when I was seventeen years old. I didn't feel good. I felt like I was in two worlds and something was pulling me from each side. I almost went insane. From my religion and the white religion, they were pulling me apart."[61]

Navajo poet and educator Ester G. Belin expressed concern about the options open to young Navajos and about how many of them become confused: "My English voice and Western thoughts rival the small Navajo vocabulary in my head. TV and other media open a new dimension of crossblood simulation. Rerouting tribal identity with capitalist influences. Every little kid I worked with knew who Michael Jordan and Shaquille O'Neal were and how much money they made. Very few knew the name of our tribal president. In my generation and before, access to outside influences was not as disarming. Urban streethood appeals as much to rez kids as do traditional ceremonies. Our nationhood competes with itself."[62]

Many Natives who are able to pass as both Native and white use their appearance and social knowledge to their advantage. Root defines one form of identification as "tokenism"—a process by which a person's ambiguous appearance and cultural background allow that person to be hired to fill a minority quota because she is seen as less threatening than a full-blood.[63] While Root asserts that the hiring agency assigns the identity for the person, often persons of ambiguous appearance will seek employment at an institution that desires an individual of the race those persons want to be. The hire validates their identity desires and gives them a title they can record on their resume for the future, such as Director of American Indian Programs. These people often claim Indianness as their "articulated identity," defined by Teresa Kay Williams as the identity "one calls oneself publicly. It may or may not be in concert with one's intuitive or experiential identity."[64] Or, as Hachivi Edgar Heap of Birds, a Cheyenne-Arapaho artist and educator, explains it, these people "don't want to be Native; they want to remain themselves while pretending to be Native."[65]

Frederick Elkin reminds us that ethnicity is not "an ascribed characteristic." Often females with only a modicum of Native blood and little or no connection to their tribe utilize their Native heritage for gain, "perhaps from fellow ethnic group members, perhaps from others."[66] Non-Natives, like some bogus "spiritual leaders," may espouse a Native heritage in order to achieve financial gain; some non-Native academics receive scholarships and positions at universities and publish under the auspices of being Native.

Further, entire ethnic groups may express their "collective identity" to achieve ends in the larger society. A tribe surely does, but on a smaller level, so do Native groups such as school clubs, community organizations such as American Indian centers, and religious groups such as the Native American Church or fraudulent Native "religious" organizations.

*Solution 3. Identification as a New Racial Group*
Although the U.S. government allowed citizens to identify themselves as multi-heritage by marking more than one racial or ethnic category on the most recent census, many mixed-heritage people identify themselves as a "new race," such as the Hapa Haole in Hawaii and the Métis in Canada, or as "multi-heritage," "multi-racial," or "biracial" so they will not have to choose a specific race or culture.[67]

Many multi-heritage Natives prefer this type of classification either because they know little or nothing about their racial heritages or because they cannot decide which one to designate as the primary racial reference group. The option to choose more than one race has incurred debate among those who believe that people should make a decision about their racial choice; they argue that not choosing one's obvious heritage (i.e., because one looks black one is black, as in the case of Tiger Woods) is a denial of self. Others argue that choosing the mixed category or choosing a race other than "black"—if one is indeed part black—will decrease the number of blacks in the country.[68]

*Solution 4. Identification with a Single Racial or Cultural Group*
This resolution is different from solution 1 because the person actively seeks identification with one group regardless of what society thinks, of her siblings' choice, or of whether she physically looks like other members of that group. This resolution is positive if the person is accepted by the selected group, does not feel marginal to the group, and does not deny other aspects of her heritage.[69]

Numerous complicated and interwoven factors influence a person to decide what identity she can realistically pursue. For example, since contact, American Indigenes have been romanticized, reviled, admired, feared, and hated by Euro-Americans. These Euro-American views of Natives and the negative and positive images of Natives that have become a part of American culture continue to exert powerful effects on the self-image of Native people.[70]

The status of the racial reference group often determines whether an individual wants to remain a member of that group. Natives and blacks historically (and often presently) were not treated as equals by Euro-Americans. By 1900 white Americans believed Natives to be "vanishing red men," doomed to disappear as a separate ethnic group. Many Natives subscribed to this ideology and attempted to blend into the dominant society. For example, Caucasian-looking Native women among the Cherokees often lived apart from their tribe, some as far away as Hawaii. These women had "passed" from one race to another, finding more advantages from living in the white world than in the Native world.[71] Their appearance allowed them that option. Not all who opt for a designation besides "Indian" choose to identify as white, however. Native students in the Dallas, Texas, school district often are negatively stereotyped and ridiculed, so many refer to themselves as Hispanic instead. "If they know they are American Indians and they are embarrassed by classmates," says Choctaw Peggy Larney, director of the American Indian Education Program, "they don't want to be identified. If they are half Hispanic and half Indian, they go with Hispanic so they won't be made fun of."[72]

Natives hear and see negative stereotypes that indicate Natives are inferior to whites. Television, movies, cartoons, books, and teachers contribute to the stereotyping of Natives as heathens, savages, ignorant, and lazy. Children learn from juvenile literature that Natives are much like animals: primal, simple, and stupid. On television everyday are classic Westerns that portray Natives as violent antagonists who were impediments to western civilization, and sports teams such as the Washington Redskins and the Atlanta Braves feature mascots that are warlike and ugly. Elma Wilkie, a Turtle Mountain Ojibway Metis, expressed concern about what is taught in schools: "Our children, when they start to wonder about themselves, spend a lot of time looking in the mirror, searching for their identity. This is about the time they start to believe about dirty Indians and scalping savages, pagans and shortly after this so many drop out of school, and the rate of dropout is so high no one likes to talk about it."[73]

Some stereotypes appear complimentary but are actually damaging. Disney's *Pocahontas*, for example, portrays the title character as a woman who wears minimal clothing, sings with animals, and is shaped like Barbie. The film angers many Native women, who argue that the character's unrealistic body image contributes to feelings of inferiority among Native girls.[74]

The two most prevalent images of Native women—the princess and the squaw drudge—still affect Native women's self-esteem. The "squaw" is the dirty, subservient, and abused tribal female who is also haggard, violent, and eager to torture tribal captives. Her opposite is the "princess," the attractive daughter of the chief who often is willing to leave her tribe to marry a white man.[75] Although modern scholars are not particularly enthusiastic about the princess image, moviemakers continue to cast beautiful women (often non-Native actresses) as Natives, as do producers of make-up and clothing advertisements in magazines. Young Native women are also confused as to why Native women such as Pocahontas and Sacajawea are revered as "heroines" when history shows that their claim to fame is based on aiding those men who helped overrun Native lands.

The impact of negative stereotypes upon Native people is profound. Wilma Mankiller, a victim of stereotypes, agrees that "There are so many stereotypes about us that we begin to believe that crap ourselves. When people know there's discrimination, and they can feel it, they've got to internalize some of that eventually. They've got to. So we've got to learn!"[76]

On the other hand, positive stereotyping might account for some non-Natives' and mixed-heritage peoples' decisions to become Natives. Individuals with little knowledge of Natives might become enamored with images of Indians as physically attractive, valiant warriors and mystical environmentalists who are "one with nature." Positive imagery of Natives in the 1960s and 1970s probably accounts in part for the dramatic increase in the number of Natives on the 1980 census.[77]

Positive stereotyping also accounts for the number of people who claim to be part Native—regardless of how much they know about their ancestors. Actors Val Kilmer, Chuck Norris, Kim Basinger, Cher, and Connie Selleca claim to be part Cherokee or Choctaw. Illustrating the vague knowledge many people have of their "Indian ancestors," disco queen Gloria Gaynor writes in her autobiography, *I Will Survive*, about her relatives: "The only thing I do know is that my great-grandmother on my mother's side was a full-blooded Blackfoot Indian, with hair down to the bend of her knee."[78]

In their 1987 article "Dimensions of Native American Stereotyping," Jeffrey R. Hanson and Linda P. Rouse propose that stereotypes are not static but change in form and prevalence depending on historical and sociocultural circumstances.[79] For example, in areas of the United States where Natives and non-Natives clash over treaty hunting and fishing rights and other economic resources, stereotypes of Natives are more negative. In a subsequent article Hanson and Rouse assert that "factual knowledge is not sufficient to counter status-based prejudice."[80] Indeed, those who have vested economic and social interest in preserving images of Natives as inferior beings rarely will acknowledge Natives as equals. In areas of the country where Natives are not viewed with favor, Natives' *perceived level of discrimination* plays a role in whether they want to pursue their Native identity in that area or whether they prefer to express their Native identity elsewhere.

A stumbling block to identifying with only one group can appear if the person's self-perception is different from others' perceptions of her. Just because a person—mixed-blood or full-blood—desires to join a particular racial or ethnic group does not mean that she has a guaranteed entrance into that group. One factor that hinders a person's acceptance by Native groups is standards that set varying requirements for tribal membership; those who do not meet the requirements are not considered tribal members. Until the late nineteenth century most tribes used cultural knowledge, appearance, and familial connections as prerequisites for tribal membership. By the turn of the century, however, the federal government required tribes to use race as the determining factor of Indianness.

Now, almost always, tribes require that proposed enrollees supply proof that they are directly related to a member of the tribe who is listed on the current tribal roll or on specified historic tribal rolls. Some tribes, such as Oklahoma Cherokees and Choctaws, allow membership regardless of a person's blood quantum. As a result, today there are enrolled members of the Five Civilized Tribes with less than 1/512 Indian blood, and few have cultural connections to their tribes. Other tribes require their members be at least half-blood. Others allow entrance only if an individual's mother is a tribal member.

Federally recognized tribes—those tribes whose existence as a unique political entity is acknowledged by the federal government—are granted specified rights such as self-government and benefits including health care and education, housing, and resource development programs.[81] Tribal membership bestowed by a tribe that is recognized by either a state or the federal government is important for most Natives. The Indian Arts and Crafts Act of 1990, for example, requires that anyone producing and selling "Indian products" be a member of a recognized tribe, thus excluding numerous self-proclaimed Native artists who have been creating "Indian" works for years.[82] In Texas, at least, individuals who wish to legally utilize peyote in Native American Church ceremonies must prove that they are at least one-quarter Native blood, which also means they must be tribally enrolled. In addition, the Bureau of Indian Affairs and the U.S. Department of Education recognize as Natives only those who are enrolled in a recognized tribe.[83]

Other factors that limit individuals' ability to choose to be Native are lack of cultural knowledge, residence apart from the tribe, ethnocentrism, and what I term "culturalism." Culturalism exists when tribal members view each other with disdain because of their cultural adherences. Root claims that all racial groups have prejudices. When these prejudices are "projected" onto a multi-heritage person, then the racial group becomes the "creator of marginal status."[84]

Racism and suspicion often exist among members of a single tribe. Economics, politics, and social aspects of kinship systems, clans, religion, and interaction with non-Natives are major factors affecting how tribespeople feel about each other. Traditionalists may believe that progressives are "less Indian" because of their cultural naiveté and that multi-heritage peoples claim tribal membership only for land and annuity purposes. Some individuals claiming to be Native are not accepted unless they can prove kinship ties to their tribes. Those who look phenotypically non-Native will especially have difficulty asserting their identity without a link to their tribe. Mixed-heritage members may see traditionals as "uncivilized" and "backwards." For example, a mixed-heritage Cherokee woman of one-quarter Cherokee blood remarked in a 1930s interview that, while growing up, "we were never allowed to associate with the uneducated class of Indians."[85]

Mary Brave Bird, a Lakota woman who looks phenotypically Native yet does not speak Lakota, recalls that when she married Leonard Crow Dog, "I was not well received. It was pretty bad. I could not speak Sioux and I could tell that all the many Crow Dogs and their relations from the famous old Orphan Band were constantly talking about me, watching me, watching whether I would measure up to their standards which go way back to the old buffalo days. I could tell from the way they were looking at me, and I could see the criticism in their eyes. The old man told me that, as far as he was concerned, Leonard was still married to his former wife, a woman, as he pointed out again and again, *who could talk Indian....* I had to fight day by day to be accepted." Finally Mary became ill from the stress: "I broke down. I got sick. I was down to ninety pounds. My body just collapsed." It was not until after she went through a peyote healing ceremony and was called "daughter" by those who had previously doubted her that she recovered.[86]

Navajo filmmaker Arlene Bowman experienced deep emotional distress when her Navajo family shunned her because they saw her as "wealthy" and because she was unable to speak Navajo. Her documentary *Navajo Talking Picture* was difficult to make because of the emotional wounds she suffered at the hands of her immediate family. Ultimately she completed her academic degrees and is comfortable with her identity.[87]

Current leadership of tribes often dictates how tribal membership is defined, how annuities are dispersed, and who receives tribal jobs. Native persons who are out of favor with the current political tribal power, who are successful by the whites' standards but not by tribal standards (such as by completing a university degree or earning a substantial salary and accumulating material wealth), or who marry a person from an "inappropriate" racial group may find it easier to live apart from the tribe or to completely distance themselves and not enroll their children.[88]

Another factor in choosing identity is the most obvious feature of one's racial heritage: appearance. Appearance, the most visible aspect of one's race, determines how Native women define themselves and how others define them. Black scholar John Hope Franklin writes in the introduction to *Color and Race* that, "If color and race constitute the bases or the justification for conflict between peoples of different areas and races, they also constitute the bases for differentiation and preference within a given society or even within a racial group."[89] This does apply to Natives as well as blacks.

An Indigenous woman's appearance, whether phenotypically Native, Caucasian, African, or mixed, either limits or broadens her choices of ethnic identity, determines whether she will be accepted or rejected by others, immediately places her in a social class, and dramatically affects her self-esteem. The color of one's hair, eyes, and skin are the barometers used to measure how "Indian" one is, and they either limit or broaden one's choice of ethnicity. An individual who doesn't "look Indian" is often suspect for claiming Native identity regardless of her cultural knowledge.

The idea that a Caucasian appearance is "better" serves as a point of contention among many people of color.[90] Like blacks, darker-skinned Natives often distrust lighter-skinned ones, arguing that their non-Indian blood makes them out of touch with the realities of Native life. Because it is assumed that light-skinned Natives have a choice as to which "world" they live in, their dedication to fighting the various social, political, religious, and economic oppressions faced by "real" Natives is questioned. Persons who look Caucasian, were raised in white society, and have little, if any, connection to their tribe but still claim a Native identity will be looked at with suspicion.

An interesting ideology opposing that of lighter-skinned Natives who wish they were more readily identifiable as Natives (i.e., wish they had darker skin) is Margo Okazawa-Rey, Tracy Robinson, and Janie Victoria Ward's claim that when light-skinned black women degrade darker-skinned black women their "identification with the racist oppressors is complete."[91] This may be true for Natives in some cases. One example is again the progressive Cherokee female seminarians of the 1870s who were lighter in color than their tribeswomen and used words like "heathen" to describe girls who were darker skinned and therefore presumably inferior. That some Indians preferred to mingle only with their own "color group" is reflected in the comments of a Choctaw woman, reminiscing about her school days at Tuskahoma, Oklahoma, in 1910: "I have never been so scared in my life. I shake when I think about it. There were so many fullblood girls blacker than anybody you ever seen. . . . I don't believe they were all just Indian, they were mixed with this other race. . . . I cried and I cried and I cried because I was up there with them black kids. I just don't like the looks of [those] people. . . . that bunch of little old black kids I tell you just looked like flies flying around."[92]

In the 1960s, the formation of the American Indian Movement

(AIM) inspired many Natives to reacquaint themselves with their cultures. Even older, traditional Natives who were leery of AIM began to reassert their Indianness. Many of the men began growing their hair: witness the before and after photographs of Native political leaders who became "re-Indianized" with the advent of the movement. During the 1960s and 1970s, numerous other young Native men began growing their hair, camouflaging the short length with leather wraps. One young man, a Muscogee/Kiowa who became re-Indianized after an argument with his adoptive white parents, commented in 1989 that his waist-length wraps represented how long he wanted his chin-length hair to grow. He also began laying in the sun to enhance his already dark skin color.

Appearance plays a crucial role in status and ease of travel among cultures, and consequently many multi-heritage Natives have numerous "worlds" open to them while most full-blood Native and multi-heritage, black and Native peoples do not. For example, mixed-heritage Chickasaw writer Linda Hogan admits that her ambiguous appearance has sometimes been an advantage: she could "pass for white . . . go to powwows and to the opera with equal ease. . . . I feel that my life's been really rich for me, with a lot of different kinds of experience and people and traveling, and it's really good."[93] Another example is the prominent mixed-blood Chippewa writer Louise Erdrich. In "Conversions" she recounts her ambition to be crowned "Queen of the Wops" (homecoming queen; the Wops were her high school mascot). In no place in her high school reminiscences does Erdrich mention that she is Native.[94] Dagmar Thorpe made a conscious decision to live as a Native even though she appears white: "I am fair and light complected and could have chosen to live my life in mainstream America or the life which I have. I have chosen to align myself with and live the worldview of Native people. The reason I made that choice is that Native thinking embraces spirituality."[95]

Some multi-racial Natives only have to alter their hairstyle and stay out of the sun to look white. Many women prefer to pass from one race to another, finding more advantage living in the white world than in the Native world, and their appearance allows them that option.

### Stage 3. Immersion-Emersion

Cross and Parham agree that blacks at this stage attempt to develop a thorough black frame of reference. For Natives, like blacks, it can be a volatile stage, often causing anxiety, depression, and frustration over attempts at becoming the "right kind of Indian." In Cross's words, "the person begins to demolish the old perspective and simultaneously tries to construct what will become her new frame of reference."[96]

Many Natives at this stage engage in aggressive behavior. They seek information on Natives (not necessarily of their own tribe) and enthusiastically participate in powwows and religious ceremonies. They protest against racial injustices (often violently), deny the non-Native racial and cultural aspects of themselves, and become hostile toward non-Natives (whites especially) and other Indians who do not conform to their ideas of "Indianness." Those insecure in their economic or political worlds adopt a "Redder Than Thou" attitude and question whether other Natives are "really Indian."

Although the founding members of AIM were young, incarcerated, and/or victimized by poverty, racism, and self-doubt, AIM and the Red Power Movement—like the Black Power Movement—touched individuals of all classes, identities, and motivations. The male "radicals," however, are the ones who garnered media attention and have subsequently demonstrated through their rhetoric and actions that during AIM's formation many of them were indeed in the immersion stage of their life. Many of these men publicly discuss women's traditional roles in the tribe as exalted and crucial to tribal survival, but they also will physically and verbally abuse them.

The Cherokee seminarians, on the other hand, began a "Whiter Than Thou" campaign and judged their fellow Natives (Cherokees and members of other tribes) on the basis of their degree of assimilation. Whether or not a person was Christian, educated, and striving for the white ideal played a large part in how these young men and women evaluated that person as a human being. In the encounter stage, the Cherokee students were convinced, according to one alumnus, that the "white way was the only acceptable way," and they began strategizing to become more like the whites their teachers so overtly praised and less like the Natives the teachers criticized.

After the Civil War thousands of blacks were freed in Indian Territory, and in an attempt to stay out of the "people of color" category, Natives kept themselves segregated from blacks—in schools and neighborhoods and at social events. E. Franklin Frazier's analysis of the "Black Bourgeoisie"—those blacks who viewed themselves as inferior because they judged themselves by white standards—is a helpful concept in understanding why some mixed-race Native women felt themselves lacking in comparison to whites yet at the same time believed themselves to be superior to other Natives and to blacks.[97] Another helpful thesis is that some blacks (and Natives) tried to imitate the oppressors in order to survive, and those who were light-skinned had an advantage.[98]

### Stage 4. Internalization

At this point a person develops inner security about her identity. She is able to discuss racial issues in a rational manner with members of other racial or ethnic groups. "In short," Parham writes, "the person becomes *biculturally* successful."[99] The person has come to a satisfactory conclusion as to who and what she is. Writer-musician Joy Harjo, for example, writes of her resolution:

I've gone through stages with it. I've gone through the stage where I hated everybody who wasn't Indian, which meant part of myself. I went through a really violent kind of stage with that. And then I've been through in-between stages and I've come to a point where I realize in a way that you have to believe that you're special to be born like that because why would anybody give you such a hard burden like that unless they knew you could come through with it, unless with it came some special kind of vision to help you get through it all and to help others through it because in a way you do see two sides but you also see there are more than two sides. It's like this, living is like a diamond or how they cut really fine stones. There are not just two sides but there are many and they all make up a whole.[100]

Just because a person has realized a satisfactory identity, that does not mean that everyone agrees with her choice. The person will continually have to defend that choice. Mary Brave Bird comments about how she copes with being mixed-blood: "I am an *iyeska*, a half-breed, and there are some on the res who won't let me forget it. The full-bloods, the *ikche wichasha*, the 'wild, natural being,' often look down upon the half-breeds as no longer living in the traditional way, as being 'apples,' red on the outside and white inside. The half-breeds, in turn, look upon the full-bloods as backward. All this doesn't mean much. *Ikche wichasha* or *iyeska*, we are all no longer living like the old Indians—we all go to the same stores and supermarkets and have to compromise, with one foot in the white and the other in the Indian world. Also, at Rosebud, we are all related in some way.... I am a half-breed. So what?"[101]

What about those individuals who never reach an equitable solution as to their identity? Do they mirror Everett Stonequist's model of a "marginal" person—one who lives a life of frustration, unable to fit comfortably into any group?[102] Whether a Native person can be at peace with herself can only be answered on a case-by-case basis. As a female Ojibwe counselor at Northern Arizona University has observed, "Every Indian person I know has an identity issue." Paula Gunn Allen concurs: "Alienation is more than the experience of the single individual; it is a primary experience of all bicultural American Indians in the United States—and, to one extent or another, this includes virtually every American Indian here."[103] As the few examples of the Cherokee seminarians, Native adoptees of white parents, and the willing victims of prejudice and stereotypes illustrate, just because a person is visually recognized as a Native does not mean that she is satisfied with her identity.

In addition to their group's perceived level of discrimination, rejection of one's identity choice by Natives and non-Natives, unfamiliarity with tribal culture and residence away from the tribe, social status of the group, and appearance, another reason for Native peoples' identity insecurities may be that they almost always have "internalized oppression" because they often reject a part of their racial heritage that is also a part of themselves. Natives may believe that in order to achieve approval from one group they must embrace only the aspects of their personality that conform to that group and reject the other parts. Rejected parts, as Root points out, cannot easily be forgotten. Parents, extended family, and physical attributes remain powerful reminders of what the individual is attempting to abandon.[104] Even parts that are not rejected are consistently evaluated and compared by the individual and by others. For instance, after I passed my comprehensive Ph.D. exams in 1988, a white professor asked me, "Have you considered that it's your white blood that makes you successful?"

There are several other aspects of self-identification that sociologists assume apply to all multi-heritage peoples but that may not apply to individuals claiming to be Natives. For example, Root asserts that individuals have the right to identify themselves according to how they want to be identified. She also believes they should develop strategies for coping with resistance to their proclaimed identities so that they do not "internalize questions as inferring that there is something wrong with them."[105] This statement, however, raises a question—What if their identities are fabricated?

In addition, one of the most hotly contested aspects of Native identity today concerns whether a person with minimal Native blood, no tribal cultural knowledge, and a lack of kinship and familial ties should identify as Native. Not everyone who claims to be Native agrees that they need to be tribally enrolled or even recognized by their tribe in order to identify with them. It may cause stress to the "Indians" whose tribes will not claim them, but tribes that must contend with unrecognized individuals who insist that they should be members of the tribe may also feel stress. As a number of Native writers have noted, it is a violation of tribal rights not to allow tribes to determine who their members are.[106]

While the economic, political, and social forces affecting Natives' identity choices and development often can be readily categorized, the vast differences among tribes and individual Natives, in addition to the complexities that they face, mean that one empirical study on Native identity cannot contribute many definitive statements to the literature except to show that the subject is complicated. Even studies focusing on specific groups of Natives at a definite point in time and place must incorporate a myriad of variables that the researcher may have trouble comprehending. For instance, many non-Natives are puzzled as to why a person of mixed blood would call themselves Native and not a member of another group. In response, Mohawk poet Peter Blue Cloud echoes the sentiment of many Natives: "They wouldn't understand even if you explained it."[107]

Indeed, non-Natives have a great deal of difficulty understanding "Indianness." Not all individuals claiming to be Indian "look Indian," nor were many born into tribal environments. Many are not tribally enrolled, while others are not racially "Indian" at all. Some Natives who appear Caucasian or black may go back and forth, assuming Native, white, and black identities depending on their current need, while others who have lived most of their lives as non-Natives may decide to "become Indians" at a later age. Some individuals are Native by virtue of biological connection but know little about their cultural mores because they lacked interest, there was no one to teach them, or, due to the time period, location, and degree of racism, prejudice, and stereotypes, it was not (or is not) socially or economically profitable to pursue a Native identity.

Some Natives are racially full-bloods but culturally "mixed-bloods" or the other way around. Some are dark-skinned, others have blond hair and blue eyes. Some speak their language but do not practice their religion. Some may do both. Some Natives live in terrifying poverty, while others are physicians, lawyers, professors, or workers in many other professions. Some are poor but happy.

The terminology of "Indianness" is confusing. Because of assimilation, acculturation, and intermarriage with non-Natives, Natives have a variety of terms to describe themselves: full-blood, traditional, mixed-blood, crossblood, halfbreed, progressive, enrolled, unenrolled, reIndianized, multi-heritage, bicultural, postindian, First Nations, Indigenous, or simply, "I'm [tribal affiliation]." Reflecting internal debate over identity, many individuals will also offer that they are secure, confused, reborn, marginal, or lost. Those who are hopeful about being accepted as Natives declare that "I just discovered my grandmother was a full-blood" or "I'm part Indian but I'm not sure what kind," and so on.

For decades anthropologists have investigated how Indigenous groups acculturate to the ways of white society. Only in the past ten years have sociologists and psychologists conducted significant studies on individual Indigenous identity issues, and it appears that much more research is needed.

# 3. ACTIVISTS AND FEMINISTS

## 9

## 1970s Activist Anna Mae Pictou-Aquash

I am the one who fought for you
And I know I'd do it all again.
I would never blame any one of you
If there was nothing you could do.
But remember what went into my name when I died for you.
And I'd do it again in a heartbeat.
I'm Anna Mae Pictou.
– "I'd Do It Again in a Heartbeat," music and lyrics by Shannon M. Collins, executive director of the ANNA Foundation.

Numerous Indigenous women have been involved in the activities of the American Indian Movement (AIM) since its inception in the mid-1960s, but men, including Dennis Banks, Russell Means, Leonard Peltier, Vernon and Clyde Bellecourt, John Trudell, and Leonard Crow Dog, have garnered most of the attention. Indeed, some of the works written about these men border on hero-worship. The media and scholars have largely ignored the role of women in the movement. Only recently, in a few articles and the books *Lakota Woman* (1990) and *Ohikita Woman* (1993), have female participants in AIM, the Wounded Knee occupation, and other Native activist organizations been heard.

The life of Anna Mae Pictou-Aquash demonstrates what it means to be a modern Native woman aggressively fighting racial, cultural, and gender oppression. She and other activist Indigenous American women also illustrate that there are a variety of definitions of "feminism," even among women of the same cultural, racial, and class group. Anna Mae is particularly notable because she desired to create a fair world for all Indigenes in addition to empowering Native women. Additionally, Anna Mae has emerged as a martyr for Native women and men who are freedom fighters, a symbol of both the courage of Native women and the possible fate of outspoken individuals who displease their government and members of their own organization.[1]

Anna Mae was born on 27 March 1945, the third child of Mary Ellen Pictou and Francis Levi, on the poverty-ridden reserve of Shubenacadie in Nova Scotia. Shortly after Levi abandoned his family in 1949, Mary Ellen married Noel Sapier, and they moved the family to Pictou's Landing, a northern area of the reserve, where Anna Mae learned about her tribe's history. Like most other members of the Mi'kmaq tribe, Anna Mae's family lived in poverty, and when she was eight, she developed tuberculosis of the eyes and lungs. When she recovered, she began attending school in an off-reserve institution. Although Anna Mae maintained an A average, blatant racism and negative stereotyping of Natives left her despondent, and she dropped out.

In 1956 Anna Mae's stepfather died of cancer. Her mother soon married a man on another reserve, and Anna Mae, her sister Mary, and her brother Francis moved in with their married sister Rebecca. They struggled through their adulthood without electricity, plumbing, or a regular source of food except for clams and fish. Anna Mae worked at low-paying jobs such as potato and berry harvesting. In 1962 she decided to move to Boston with another Mi'kmaq, Jake Maloney. She found work in a factory, and by 1965, she and Jake had two daughters, Denise and Deborah. Although they were fairly successful in their Boston life, they missed Nova Scotia, and several times they moved back and forth between Canada and Boston.

Anna Mae was not satisfied with her life as a suburbanite, although she enjoyed learning karate, which her husband later taught. She yearned for the company of other Natives, so she became involved in organizing an Indian community center that eventually became the Boston Indian Council, an establishment designed to support Natives who had moved from reservations to the intimidating city. Jake Maloney was not interested in Anna Mae's activities, nor was he faithful. After she discovered his affair with a white woman, they separated.

Anna Mae was not the only frustrated Native to emerge from the 1950s. Natives living in cities and on reservations had a difficult time: they faced poverty, racism, and identity confusion. Many, including Anna Mae, drank to cope with stress; others vented their frustrations in less legal ways. Throughout the 1960s many incarcerated Natives were angry young men with histories of crime and identity crises. Ojibwes Clyde Bellecourt and Eddie Banai, who were jailed in Minnesota for robbery, believed that if Natives were organized they could address the serious issues facing their people. They coordinated regular discussions with Native inmates in order to familiarize themselves with their tribal cultures.

After Bellecourt's release in 1964, he and other Minneapolis Natives, including Dennis Banks, an Anishinabi who had attended an Indian boarding school, served in the Air Force, and been convicted for burglary, helped to form Concerned Indian Americans. Dissatisfied with the acronym CIA, they changed the name to American Indian Movement.[2] AIM's first goals were to help Natives by obtaining better living conditions and to create street patrols to monitor excessive police arrests. Meanwhile, "Red Power" movements and "fish-ins" were taking place on the West Coast and in the New York area. AIM obtained considerable financial support from churches and community action groups and organized a "survival school" for young Natives in Minneapolis so children could learn about white society and their tribal cultures simultaneously. The movement adopted the upside-down American flag as its symbol, a version of the international distress symbol that was controversial and did not sit well with Native veterans.

While working at the Boston Indian Council, twenty-five-year-old Anna Mae attended her first AIM activity, a protest of Thanksgiving in which Natives boarded the *Mayflower II*, a replica of the ship that brought Pilgrims to Plymouth. Soon after, she moved to Bar Harbor, Maine, to work in the Teaching and Research in Bicultural Education School Project (TRIBES), a career she enjoyed. When lack of funding closed the school in 1972, and she and her daughters moved back to Boston. She enrolled in the Wheelock College New Careers program and obtained a satisfying job as a teacher's aide in an all-black child care center. Despite her lack of formal education, Brandeis University offered Anna Mae a scholarship, but by that time, she was thoroughly dedicated to Indigenous causes and declined it.

Anna Mae met an Ontario Ojibwa artist, Nogeeshik Aquash, who moved in with her and her daughters. Anna Mae and Nogeeshik participated in the first part of AIM's March on Washington, also known as the Trail of Broken Treaties, a protest designed to call attention to the federal government's disregard of rights guaranteed by treaties.[3] AIM members eventually occupied and partially destroyed the Bureau of Indian Affairs building, a move that garnered AIM a dubious reputation as a violent organization.

While AIM appealed to many Natives across the country, it also repelled many traditional Natives, who viewed AIM as comprising young, glory-seeking Natives with little knowledge of tribal culture. Non-Natives labeled it a group led by ex-cons and communists espousing an anti-white attitude. Disagreements among its leaders emerged almost immediately, and fractures in the movement continue today.

Regardless of its detractors and internal problems, AIM continued to grow. Many Natives, frustrated with their lives and with a government that appeared uninterested in their problems, were enthused by AIM. Like Anna Mae, many Natives perceived AIM as an organization that served as a vehicle not only to alert Americans to the issues Natives faced but to solve those problems. Association with AIM also became a source of identity and pride.[4] Offshoot chapters sprang up across the country, and the organization became important enough for the FBI to begin planting informers—Natives and non-Natives alike—in its midst.

In January 1973 a young Lakota, Wesley Bad Heart Bull, was fatally stabbed by a white man, who was charged only with involuntary manslaughter. Incensed, AIM members and supporters burned down the courthouse in Custer, South Dakota. At the same time, opposition by Pine Ridge Reservation Oglala Sioux to the Oglala tribal chairman, Richard Wilson, was growing. They claimed he was a "one-man council," a nepotist, and a "dictator," who controlled the tribal government.[5] When Wilson realized that tribal members had appealed to AIM for help, he banned AIM from the reservation. On Tuesday, 27 February 1973, urged on by Pine Ridge residents (mainly traditional Oglala women), about two hundred AIM members took control of the hamlet of Wounded Knee. Within hours after Wilson asked the government for assistance, armed marshals sealed off the town while AIM fortified its position. The government sent reinforcements in the form of FBI agents, military troops, and weapons. Natives held their location inside a church for seventy-one days, exchanging gunfire with outsiders, accepting food drops from daring pilots, and watching negotiations move forward and then falter.

Meanwhile, debates over the purpose and intent of the takeover raged across the reservation. Many residents of Pine Ridge were grateful to see AIM attempt to rectify what they believed to be an overbearing, despotic tribal government. Others were dissatisfied with AIM's presence, arguing that most of those involved in the takeover were not even from South Dakota, nor did they know about their own tribal cultures, much less about Lakota culture. They conceded that some of the AIM members truly wanted to help, but others, especially the leadership, were purely attention-seekers.

When Anna Mae and Nogeeshik learned of the takeover she resigned her job at the General Motors plant in Massachusetts. She left her two children in the care of her sister Mary, then traveled to South Dakota. Upon arrival, she and Nogeeshik busied themselves secretly bringing food and medical supplies through the government barricades.

Anna Mae remained active within Wounded Knee, cooking, cleaning, and assisting in the delivery of Mary Brave Bird's baby Pedro (Mary later married and divorced Leonard Crow Dog). The day after the birth, 12 April 1973, caught up in the excitement of Wounded Knee, Anna Mae and Nogeeshik married in a traditional Lakota ceremony conducted by Wallace Black Elk.

Although the male AIM leadership at Wounded Knee depended on women to cook and clean for them, they preferred that women stay in the background. They did not seem impressed with the "masculine" roles many women played in the takeover. Anna Mae was one of the few women to walk the nightly patrols and dig bunkers. She also was physically fit, thoughtful, and organized and often spoke of pursuing her ambitious book project, "A People's History of the Land," the Natives' versions of their tribes' histories and cultures. One participant at Wounded Knee later commented that Anna Mae had a bent for adopting the mannerisms of others around her, and according to her sister Mary Lafford, "After a while she showed men themselves and they didn't like it."[6] In addition to her ideas about how the leadership structure should be organized, it appears that Anna Mae's aspirations, emotional strength, and intellect, in addition to her martial arts background, were intimidating to some males, and she lost support from those who were most insecure.

Many women were and are members of AIM, but the organization always has been dominated by men. At Wounded Knee men negotiated with government officials and media coverage ignored the women's participation during the takeover. This is not surprising considering the stereotypes non-Natives hold of Native women as either the "squaw drudge" or the "princess"—neither possessing leadership abilities. The press focused on the flamboyant AIM individuals, most notably Russell Means, a mixed-blood Oglala who had previously worked as an accountant and ballroom dance instructor. His dress of braids, beads, and jewelry in combination with his angry rhetoric catered to the press's stereotypical image of the Plains Indian warrior. He appeared to gain momentum with every interview and photograph, causing one of his confidants to remark that "the press created Russell Means."[7]

After the siege was over, Russell Means, Dennis Banks, and others were indicted for their roles in the takeover, and for years afterward faced a variety of charges.[8] The Aquashes returned to Boston to continue their activism. When they could not obtain funding to open a survival school, they moved to Ottawa, where Anna Mae organized a successful fashion show at the National Arts Centre in 1974. Always resourceful in locating funds for AIM, Anna Mae revitalized the "ribbon shirt," originally created by northeastern tribes to spruce up the ordinary clothes brought by missionaries. She intended to sell the shirts, but spouses and boyfriends of the seamstresses received all the shirts as presents. Anna Mae was later involved in the Menominees' takeover of the Alexian Brothers Catholic Monastery in Wisconsin, enough activity for the FBI to keep her under observation.

While Anna Mae was active in South Dakota, her ex-husband had taken custody of their children, a move Anna Mae did not object to until the girls decided to live with their father permanently. Although she knew that Maloney could afford to buy Denise and Deborah things they wanted and needed, their decision still grieved her, and she dove into her work for AIM. She traveled extensively, forged support groups, raised funds, and ferried messages. She set up AIM's West Coast branch, a move that signaled not only AIM's national influence but also Anna Mae's prominence in the movement.

In 1974 Anna Mae and Nogeeshik separated after months of his verbal and attempted physical abuse, usually brought on by his drinking. Among Lakotas, being married by the pipe is sacred, and the expectation of couples married in this fashion is that they cannot divorce; those who do are accused of "playing with the pipe." Yet abuse of women by men (and sometimes the other way around) is so commonplace that one partner often will break the sacred trust. Although she was not Lakota, Anna Mae respected the meaning of the pipe, and she felt guilt over her broken promises. Guilt and disappointment led her to drink, which often resulted in outbursts of anger. This behavior only added to her sense of failure, since she and fellow activist Leonard Peltier had taken a strong stance against drinking after Wounded Knee and often chided AIM leaders about imbibing.

"We broke even," said John Trudell about Wounded Knee. At the same time, AIM was instrumental in bringing attention to Native causes. The methods members used to get their points across were often ineffective, but AIM gave identity and pride to many Natives of all ages. Men and women across the country experienced a surge of interest in their cultures. Men began growing their hair and wearing clothing like the AIM leaders. "City Indians became new reborn Indians," said Pine Ridge resident Milo Yellow Hair about the Natives who flocked to the reservation in search of their Indian heritage. "We were like the library that never got used." The AIM leaders also directed America's attention to problems Natives faced across the country in addition to illustrating that Natives were indeed still alive and not living in the past.[9]

Wounded Knee changed little for Natives in South Dakota, however. Poverty, crime, and health problems still raged, and in 1975 the "reign of terror" began against AIM and its supporters on the Pine Ridge Reservation. Members of Wilson's political faction beat, shot, and terrorized residents almost on a daily basis. By the end of the year, at least forty-seven Natives were dead, most under mysterious circumstances. FBI intrusions, imprisonments, violent unsolved deaths, and discoveries of infiltrators resulted in collective paranoia. AIM members and residents of Pine Ridge found it difficult to trust anyone—including each other—and even unlikely persons were suspected of being informants for the FBI. One man, Douglass Durham, had worked as Dennis Banks's personal bodyguard for more than a year. He was privy to AIM's important plans and had worked in several AIM offices across the country. While Anna Mae and Durham were working at the St. Paul AIM office during the Banks and Means trials, Anna Mae observed his abusive nature toward women and noticed that he was dyeing his hair black. She sensed Durham might be an informant, and in February of 1975 Durham was indeed revealed as an informer, thus prompting further fear and concern among AIM and its supporters.[10] Not surprisingly, the prominent AIM leader Anna Mae Pictou-Aquash also came under suspicion from numerous AIM leaders and members.

Anna Mae's difficulties were compounded when she became intimate with the organization's leader, Dennis Banks, which garnered her the nickname "Dennis's West Coast Woman." The main problem with their relationship was that Banks was married to a young Oglala woman, Kamook, who was not only Anna Mae's friend but was pregnant with Banks's child (by 1975 Banks had fathered fifteen children with a variety of women).[11] The revelation of Anna Mae's relationship with Dennis Banks was devastating to Kamook, their friends, and to Anna Mae. Because of the combination of emerging rumors about her being a FBI informer and her exposed affair, in addition to her being a member of West Coast AIM and not Dakota AIM, Anna Mae endured ethnocentrism at the hands of other Native women. She had already faced snubs by Lakota AIM women at Wounded Knee known as the "Pie Patrol" because she was a Canadian Native. Anna Mae gave them "a piece of her mind," according to Mary Crow Dog, but ostracism by women she had wanted to work with must have cut deep.[12] So did the accusations from the AIM spiritual leader, Leonard Crow Dog, that she was an FBI informer.

Anna Mae's emotions were on edge when, at the AIM National Convention in Farmington, New Mexico, she was interrogated by AIM members Dino Butler, Leonard Peltier, and Bob Robideau, some say at the behest of Vernon Bellecourt.[13] Peltier commented years later that he did not really believe she was an informer but that if she was, "She was involved in a lot of stuff, and she could have done a *lot* of damage."[14]

Dismayed and saddened that her colleagues were suspicious of her, Anna Mae almost returned to Nova Scotia but decided to stay in South Dakota in order to help the elderly Oglala women. Many of these women knew Anna Mae had experienced in Canada what they had experienced in the United States, and they accepted her. According to Roselyn Jumping Bull, Anna Mae once told her, "After I realized how you people live I didn't want none of the things I had before. I left everything because I wanted to show you how I love you people and want to help you." Jumping Bull explained shortly after Anna Mae's death that "None of the other girls ever talk like that—she's the only one."[15]

Anna Mae had learned about her tribe's culture while she was young, and unlike the AIM leadership and many of its male and female members, she had lived in a tribal environment all her life. She spoke her tribal language, was aware of her tribe's history and customs, and understood the traditional strength of Mi'kmaq women. It may have been unsettling for her to possess a strong desire to return to traditional gender roles (in addition to equality among races) and to live in the harsh reality that included racism against Indians by whites, misogyny among many AIM men, and acceptance of the men's behavior by many of the Native women with whom she worked. Anna Mae chose to work with AIM rather than her own people because she believed that AIM could address a range of Native grievances and serve not only displaced and confused Natives but also people like her, who were secure in their tribal and ethnic identities.

It would not be easy and she knew it. The "reign of terror" which had induced paranoia soon reached Anna Mae personally. On the morning of 26 June 1975, two FBI agents, Ronald Williams and Jack Coler, arrived on the Jumping Bull property at Pine Ridge with a subpoena for teenager Jimmy Eagle, who was accused of stealing boots. Shots were fired from within the ranch house, and shortly afterward the two agents and a young man, Joseph Killsright Stuntz, were dead. Soon armed agents arrived at the Jumping Bull property, and under orders from their leader, Norman Zigrossi, the team swept the reservation with M-16s, helicopters, and dogs and proceeded to interrogate anyone they pleased without warrants. Angry that they could not locate the culprits, the FBI created a list of individuals they believed could inform them of who did the killings, and Anna Mae made the list. In September, while Natives were camped at the property of Al Running and at Leonard Crow Dog's Paradise, dozens of armed agents raided the properties, destroying many sacred cultural items in the process of searching for suspects in the killings of the FBI agents. Anna Mae was one of those arrested at Crow Dog's.

After being transported to Pierre, South Dakota, she was interrogated for over six hours about the deaths. She insisted that she was in Iowa at the time of the shooting, but agent David Price persisted, telling her that if she cooperated in helping find the killers she would be given a new identity and a place to live. He also warned her that if she did not cooperate and tell them who the killers were he would "see her dead within the year." Her reply, one of many forebodings of her death, was, "You can either shoot me or put me in jail. That's what you're going to do to me anyway." She was released on bail and promptly fled underground.

In November 1975 Anna Mae, along with Dennis Banks and Leonard Peltier, were sought on fugitive warrants. On the evening of 14 November two vehicles (one owned by Marlon Brando) were stopped by a state trooper in Oregon. Anna Mae was arrested, put in handcuffs, and shackled to the pregnant Kamook Banks. She was extradited to South Dakota, where she faced charges of transporting and possessing dangerous weapons. Because she had not been indicted on earlier charges, the judge released her on bail, and she went underground once more.

In the fall of 1975 Darrell Dean "Dino" Butler and Robert "Bob" Robideau were arrested, but another suspect in the July shooting, Leonard Peltier, fled to Canada to avoid arrest. Because of the false testimony of Myrtle Poor Bear, who claimed to have seen Peltier kill the two agents, Peltier was extradited to the United States and was convicted of murder. Butler and Robideau were acquitted in June 1976, but Peltier remains in prison.[16]

Anna Mae called her sisters in Nova Scotia, speaking Mi'kmaq in case of wiretaps. She told them that she expected to be shot "sooner or later" and said that if anything did happen to her, she wanted Mary to raise her two daughters. She was thirty years old, and it was the last time her family spoke to her.

On the unusually warm winter afternoon of 24 February 1976, in the northeast corner of the Pine Ridge Reservation in South Dakota, a small Indigenous woman lay curled, sleeping it appeared, at the bottom of an embankment on the property of cattle rancher Roger Amiotte. She was not adequately dressed for the cold winter nights and considering the distance from the closest town, Wanblee, her wardrobe of ski jacket, blue jeans, and sneakers was very curious. Her inappropriate attire did not matter, however, because she had been dead for at least two months.

Upon finding the body, Amiotte immediately called the Oglala tribal police, who responded within twenty minutes. Within hours, so did a large number of deputies and four FBI agents, several of whom were a hundred miles away when they got word of the discovered body. *Why all these authorities?* wondered Amiotte. Bodies were frequently found across the reservation during the turbulent years of unrest between the FBI and Natives, and no other deceased Native had drawn this kind of attention.

The woman was taken to the Pine Ridge Hospital, where, after a cursory autopsy, the pathologist resident at the nearby Scottsbluff, Nebraska, hospital reported that she had died of exposure. Instead of fingerprinting her, he severed her hands at the wrist and, at the behest of the FBI, sent the extremities to Washington DC for identification. Physicians at the Pine Ridge hospital were puzzled at the pathologist's conclusion, as they had seen a bloody flow from the base of the dead woman's skull, which is consistent with a traumatic injury. Nevertheless, without waiting for identification or announcing that a woman's body was in the morgue available for identification by potential family members, the unidentified woman was named "Jane Doe" and buried in a local Catholic cemetery.

The day after the burial, word came from Washington that the hands belonged to Anna Mae Pictou-Aquash, aged thirty. On 5 March Anna Mae's sisters in Canada were notified of her death. The older sister, Mary Lafford, was doubtful of the coroner's conclusion that Anna Mae had died of exposure and demanded through AIM attorney Bruce Ellison that the body be exhumed and an autopsy be performed. This time, a Minnesota pathologist quickly discovered that Anna Mae had been shot in the base of the skull at point-blank range with a 32-mm handgun. He also proposed that Anna Mae had been raped. He was surprised that the cause of death had not been noticed during the first autopsy. Indeed, so was the U.S. Civil Rights Commission, whose report referred to the oversight as incredible.[17]

On the cold, snowy day of 14 March 1976 Anna Mae was reburied on land belonging to Wallace Little, forever next to the grave of Joe Killsright Stuntz, the young Oglala man who was killed during the shoot-out between Indians and FBI agents. Her grave was prepared by young Oglala women, one of whom lay in the grave to determine if it was long enough. They adorned the Mi'kmaq woman's mutilated body with moccasins, a ribbon shirt, jeans, and a jacket with the AIM crest and upside-down American flag, then wrapped her in a star quilt. Instead of placing her in the government-issued coffin, the men assisting in preparations smashed it to bits. A young pregnant woman gathered sage, and six youth served as pallbearers. No male AIM leader was present at the burial, nor were her ex-lovers or ex-husbands.

Although some leaders were unable to attend, Russell Means and his brother Ted, along with several AIM members, drove past her funeral on their way to a basketball game a few miles away. After her mourners departed, the black, red, yellow, and white streamers attached to poles signifying the sacred directions blew in the wind. Wind blew hard and bitter, the way it responds, elders say, after a murder victim has been moved from the grave.

Paula Gunn Allen's truism, "You cannot be political without being spiritual," applies to Anna Mae Aquash more than most activists.[18] Throughout the last months of her life, Anna Mae spoke often about her premonitions of her death. Shortly after the publication of *Voices from Wounded Knee, 1973*(1974), which included a picture of Anna Mae and Nogeeshik at their wedding, Anna Mae took to heart what one of the elders told her after looking at her photograph: that she had no future and would die soon. Later, Anna Mae confided to her friend Bernie Nichols that she had dreamed she flew to the Spirit World in the form of a bird.[19] Prior to her trial in Pierre, Anna Mae commented to Nilak Butler (Dino's wife) that "the only way I could get away with anything, with all the fingerprints they [the FBI] took, would be to have my hands cut off."[20]

Intense debate over who killed Anna Mae emerged soon after her burial. FBI director Clarence Kelley stated that he was satisfied the FBI had nothing to do with her death. Another agent active in the 1970s events, Zigrossi, suggested that the AIM leadership had ordered her death, believing she was an informant working for the FBI. Her former lover, Dennis Banks, fearful that if that was true, "it would crush our movement," launched only a half-hearted investigation of events. AIM leader John Trudell, who lost his wife and three children in a mysterious trailer-home fire twelve hours after he gave an anti-FBI speech in Washington DC, argued that the FBI ordered Anna Mae's death in order to avenge the death of their two agents. "I think getting Anna Mae and Joe Stunz made it two-to-two," he said.[21] Nogeeshik Aquash, still involved in the struggle for Native rights, tried to find his ex-wife's killers. After years of collecting information about AIM and the FBI through the Freedom of Information Act, Nogeeshik, wheelchair-bound following a car wreck, was killed in a suspicious fire that destroyed his Sault Ste. Marie home along with his documentation.

Despite cursory probes and exculpatory pronouncements, little real investigation into Anna Mae's murder took place for years, and the last days of her life are unclear. In the early 1990s, Robert A. Pictou-Branscombe, a highly decorated Mi'kmaq combat Marine veteran, began pursuing information about his cousin. He concluded that in very early December she was questioned persistently by AIM members about being an informer. Then she was taken forcibly to South Dakota, where she was executed. Theda Nelson Clark, Arlo Looking Cloud, and teenager John Boy Patton, at least, were involved in the execution. From 1994 to 1998 reporters from *News from Indian Country*, a Wisconsin-based newspaper, interviewed a variety of people, including journalists, AIM members, and residents of Pine Ridge. They concluded that the FBI, using COINTELPRO (the bureau's counterintelligence program) tactics, "bad jacketed" Anna Mae, or purposely framed her as an informant for the FBI in order to create confusion among the AIM organization, and this in large part contributed to her death. One AIM member accused Trudell of instigating her execution, while others think the Bellecourt and Means brothers played a role in her death. After all, they reason, the latter had not been supportive of Anna Mae's efforts for AIM.[22] In March 1999 Detective Abe Alonzo of the Denver Police Department received permission to investigate Anna Mae's death. By June, Alonzo had narrowed the field to the same culprits that Pictou-Branscombe had identified.[23] In an October 1999 press conference, Pictou-Branscombe accused the AIM leadership of conspiring to have his cousin murdered. One month later, on 3 November, Russell Means announced in an emotionally charged statement delivered in Denver that Vernon Bellecourt had ordered Anna Mae's execution in a phone call to which other AIM leaders were privy.[24]

Hostility toward Anna Mae stemmed from many sources. The FBI probably did plant false rumors throughout the AIM structure that Anna Mae (and others) was an informer for them. But there are other reasons for the profound distrust and acrimony that led to her death. AIM members might have experienced the "siege mentality" common to combatants during times of war. Extraordinary circumstances produced heightened sensitivity and even irrationality that sometimes was directed toward those who did not seem to fit in. Anna Mae was an "outsider," a Canadian Indian, whose strong personality attracted attention to that status. The rumor that Peltier confided to her the identity of the people who killed the FBI agents and her knowledge of AIM's "secrets" made her a potentially dangerous person. Furthermore, many AIM members, including some of the AIM women, were jealous of Anna Mae's strong female character and her position within the AIM hierarchy. Whatever the mix of charged emotions, tragedy resulted.

Even in death, Anna Mae Pictou-Aquash has become a part of the movement. Dennis Banks acknowledged her pervasive influence in response to an interviewer's question about the last time he saw Anna

Mae: "I see Annie Mae today in every brave woman. She represented the troubles going on in the Indian community for centuries, and I've often felt that women such as these are the real warriors."[25] In May 1999 the ANNA Foundation, an international non-profit organization, was incorporated in Arizona by her family in order to continue what Anna Mae started: crusading to "preserve the Native languages, cultures, and traditions of the American Indian people." The ANNA Foundation supports a variety of individuals and programs, such as those pursuing university degrees or careers in art and entertainment and health and wellness and drug and alcohol rehabilitation programs.[26]

Despite the frustrations many Oglala women feel about Anna Mae's martyrdom and the belief that "she didn't do any more than the rest of us," the reality is that she has become a symbol of Native female activism. She dealt with chauvinism among male AIM leaders, she survived verbal and physical abuse by both her husbands, and she was ostracized by Lakota women who disapproved of a Mi'kmaq woman encroaching into their South Dakota AIM territory. Anna Mae kept striving for racial equality that, in theory, could eradicate gender oppression among Natives. If she had not been executed, her family firmly believes she would still be fighting for Native rights today.

Anna Mae lived up to her expectations for herself, which she outlined in a letter to her sister Rebecca written in the last month of her life: "My efforts to raise the consciousness of whites who are so against Indians in the States were bound to be stopped by the FBI sooner or later. . . . But I'm not going to stop fighting until I die, and I hope I'm a good example of a human being and my tribe."[27] She is remembered. The Indigenous Women's Network, for example, presents the annual Annie Mae Awards to honor the lifetime achievements of activist Native women. No matter where they struggle, Native women such as Anna Mae Pictou-Aquash, who often have not been the most visible or vocal of Native activists, prove through their actions, beliefs, and strength that they were, and still are, the foundations of their Nations.

**10**

Interview with Denise Maloney-Pictou
and Deborah Maloney-Pictou

Anna Mae Pictou-Aquash was a prominent American Indian Movement (AIM) activist in the 1970s. A Mi'kmaq from Nova Scotia, Anna
Mae had a long history of working for Native rights. She helped form
the Boston Indian Council and worked in Maine teaching Native students. In the early 1970s she participated in AIM's activities because
she believed that she could help secure equal rights for Natives. She
participated in numerous activities, including the boarding of the
*Mayflower II* to protest Thanksgiving, the march on Washington, and
the takeover of Wounded Knee in 1972–73. After Wounded Knee Anna
Mae worked for a while in the St. Paul, Minnesota, AIM office.

After the takeover at Wounded Knee ended, conditions remained
dire for South Dakota tribes. Poverty, crime, and disease raged among
them throughout the 1970s, and residents of the Pine Ridge Reservation experienced a "reign of terror" in which members of Oglala tribal
chairman Dick Wilson's political faction beat, shot, and harassed his
opponents almost on a daily basis. A "siege mentality" was beginning
to show among AIM members by 1975. On June 26 of that year, two FBI
agents, Ronald Williams and Jack Coler, arrived at the private Jumping
Bull property in South Dakota to arrest a young Native man accused
of stealing boots. A firefight ensued, and Williams, Coler, and one
Native man, Joseph Killsright Stuntz, were killed. One suspect in the
shooting was Leonard Peltier, who was arrested and imprisoned for
life for killing the agents.[1] Although Anna Mae was not present at the
shooting, the FBI was convinced that she knew who the killers were
and interrogated her intensely before releasing her. Later that year
she was arrested on a weapons charge and then was quickly released,
leading AIM members to believe that she was an informer for the FBI.

In the winter of 1976 Anna Mae's body was found in a remote area
of the reservation, although she was not immediately identified. The
initial autopsy concluded that she died of exposure. Her hands were
severed and sent to FBI headquarters for identification, and she was

buried in a local cemetery as a Jane Doe. After her fingerprints were identified, Anna Mae's family demanded a second autopsy, which revealed she was shot in the head. Immediately, AIM accused the FBI of instigating her murder, but the FBI denied the allegations and suggested that AIM members executed her because the leadership believed she was an FBI informer. For almost twenty-five years the case was not seriously pursued. Then, in the early 1990s, Anna Mae's cousin Robert A. Pictou-Branscombe, a former Marine and Vietnam veteran, , began a personal investigation into the death of his cousin.[2]

After years of inquiry that brought him face-to-face with the individual who says he was the shooter, Pictou-Branscombe has announced that Anna Mae was murdered by three Indigenes at the behest of the AIM leadership. It is Pictou-Branscombe's belief (and, indeed, the belief of many others) that Anna Mae was executed in part because she knew who the FBI informers were among the AIM members and because she knew who killed the two FBI agents at the 1975 shoot-out on the Jumping Bull property. Some have also asserted that if Anna Mae's murder is solved then Peltier will be exonerated. This has, of course, ignited an enormous controversy among everyone involved, all denying that they played a role in her death.[3]

Most discussions and textualized documents about Anna Mae revolve around her involvement with AIM. What is usually ignored, however, is that Anna Mae had a life outside of fighting for Native rights and that she had a family. Her two daughters, Denise and Deborah, were very young when their mother was killed, and they remained quietly in the background until recently. Now, in their thirties and with families of their own, they have stepped forward to talk about their mother and their desire for justice.

This conversation I had with Anna Mae's daughters took place via phone on Thanksgiving eve, 1999. Denise was on the line from Ontario and Deborah from Nova Scotia. Both are now vocalizing their desire to have their mother's murder solved. We talked about many things: Anna Mae, education, the importance of family, and what the memory of their mother means to them. I was not interested in printing intricacies about who killed Anna Mae. Although we did talk about many aspects of Anna Mae's murder, much of the information is not appropriate for publication at this time, and we collectively decided to omit portions of our conversation. I was more focused on finding out what it means to be the daughters of Anna Mae Pictou-Aquash and how they have adjusted without her.

Denise and Deborah (who prefer to use the last name Maloney-Pictou for print) are two very well-adjusted, intelligent, and happy women. We laughed throughout the interview, and I thoroughly enjoyed our three-way conversation. My tape recorder and telephone conference call feature were never particularly efficient, and at one point my smoke detector went off, but we managed to create an interview that I hope will give readers better insight into Anna Mae and especially into two interesting women who deserve to have their voices heard.

DM: Shannon told me that the first time people were to see you in a public setting would be at the July 2000 memorial to your mother that will take place in Nova Scotia.[4] Then I saw your faces on an October cover of *Indian Country Today* [in a photograph] that was taken at the news conference in Ottawa.[5] I'm wondering if you planned to have your photos taken?

DENISE: That was decided within about two hours.

DM: Have you gotten a lot of response?

DENISE: No, I think we didn't really understand the importance and the weight that this particular news conference was going to carry. We were there supporting Robert to go to Parliament. But, knowing how the government is and knowing how the Canadian media can be, it was suggested that maybe they would take it a little more seriously if one or more of Anna Mae's daughters were there. Again, we had that fear issue that we had to contend with because you know, the circumstances under which she died and all of the complexities of everything that's coming to light now. At the time we didn't know who these people were, where they were, you know. We both have families to think of.

DEBBIE: We talked to Dad [Jake Maloney, Anna Mae's first husband] about it.

DENISE: That's right. We had talked to our dad about it, and he basically reassured us and told us that it was time we took the bull by the horns and took a stand. People needed to know what her daughters felt and what they wanted done. And in talking to him, we felt reassured, and we both made the decision to go.

DM: What does your dad think about all this?

DENISE: He's very supportive. And I think he always knew this day would come. That we would basically take ownership of our mother and do what was right as a family member in getting justice and finding out the truth of what happened to her.

DEBBIE: I think a lot of family members knew that. And they knew it would come when we were ready. Because they're coming out now and telling us that this day would come.

DM: I acquired a variety of documents about your mother this summer from an unexpected source. Did either of you see these documents before they were sent to you?

DENISE: Not to my knowledge. Did you show that to any of the family, Debbie?

DEBBIE: Mary [Anna Mae's sister] had never seen it or heard of [one of those items] when I read it to her. And I didn't check with Rebecca [Anna Mae's other sister].

[At this point we discussed the origins of the documents, who had them and why, and why they were not sent to the family.]

DM: I'm wondering if the information that is new to you makes you look at things differently?

DENISE: We're very skeptical at everything we receive and hear because you've got everybody coming out of the wall, from every angle, so we take everything with a grain of salt. It's hard to say that we can really 100 percent believe anything. Why would people have these items and not pass them on to the family knowing full well that it was meant for the family? To me that's very hard to understand why they wouldn't hand that over after twenty years. There's lots of questions at every level. I think that Debbie and I are tired of asking questions and are starting to become very focused on what our mission is in finding out the truth and getting justice for her death. And I think that's what really needs to be done, is to remain focused and it's time to put the blinders up and to have an open ear, but yet not necessarily be so gullible and believe everything that's thrown in front of us right now. Because obviously there are lots of stories out there that aren't true.

DM: Do think people are intrusive for wanting to know about your mother?

DEBBIE: I don't feel that.

DENISE: No, I've never felt that at any level. In kind of a bizarre way, we've been running alongside of them trying to find out just as much information as they are. Their questions have helped us learn more about her. More often than not, in every aspect we learn something new.

DM: What happened to all of her possessions?

DENISE: We have no idea, and I read somewhere in a book or a passage, and it made me very angry, that someone had been rifling through her personal belongings—her purse of all things—and they were talking about holding on to a piece of soap that was in her purse wrapped up in a piece of foil. And I thought, "My God." I tried to find the date when this was written and [was] thinking "what is wrong with these people?" And that aspect of it makes me very angry. I can't speak for Debbie.

DEBBIE: Yes, I feel the same way.

DENISE: Those personal things were supposed to be sent back to her family and they never were.

[Another discussion ensued about items some people have that belonged to Anna Mae and now rightfully belong to her family.]

DM: I would think that considering the way Bob [Robert Pictou-Branscombe] analyzes everything, he's probably got that on his list. What are you going to tell your kids and grandchildren about your mother?

DENISE: I'm always the optimist here. I'll going to tell them that the truth shall prevail. [laughter] That's what I'm gonna tell them. My God, I actually believed my mother when she said there was justice in truth and every other adult that came thereafter who told me, "Don't lie. Tell the truth, you'll always come out winning in the end." I may live in some kind of fantasy world, but that's what many people tell their children every day, and we turn around and blatantly lie. The truth only works if you do this, or if you pay this person off, or you're friends with the particular group of people. That's what I would tell them.

DEBBIE: We've never ever seen or heard of our mother in a bad light.

DENISE: No, never.

DEBBIE: Nobody has ever said anything negative about her. Even before all of this came out recently, and even when she was still living and we were living with our dad and with our stepmom. Nobody ever said anything negative about her. And we truly believe there wasn't anything negative about her.

DENISE: There have been petty things said, but nothing to do with her character or her person or who she was and what she stood for or what she lived for.

DM: Some of the AIM leadership are acting remorseful over her death, at least for print. Did any of them write you letters of condolence after her death?

DENISE: Nooooo. Nothing. [much laughter]

DEBBIE: Someone recently offered their condolences after twenty-something years, and we laughed because it's way too late for that.

DENISE: That's right. Too little, too late. That's just the way we look at it. I don't think we're being harsh or vindictive or hateful. And as Debbie has stated before in press conferences, if these people want to talk to us, talk to a grand jury. We don't want to hear your confessions. We don't want to hear your excuses. After the dust settles, if people want to still come forward and talk to us, then maybe we'll talk to them. But really, with all of this circus that's going on right now it's really hard for us to decipher who is being genuine and who isn't. All of our contact right now is through phone or through e-mail. We refuse to talk to anybody face-to-face right now. It's for our own safety. [laughter]

DM: Well, you're mothers and you must think of that.

DENISE: Exactly. That does come out. And we're very protective of her memory. We don't want people running around wearing their memories or their recollections or their stories that they've heard from three other people as some kind of badge of authenticity, that they have some sort of truth to say that we haven't heard already. Really, we haven't heard anything new from anybody that has tried to talk to us before. There's nothing so earth-shattering or so new that would lead us to believe that they were seeking the truth or that they were saying anything that would validate that they were her friends. Anybody can say that they were anybody's friend. It's a matter of our word against theirs.

DM: Have you seen the Brookes movie about Anna Mae?[6] Some of the people in the film showed some very bad acting in pretending that they didn't know what happened to your mother. What did you think of the movie?

DENISE: It's no different from what these people are saying now, really, for me. It's hard for us because everybody is saying something, but they're all blaming each other. And we don't know them from a hole in the wall. None of the people up in Canada, her family members, knew anything really about AIM or about the people she was with, who she said were her friends. So who do we trust? We're at their mercy basically—or so they think we are. And I think that one way to protect ourselves is we've become quite skeptical of everyone. We know how news travels in Indian country. We know that it's a close-knit community. So we know that these people would have heard rumors, they would have heard comments.

DEBBIE: What's really surprising is when you look at something as simple as the fact that there had been three or four grand juries in regards to that case, then you know there is enough information there, somewhere. Somehow, this case is slipping through the cracks each and every time. Now, if there is enough information to bring us to grand jury that many times, then why don't they tell us what they're missing? What do they need? Put it plain and simple. This is what we need, these are the witnesses that we need.

DENISE: That's right.

DEBBIE: But nothing like that has ever been put out there by the investigators. It's never been on *Unsolved Mysteries*. [laughter] It's never been on any news program. [laughter] No, really. That's really frustrating. So there is information out there, there are witnesses out there, there are people who know things. And we're just hoping that . . .

DENISE: And the worst thing is that we know that they know. [laughter] That they know that we know that they know. [laughter]

DM: Russell Means has said that he's going to make a movie with a character named Anna Mae in honor of your mother. So who do you want to play you two? [much laughter]

DEBBIE: I don't want to be portrayed at all.

DENISE: No, neither do I. I don't. See, we don't know about this at all. This is all new to us. That just gives you an idea of the position that we've been in for the last twenty-three years. And I get worked up about this because I'm not saying that the story shouldn't be told. The more the merrier as far as I'm concerned. I don't want any monetary compensation. Debbie and I've never thought that. But it would be nice to know instead of reading in the paper that there's a movie out about your mother. Or a new book out about your mother or a new article on your mother instead of having a friend call you up and say "Hey, did you know . . . ?"

DEBBIE: That's happened a lot and it's embarrassing.

DENISE: Yes, it's embarrassing. And it makes me angry because people get lost in the legends and they forget that my mother was a person. They forget that she was a mother and that she had a family. And really, that's the best way I can describe it. I'm not in any way discrediting what my mother did and how important she is to the Native community and to women. I'm right out there with her. Quite honestly, that's just my personality. I don't know if it's genetic or what it is, but I'm the first one to get out there and start arguing with somebody about the rights of women, and Native women in particular. And children and education and everything she stood for. We were nine and seven when we saw her last or when we lived with her last. And you can teach a child a lot in nine years and in seven years about what's right ethically and what's wrong. And she did give us a sense—which we're realizing right now how similar and how familiar it is to how she was—through what everybody else's accounts were about who she was as a person.

DM: It seems some people are appropriating her. They're taking over her memory and doing with it what they want.

DENISE: That again, I don't think that her memory, or what was her, is ours to own as far as restricting people on what they want to say. Everyone has a take on what their experience with her was. And that is theirs. We weren't there. Quite honestly, I have to question people who have never met her, writing and doing things and going on accounts again, or hearsay, that seems to be the big word today. I find it very frustrating. I try not to think about it too much because I know that it's been done for twenty-three years and there's not really a heck of a lot that's going to change people. My only hope is that the people who did know her and the people [who] are learning about her now are knowing that the information is not always the truth just because it's written down or is seen on a screen.

DM: Has what happened to your mom made you two closer? I realize that you've always been close, but have you been getting closer?

DENISE: [laughter] No. There's no way we could possibly get any closer. We share the same brain—we always have, we always will. Before any of this happened we talked to each other almost daily on the phone. And we still do. I remember my mother looking at both of us and saying that "You know, for the rest of your life you'll never have anyone else but each other." That's what she said to us. My father instilled that as well, growing up, how important the other was, especially when we were in knock-down drag-out arguments in teenage-hood. She said, "One day, you're going to look over and you're in the worst place you can be and there's your sister standing there for you." We've always had that connection since I can't even remember. Must have been since birth, or since Debbie was born, that's for sure. We're very protective of each other growing up and even today.

DM: When young kids loose a parent, particularly their mother, they often have many difficulties, but you two have kept it together.

DENISE: It's because we had each other and because of the relationship we had.

DEBBIE: Even when we were with her, and living with her, I remember relying on Denise so much. She was always like my mother. In the middle of the night with sirens going by 'cause we lived in the city, I would always crawl in bed with her. Or if I needed something or wanted something I would always go to her. Not so much now [laughter], but I've always gone to her.

DENISE: There was a time when Mother first went to Wounded Knee that she took me aside and looked me in the eye and told me that I had to watch out for Debbie. She was putting me in charge. So of course, when you're nine years old, you're thinking, "Yahoo." [laughter] "I'm the boss." And I've always been that since that day on. [laughter] You can ask my husband. [laughter] I've never let go of that handle.

DM: So which one of you is the martial artist? [laughter]

DEBBIE: That's Denise.

DENISE: Everyone thinks I am, and I don't deny it. I've been around it my whole life, with my dad being a martial artist. Everyone assumes we took classes, and then of course my husband happened to be one of father's students, and when we got married and moved here to Ontario we started our own school, and I fell into the routine because I had been around it my whole life. I obviously set them straight when people ask me. I don't wear a sign saying, "I don't have my black belt." So it goes with the territory.

DM: It's probably good to let them think that right now.

DEBBIE: Exactly. [laughter]

DM: To be metaphysical, it appears that your mom is still at work.

DENISE: Oh yeah. We've known that for a long time. With me being classically trained as a scientist, I denied that for a long time. But there's just too much going on that's flowing in the right direction. To put a focus on what we're doing: I think that's what truth is. That's how truth goes. That's how justice goes. I believe my family when they said the truth shall prevail. It will come out.

DM: Your mom really valued education.

DENISE: Both of us are educated. I've become a professional student. [laughter] I love it; I love learning new things. It's the solution to a lot of things that are wrong today in our society and in the way people think and in the way the treat each other. It's because they're not educated. They don't know, they become very involved in their own little realms. There's nothing wrong with that, but you always have to have an open mind and be willing to learn. That's a part of life—learning. My mother was an advocate for Native schooling. And you have to consider how it was twenty-three years ago. Blatant racism in the school system. Debbie and I experienced it when we were growing up. I shudder to think that my child will have to experience it one day. On the other hand, I know that I am hoping to give him the ammunition and understanding as to why people think that way so that it won't hurt him. That he will understand their shortcomings and their misunderstandings and their inability to understand their fear. We see it everyday on the news.

It's not as bad as it was twenty-three years ago or even when we went to school. We didn't experience anything that harmed us physically. It left a couple of mental scars but nothing serious, and I don't think any child should have to go through that. And I know my mother was an advocate of teaching Native heritage and preserving Native cultures, and I think that her mind back then was that the only way to attain that is to pull your kids out of the regular system and home school them and teach them your ways. It can be done through the regular school system, too.

DM: Russell Means spoke at NAU recently, and he said that Indian parents should take their children out of school at third grade. Do you think Russell is right?

DENISE: No, I think Russell is still thinking back a few years. Some traditionalists don't realize that isolating ourselves from the rest of the world can mean the extinction of tradition. We have to make it part of our everyday lives by integrating it into our everyday teaching routines. Teaching at home may have been a good idea twenty-three years ago when racism was very much a part of our school systems. Running and hiding from the problems doesn't help to solve them. If the next generation is going to be in any way successful in breaking down some barriers then they need to educate themselves in the same way the rest of the world does or they won't be equipped to fight the battles.

DM: Your mom was ahead of her time in many respects. She apparently was a deep thinker and had aspirations of writing a book on the histories of tribes from the tribal viewpoints. Her intelligence and aspirations set her apart, and that may have brought about a lot of jealously.

DEBBIE: There's intimidation, too. Does weird things to people anyway. We weren't there, we don't know who the other women were who were around her. We have no idea because she never spoke of them. She never said, "My good friend so and so . . ." So I don't know what to say about that.

DM: I've met some of the women who were there; your mom's name never comes up because they're very closemouthed about this. Even more so recently and with good reason, it appears. What is your identity as Mi'kmaqs? How do you see yourselves as Indian women? Are you traditionals? Progressives? Activists?

DENISE: Aggressive activists. [laughter] I'm sitting on the fence. I definitely have an activist mind, but I do tone it down a bit right now. I'm not saying that it's always going to stay that way. I don't like to put labels on myself or anyone else. I know in my heart that there are certain values that I live by, and I have a certain philosophy that I try my best one day and then take a couple of steps back the next day and then I try even harder the next day. I do know myself as progressive, definitely. And I know—and here's one little piece of information—one of the reasons I don't care to talk to any of the original AIM leaders is that in my heart I know that my mother was progressive. I don't want to say she was a feminist. She was more of an activist. She knew that she had certain rights as a human being, not necessarily as a woman, but as a human being. And a lot of the thinking back then obviously didn't accept that attitude, and I know she ticked off a lot of men. Just knowing that, and listening to these gentlemen—if you want to call them that—talk, I can hear exactly what my mother would have said. Not because of her ways, but because of the comments that come flying out of my mouth and out of my brain when I listen to these people talk. That's how I know, because every time I hear something new I never sit down and say, "Well, that's the way things are."

DEBBIE: If you were to look Denise and I, our personalities combined would make what our mother is. I'm opposite from what Denise is; I'm quiet. [laughter] When it comes to serious things that need to be addressed, things that need to be said, I'm the one that takes the bull by the horns. Denise is the one who has her fire. I'm the one who has Mom's passiveness, and I'm more the one not necessarily focused on the small details, but . . .

DENISE: Yeah, you are. You are focused on the small details. You keep me on track. [laughter]

DEBBIE: I'm very realistic.

DENISE: Yes, definitely.

DEBBIE: I'm the passive side of her, I'm the compassionate one. The soft one, the thoughtful one.

DENISE: Yes. Yes.

DEBBIE: And the one when it comes down to emotions—well, I can't even say emotions now anymore—cause you're the one who first cried at the press conference. [laughter] I'm always accused of being the emotional one.

DM: Y'all laugh exactly alike.

DEBBIE: Yes. But I'm the softer side of Anna Mae.

DENISE: She has our mother's heart. I know I have my mother's fire, I've always had it. And that's what I remember about my mother. I remember her being very passionate and very focused and very adamant about certain things. Like her telling me a hundred times, "Don't you lie." This was engraved into my mind: "Whatever you do, don't lie." It's just amazing, as Debbie said, how much of our personalities have taken qualities of her own that we didn't even know about. Like we said, learning about her through different people and from what Robert has done, and from obviously talking to family. These avenues were all very kind and considerate in waiting until we were ready; they didn't push it on us, they never asked questions. We had aunts and uncles who said we needed to wait until you guys were ready.

DEBBIE: And we weren't ready until now. We went through a stage where we were fearful, as teenagers growing up. And then we went through a stage when we were angry. It was not until we got settled and we became mothers ourselves and we're okay with our lives that we needed to fix the missing piece. And that's what we need to do now.

DENISE: That's right. For her grandchildren as well. And for the rest of her family. She had family! She had sisters and brothers and nieces and nephews and brothers-in-law and sisters-in-law. She had a full life, and she wasn't just a legend. She was a human being. She was like you. AIM was only a small part of her life.

DEBBIE: That's right.

DENISE: Wounded Knee was not her whole life. Wounded Knee did not make my mother. My mother was who she was before she got to Wounded Knee. And everyone that really knows her knows that. And that's the big qualifier. [laughter] If you print that, then now everyone's going to say, "We knew your mother before Wounded Knee." [laughter]

DM: What do you think she would be doing today?

DENISE: Probably the same thing as far as schooling goes.

DEBBIE: She would be doing exactly what we're doing. For somebody else who had been silenced. She would be fighting for women's rights. For Native rights. For schooling.

DENISE: Schooling. Education. I think she would have carried on, and I think she could have changed a lot. There are a lot of Anna Mae's out there right now and a lot of people doing what she was doing right now. It's going; they're getting it done to a certain level. It's obviously a process. It doesn't happen overnight. Education is the key, and she knew that. She knew that she had to teach people what the Native issues were and what was happening in their own country. She said that. Her sisters said the same thing. She was ahead of her time. And we all know that now because we see the same thing being done today by certain individuals that want to see progress. And that's where I come in with the progressive side of me, because I know that we do have to change our thinking and our education and our learning tactics in order to get the kind of progression that we need. We have to be open minded but still hold onto our heritages and our pasts and change with the rest of the world and the rest of the universe.

DM: Are y'all active in your tribe?

DEBBIE: Active in the sense that we've always maintained contact with the community there. We never actually lived there, although both of our parents did. We grew up approximately thirty minutes from the reserve and usually visited with family on the reserve weekly. It was difficult for both of us to maintain a consistent contact with family once we both moved away. I resided in British Columbia for almost twelve years, and it is only now that I have moved back to Nova Scotia that I am able to have more involvement in the community there. And although we had lived apart from the community there, the connection has never been lost. The Indian Brook First Nation community has wholeheartedly supported us on our quest for justice and has been there for us every step of the way. We are also at the point in our lives now where we are able to start learning more on our Mi'kmaq language and traditions. It's easier for me living here now. More difficult for Denise.

DENISE: She is right. It is more difficult for me to maintain direct contact to my family back east because of geography. Which brings me to the point that I am a true believer that you do not have to be in the thick of things to make a difference. There is a lot to be said for spirit and family. I will always be my families' relation, nothing will ever change the fact that I am a Pictou, Maloney, or Mi'kmaq. My thoughts and my heart are with them always, very much in the same way our mother is with us. We spent a lot of time building our families; we needed to have that stable foundation. You need to have that core. If you don't have that, then really, I don't think that you can go on without having some kind of resentment if you don't have some kind of sound base, and I think that's what we needed to do in order to stand up for ourselves and start saying how we felt and what we thought. I had someone ask me over the weekend, "What do you think you can do?" And I said, "I'm not sure what I can do, but I know I can do something, and I think that's half the battle." You have to know that you can make a difference, that you can make a change. You have to have that positive attitude. You have to believe that. You can't have a pessimistic or a defeatist attitude. You have to know that you can do it and then you can. Politics—I don't think we're running for office yet. [laughter] I tell everyone that I used to be very silent and not voice my opinion, but I'm very opinionated. Stop laughing at me, Debbie.

DEBBIE: Usually when I run out of my opinions I call her for some more.

DM: A lot of people might say that Anna Mae was a hard person to live up to. But it sounds like you both have.

DENISE: I don't think that we've ever felt that way, have you, Debbie?

DEBBIE: No.

DENISE: No. Because we knew her as our mother, and we've known her as our mother for thirty-five years. She stood up for common sense. We think about her on a regular basis, and I think that's what people have lost, their destination or their way off the beaten path. We're all trying to attain the same goal, the truth. And that's why we're pushing forward on this.

DM: Will you attend any of the trial if it does happen?

DENISE: I would like to.

DEBBIE: I would, too. Whether or not it's possible, it depends on what's happening at the time. We appreciate you being sensitive and considerate. This is the first time someone's been that considerate. We appreciate it. We trust Shannon. You sound a lot like her, actually. That southern accent.

DM: My drawl comes out when I'm tired. Anything else? You want to think about it. It's late there. You guys are well-protected and all that?

DENISE: Oh yeah.

DEBBIE: Yes, yes.

DENISE: That's not an issue with us anymore because we're not looking for anything that is wrong or undeserving. We're looking for fundamental things. We're looking for the truth. How basic can you get? It's not a complex thing, and that's what gets Debbie and me.

DEBBIE: And it's not as if people don't know the information. It's not as if this hasn't been said before. The question is, Why is something not being done? That's the biggest question.

DENISE: I'm the optimist here, and I do feel it in my bones that it's going to get done. That we will get the truth, and we will get justice. My reality is they can't kill us all.

DEBBIE: Right. [laughter]

DENISE: There are too many of us.

DM: This does have to end at some point.

DENISE: I've heard that comment before but in a strange way. This facet may not continue, but what this whole thing represents—and in some weird form it may be someone else's name, it may be a different circumstance, but it will continue—that quest for truth and for justice. It will continue, and that's the irony in all of this is that so many out there make half-wit comments like, "Why don't you let it rest?" "You're beating a dead horse." And all these stupid comments. And I'm like, "You people are not getting the picture." You don't understand what this is about. It's not about one women; it's not. It's about a whole era. A whole generation, a whole concept of thinking. A way of life for people who have [been] allowed to poison themselves. They're not thinking about the basics. I'm not a religious person, but the Ten Commandments pop into my mind. And I call them words to live by, the fundamental ethics of being a human being. And to living socially with other people. You just don't do that to each other.

DM: And there are many people that you'll never know about and never hear from that are just waiting to see what's going to happen. They want justice to be done. And this whole thing is meaningful to young and old people who were around when your mother was murdered and now are waiting for justice.

DENISE: What is so appalling is that I actually believed my mother when she told me the truth will prevail and that there is truth in justice, and we always tell ourselves that we're evolved in this era that we live in, and when we really think about it and we see the same things coming to light again and nothing is being done and people are running around basically in circles. It's amazing. It shows how much we are not evolved in our thinking. It's disturbing. I find this very disturbing and disheartening at times, just thinking about it. I know that people will say I live in a fantasy world or that I'm idealistic. I think that we need to be that way in order to get through things like this. I know what the reality is. I refuse to accept it as the norm. I think we have the intelligence in ourselves to change that. And that's all I have to say.

DM: Well okay. [laughter] I appreciate it. Call me or e-mail if you have something else to add.

DENISE: We haven't had anybody give us access to our interview.

DM: I've been misquoted quite a few times so I understand and will give you the opportunity to look at this. I'm not a journalist, and my livelihood isn't based on producing sensational interviews.

DENISE: We know we have had the opportunity on three separate occasions to say what we have said here today, and really, we have yet to be heard. But in all three conferences the media focused on us drying each other's tears or me breaking down in Parliament instead of what we have to say and why we're doing it. [laughter] Again, that's the media.

DM: Brings to mind the Eagles' song about "Dirty Laundry." That's what people want to publish because that's what sells.

DENISE: Right. They don't want to hear about what we're doing.

DEBBIE: I hope you can come up to the memorial that we're going to have in Nova Scotia.

DM: I would love to do that.

DEBBIE: We envision the memorial, too, and we're going to try everything in our power to make sure the memorial happens.

DM: I've enjoyed this so much y'all. And you do have lots of supporters. Thanks and Happy Thanksgiving.

DENISE: We had ours already. Canada's thanksgiving is the twelfth of October.

DM: Oh. Well, never mind.

DENISE: Christmas. That's what we're looking at right now.

DM: Merry Christmas then. [laughter]

# 11

## Activism and Expression as Empowerment

What I learned when I became involved in political issues is that our perceptions as women very much relate to our cultural, racial, traditional backgrounds. I found that my work, which is primarily political work, became spiritual work as well because the protection of our spiritual practice and sacred sites is a political issue. My work also relates to the health of our communities, women's health, and domestic violence. I consider my political work to be all encompassing because these issues are all related. – Mililani B. Trask, native Hawaiian, attorney, and elected prime minister (kia-aina) of Ka Lahui Hawai'i, the Sovereign Native Nation of Hawai'i

Today, more Indigenous women participate in tribal politics than ever before.[1] As discussed in chapter 6, although Native women traditionally did not serve as tribal "leaders" per se, they did control tribal activities by dictating the recipients of crops, declaring leaders, and serving as mothers, advisors, medicine women, midwives, and manufacturers of skins, hides, clothing, and implements. Females figured prominently in tribal religious stories as well. Many modern Native women leaders point to their tribal religions and traditions as inspiration and justification for their positions as leaders. They argue that taking leadership roles is a way of regaining the prestige and power their ancestors once held and of assuming responsibility for the welfare of their tribes.

Research suggests that white women leaders tend to emphasize certain aspects of their life more than male leaders might. Those "women's issues" are considered to be child care, reproductive rights, spousal and child abuse, health care, education, and welfare.[2] Native women, however, have the best interests of all aspects of their tribe in mind, from those issues listed above to environmental issues, including concerns over land, water, and air pollution as well as worries about how that pollution affects humans (poisons in breast milk and salmon, for example).

Mililani B. Trask concurs that ethnicity has everything to do with her political decisions: "I cannot stress enough how gender, ethnicity, and race very much impacted the way I look at the world and the way that I exercise my leadership role. . . . My background as a woman, as a woman of color, and as an indigenous woman of color has exposed me to a great deal of prejudice. . . . all these things, which might be called detriments by some people, could have been stumbling blocks, but they have given me strengths. They exposed me to racial bias, sexism, and other types of prejudices and taught me a great deal about what it means to be a leader and how leaders must fight for recognition."[3] Studies also suggest that a women's ethnic background will have more impact on her decision-making as a leader than will her gender, and the few studies on the topic reveal that men and women tribal leaders tend to focus on the same issues.[4]

Although Seneca activist Alice Jemison (1901–64) did not serve as a formal leader of her tribe, she was an outspoken Native woman who championed tribal rights. Through the American Indian Federation, Jemison relentlessly criticized the Bureau of Indian Affairs during the New Deal era. She was raised in poverty, yet because of her tribe's respect for women and her knowledge of the traditional roles Seneca and Cherokee women played (Jemison primarily identified with her mother's tribe, the Seneca), she developed the confidence to wage an aggressive verbal war against the government. She was determined to protect her tribe's civil and treaty rights, even when her commentaries led government officials to label her a "fascist" and put her under FBI surveillance.[5]

An Iroquois woman, Laura Miriam "Minnie" Cornelius Kellogg (1880–1947), also fought for tribal rights. Kellogg, a highly educated, well-traveled Oneida who attended Grafton Hall, Stanford, Columbia, and Cornell used her education and speaking abilities (both in English and in Oneida) to help found the Society of American Indians and to champion tribal rights, self-sufficiency, and the maintenance and continuity of tribal cultures. Like Jemison, Kellogg's intense pride in being an Iroquois woman gave her the confidence to speak her mind. Unfortunately, despite her gift for oratory, talent for strategizing for her people, and desire to help other Iroquois, Kellogg may have faltered in her determination to assist Native peoples, and she leaves a confusing legacy. She has been accused of swindling Iroquois people out of thousands of dollars intended for their land claims. As her biographer, Laurence M. Hauptman, put it, Kellogg "is blamed today for all that went wrong in Iroquois history during the interwar period from 1919 to 1941," yet she also "dealt with questions of Iroquois treaty rights and sovereignty as well as with other fundamental aspirations, needs, and values of her people."[6]

An Ojibwe woman, Naaneebweque (1824–64), also known as Catherine Sutton, was a Christianized, educated spokesperson for her tribe, although she lost her tribal status after she married an English missionary. In 1860 Naaneebweque and Queen Victoria discussed land ownership rights for her people, in addition to the issue of Native women losing tribal status after marrying white men. Although the queen promised support, she never gave it, and Naaneebweque's band was removed to Cape Croker, Ontario. Nevertheless, she is honored as one of the first Native land-claim activists. Recently, developers wanting to build a seniors' resort have encroached upon the graves of Naaneebweque and her family in Cape Croker, but because of the Chippewas' protests, the project was halted.[7]

A more current example, Wilma Mankiller, served as principal chief of the Oklahoma Cherokee Nation from 1985 to 1995, and she did not deal with only "women's issues." While she had enormous responsibility in dealing with female interests, she also faced issues on everything from treaty rights to emerging tribal enterprises. Under Mankiller's tenure, the tribe re-established the tribal judicial system and district courts and created new businesses. Numerous agencies presented her with awards: she was inducted into the Oklahoma Hall of Fame (1986), named *Ms.* magazine's Woman of the Year (1987), included in *Ladies Home Journal*'s list of the one hundred most important women in America (1988), and received numerous honorary degrees from colleges and universities such as Dartmouth and Yale.[8]

Like Wilma Mankiller, Comanche LaDonna Harris has also been active in all arenas of tribal life. Ironically, she became active in politics through her former non-Indian husband, the Democratic senator from Oklahoma, Fred R. Harris. LaDonna Harris currently lives in New Mexico, a fair distance from the Comanche Tribe, and tends to focus more on pan-Indian issues than on her tribe's issues. For example, she co-founded the Albuquerque Indian Center, assisted the Taos Pueblos in reacquiring Taos Blue Lake, and helped the Menominee Indian Tribe of Wisconsin receive federal recognition. She served as a member of the U.S. Advisory Council on the National Information Infrastructure, founded Oklahomans for Indian Opportunity (OIO) in 1965 and Americans for Indian Opportunity (AIO) in 1970, and assisted in founding the National Women's Political Caucus, the Council for Energy Resources for Tribes, and the National Indian Business Association.[9]

Former tribal chairperson of the Menominee Indian Tribe of Wisconsin Ada Deer has also dealt with more than "women's issues." Deer was the first woman to be assistant secretary for Indian affairs in the Department of the Interior. In that capacity Deer has been active in women's issues, and she has served as a member of the president's Inter-Agency Council on Women and has implemented the Platform for Action from the United Nation's Human Rights Committee. Deer is best known for her work for her tribe. In the early 1970s she was vice president and lobbyist for the National Committee to Save the Menominee People and Forest, Inc., and she also served as chair of the Menominee Restoration Committee, an organization that helped to restore tribal status to the tribe in 1954. She has served on a plethora of committees, such as the Girl Scouts of the USA, the National Association of Social Workers, the National Women's Education Fund, and the Wisconsin's Women's Council, and she has garnered numerous awards for her services.[10]

It is clear that Native women play important tribal leadership roles. One organization that strongly supports Native women's leadership is the Young Native Women's Leadership Conference, sponsored by Northern Arizona University and co-sponsored by the Arizona Department of Education–Vocational Equity Division. The purpose of the annual conference is to provide young Native women with role models in a variety of careers, such as politics and law enforcement. The young women not only gain information about future careers but also are encouraged to maintain close ties to their tribal traditions, which in turn helps them to develop confidence, self-esteem, and a strong sense of identity.[11]

The role model for the Navajo participants in the Young Native Women's Leadership Conference was Annie Dodge Wauneka (1910–97), the daughter of the first elected chairman of the Navajo Tribe, Henry Chee Dodge, a wealthy rancher and politician who gave his daughter a privileged childhood. She earned a B.S. degree in public health and worked tirelessly to improve health care among Navajos. In addition, she served as an effective mediator between the traditional and progressive tribal members. The tribe recognized her efforts and elected her the first woman on the Tribal Council. She also was presented the Arizona State Public Health Association's Outstanding Worker in Public Health Award and the Indian Council Fire of Chicago's Indian Achievement Award in 1959. John Kennedy presented her with the Presidential Medal of Freedom in 1963.[12]

## Land and Environment

From toxic uranium and nuclear waste to PCBs in breast milk to water, air, and land pollution to the extinction of flora and fauna integral to the subsistence and religion of Native peoples, the environments inhabited and utilized by Natives have been abused and appropriated. Often one finds that leaders of the fights to restore, clean up, and heal are women.

One of the most notable environmental activists is Winona La-Duke, a member of the White Earth Band of Ojibwe in Minnesota. A graduate of Harvard and Ralph Nader's recent vice presidential candidate, LaDuke began her activist efforts at a young age and spoke before the United Nations at age eighteen. LaDuke is the author of fiction and non-fiction works that focus on environmental and cultural issues and attempts to bring Native issues to the national political arena. Interestingly, LaDuke's father, Vincent LaDuke, known as "Sun Bear," was described by many as a New Ager who exploited Native religious traditions for profit. Winona, however, describes him as an "activist."[13]

Responding to illegal appropriation of White Earth lands by the U.S. government and the logging industry, LaDuke founded the White Earth Land Recovery Project and to date has acquired one thousand of the thirty thousand acres the group intends to purchase.[14] In 1985, along with Ingrid Washinawatok (an activist who was murdered in Venezuela in 1999 while helping to set up a school system for the U'Was), LaDuke founded the Indigenous Women's Network (IWN) for the purpose of preserving the traditions of Native women and to provide a system of support for Native activism, especially in the areas of health care (particularly sterilization, reproductive rights, and education), environmental protection and preservation (including water, wildlife, and land), and preservation of traditional cultural knowledge and traditions that often are passed through the generations by tribal women. The IWN strives to encourage Native women to use their tribal traditional knowledge to assist them in formulating successful community projects. LaDuke also serves on the board of directors of Greenpeace, USA. For her efforts, LaDuke won the International Reebok Human Rights Award in 1989, was named one of *Time* magazine's Fifty Leaders of the Future in 1995, and was *Ms.* magazine's Woman of the Year in 1997.[15]

LaDuke often espouses the concept of the "Seventh Generation," an Iroquois ideology that is used today by environmentally conscious people to consider how current decisions about the environment and its limited resources would affect the seventh generation of descendants. This concept is in direct contrast to what Salish-Kootenai economist Ronald Trosper terms the "contemporary shopping mall culture of shortsightedness."[16]

Other environmental activists include Sauk and Fox Grace Thorpe, the daughter of Jim Thorpe, the 1912 Olympic decathlon and pentathlon winner. Grace Thorpe participated in the takeover of Alcatraz Island (1969–71), and in 1992 she organized a successful protest to convince the Oklahoma Sauk and Fox Tribe to remove its application for a grant to study the feasibility of a nuclear dump on tribal land through the Monitored Retrieval Storage (MRS) program.[17]

Northern Cheyenne Gail Small has served as director of Native Action (NA) in Montana, a group organized to deal with environmental issues affecting the tribe. Most notably, Small and NA have attempted to fight the largest coal gasification complex in the country, Colstrip, by focusing on violations of leasing procedures. Small also spearheaded the effort to have the Cheyenne region classified as a "Class One" air-shed so that the coal strip-mining project that is located nearby would have to abide by the strict EPA standards. Small is similar to many Indian women who know that in order to accomplish their goals of protecting their lands and peoples, they have to do the work themselves: "We can do it ourselves. What we really need is money, not more national organizations in Washington, Albuquerque or Boulder with big federal money and no accountability to the communities."[18]

Tulalip Janet McCloud, among other women like Puyallup Ramona Bennett, became involved with fishing rights in the Northwest in the early 1960s, after the government attempted to remove non-treaty Indians from their fishing grounds on the Nisqually River in Washington, despite their reserved right to harvest salmon. McCloud and others formed the nonprofit Survival of American Indians Association in 1964. Now tribes face water pollution and depletion of their salmon (which play a major role in the religion and economy of northwestern tribes). McCloud quickly became well known and throughout the 1970s was asked to speak on women's issues, education, and religion in Europe, Australia, Japan, and Africa. She formed "women's circles" to discuss issues women face throughout the world. McCloud believes that women are "like the low man on the totem pole, yet we're holding it up." She states that "There's just no limit on whatever you can do to help Indian women bring out their creativity, and try to find resources to be able to do that. And knowing that trying to do things alone is really almost impossible, but if you're working together, you can do a lot of things."[19]

## Retaining Language

Historian Harold Isaacs writes, "That first learned language is, to begin with, the mother's tongue, with all that conveys and contributes to the forming of the self and the development of the individual personality. It opens into every aspect of life. . . . It is the language in which he learns, absorbs, repeats, and passes on all the group's given truths, its system of beliefs, its answers to the mysteries of creation, life and death, its ethics, aesthetics, and its conventional wisdom. The mother's tongue serves to connect the child to a whole universe of others now living or long dead."[20] Isaacs is speaking in general terms about language, but his assessment holds up when discussing Indigenous languages. As Tessie Naranjo, Santa Clara Pueblo, states, "It's how we survive. Your world view is embedded in the language."[21] According to Crow educator Janine Pease Pretty on Top, "Our whole world is framed by our language. It embodies so much of our culture that it's a real exploration of who the Crows are."[22] Unfortunately, only about 175 languages remain from the 300 or more that existed at the time of contact.[23] Through attendance at boarding schools, intermarriage, and exposure to the non-Indian world, many young Natives have lost interest in their tribal cultures, and many do not see the need to learn their languages. In addition, among many tribes, the number of elders who are fluent is dwindling.

Although students may learn their tribe's language and some of the culture at school, the most effective learning and reinforcement takes place at home. Since it is not always possible to learn these things at home, in many areas of Native America there has been a surge of interest in revitalizing languages. Tribes across the country encourage kindergarten through high school classrooms to incorporate Native languages. At Sapulpa High School in Oklahoma, for example, students can chose the Cherokee or Creek languages to fulfill their "foreign" language requirement. "Taking Cherokee helps me learn more about my culture and who I am," says the Indian Club princess Dana Winn. The director of the program, Laura Hurd, agrees that learning their tribal language is one way for students to recover their heritage: "In my family we lost our heritage. That's why I had such an interest in it."[24] At Leupp Public School in northern Arizona, young Navajos are taught their subjects in Navajo the first half of the day, then in English for the remainder.[25] Tribes throughout Arizona, including Gila River, Hopi, and Salt River Pima–Maricopa use the charter-school system in order to incorporate tribal customs and language lessons into the curriculum.[26]

Dixie Davis, a Yavapai teacher, attended a boarding school in Holbrook, Arizona, as a child. While there, when she attempted to speak her language she had her mouth washed out with soap, was given no food, and "they beat me up." After school, Davis moved to Los Angeles on the relocation program, then enrolled in various universities, where she studied law. Now, as a Yavapai elder confined to a wheelchair, Davis teaches the Yavapai language to tribal members at the Fort McDowell Recreation Center in Arizona. "If you lose your language, you lose your people," she says. And, she adds, "I can rap in my language."[27]

## Creativity as Empowerment

Cree singer Buffy Ste. Marie speaks of the importance of art and creative expression for Natives: "We'll sing our historical truth songs so never again will anyone be able to sweep it under the rug. But we will not be victims of it anymore. We'll also sing our songs of joy in being Indians."[28] Non-Indians have always been interested in Indigenous pottery, quill and beadwork, robes, pipe bags, masks, silverwork, rugs, weapons, and katsinas, but it was not until the 1920s that the public began viewing these creations as forms of "art." In 1975 the Museum of Modern Art's "primitivism" show spurred unprecedented interest in Indian artworks—not only items created by living Natives but also sacred cultural objects buried with the dead and religious figures left as offerings (which are not to be touched). Collectors and art dealers realized the marketability of Native art, especially historic works like pottery, and soon art lovers from around the world clamored to buy items made by dead and living Natives.[29]

Often what non-Natives perceive as expressions of Natives through Native art are not personal expressions at all but creations that Native artists know non-Natives want to see. Like other minority writers and artists who express frustration over pressures to conform to what others think they should be creating, many Natives know that in order to be truly successful they must paint images that fulfill whites' expectations, such as outdoor scenery, faces of full-bloods adorned with war paint and surrounded by feathers, and animals. Not all Native artists conform to non-Natives' demands. They create artwork that expresses their identity and emotions and that may not always mean art that looks "Indian." Others use their energies to make pieces that reflect their tribal pride.[30]

For example, throughout the eighteenth and nineteenth centuries Navajos worked to establish their craft as blanket and rug weavers. They took pride in their abilities to create beautiful striped, terraced, and diamond-patterned designs from natural wool colors in addition to indigo, blue, and cochineal. After their near-spirit-breaking imprisonment at Bosque Redondo from 1863 to 1868, Navajo weavers began producing blankets for the non-Indian market, for persons who desired art objects made by Natives but who had little appreciation for quality. Traders capitalized on the desire for these goods and began selling materials to produce the product. Produced from coarse handspun wool or three- or four-ply Germantown cotton twine dyed with aniline, the blankets became rugs and were, according to historian Ruth Underhill, "some of the weirdest and ugliest products ever made by Indians." Until 1920, the production of blankets and rugs was almost purely for the tourist trade; according to Underhill, the Navajos were "prostituting" their art for income. Their desire to create something quickly and cheaply was spurred by the traders' practice of purchasing products by weight, and Navajos soon realized that a blanket or rug heavy with lanolin and sand would bring in more money. During the "Revival Period," from the 1920s on, encouraged by the government's program in tribal cultural revivals, weavers returned to their traditional geometric designs made from handspun wool colored with vegetable dyes. Navajo females once again demonstrated their pride and identity as Navajo women by creating intricate, high-quality products, a process that has roots in their tribal traditions.[31]

Joane Cardinal-Schubert, a Canadian Indian, describes herself as "an artist, as a communicator, as a maker of visual imagery; one of the most powerful forms of communicative expression that we have." She had a difficult time in school, yet ultimately became comfortable with her identity and began expressing it through her art:

Other people knew more about me than I knew about myself. "You're an Indian!" the kids screamed at me at school. "You're a half-breed!" they said as they got older and had listened to their parents' dinner conversations. "You're a Metis!" they started to whisper in the 1970s, gentrifying the term 'half-breed' or 'mixed-blood.' In a museum in Rocky Mountain House, I found the Tree of Life chart drawn by pious Father Lacombe, who started Dunbow school near Calgary. I found the pathway to heaven known only to one Indian. The rest came along the path where one of the seven deadly sins—that of slothfulness—had been depicted. You can see this chart on the third floor of the museum. It has every Indian going to hell. I started asking questions in my artwork, drawing pictures of all those chiefs, those Canadian heroes with their Victoria medals burning a hole in their chests for generation to come. I did these paintings from 1969 to 1973. I drew and painted very personal statements then. My work began to take a more political—as some people called it—bent. . . . I started to like myself, I began to take a stand, I was proud of my heritage.[32]

Cherokee artist Shan Goshorn uses her painting and photography to educate, to show the world that Natives are not peoples of the past, and to come to terms with her heritage. "We are part of contemporary society. We have roots that are still very strongly connected to tradition, but we are people here in the 1990s, like everyone else, and we have a voice. I feel that in a different way because my mother is Indian, my father is not, but I was as comfortable sitting on either grandparent's knee, whether it was white or Indian. I really feel that my path is to try to connect the two peoples, whether it's through my artwork or whatever. And also I think that women innately have that role anyway because we're such nurturers."[33]

Numerous Native women, such as Tuscaroras Marlene Printup and Mary Annette Clause, are ardent bead workers, creating designs for clothing like their ancestors did. These women teach their children the skills because, according to Clause, "I feel that it's very important to pass our culture along."[34]

At Second Mesa on the Hopi reservation, Hopi women teach pottery, weaving, armband-making, beading, and painting to young tribespeople through the Hopi Pu'tavi Project. Funded by organizations such as National 4-H and the University of Arizona Agricultural Extension, the youth program is an attempt at teaching young Hopis their tribal language as they learn arts and crafts. Hopi women also have organized groups such as the Hopi Women's Coalition, which stresses the need for women's perspectives on issues facing the tribe and strives to find ways to improve life at Hopi; the Hopi Quilting Club, a group that seeks to strengthen the Hopi culture through social interaction; the Miss Hopi contest, which offers a female role model and emphasizes Hopi females' roles in traditional society; and Mamantuy Ogala-am', also known as Girl Power!, a conference for Hopi girls that covers topics relevant to Hopi females, funded in part by national organizations such as the Healthy Babies Coalition and the Department of Health and Human Services.[35]

Pueblo women such as Martina Martinez (Tewa) and Helen Quintana Cordero (Cochiti) are well known for their artistry. Martinez reproduced her tribe's ancient pottery, created new designs, and successfully turned "a craft into an art." Cordero created the Storyteller (the singing mother with children around her), a traditional Cochiti figure. In addition, both women have won numerous awards and prizes, and they contributed to the resurgence of pottery making within their tribes—a strong expression of tribal pride and identity.[36]

## Filmmaking as Activism

As the Abenaki filmmaker Alanis Obomsawin has noted, "Documentary film is the one place that our people can speak for themselves. I feel that the documentaries that I've been working on have been very valuable for the people, for our people to look at ourselves, at the situations, really facing it, and through that being able to make changes that really count for the future of our children to come."[37] Obomsawin has created documentaries such as *Poundmaker's Lodge: A Healing Place* (1987), *Richard Cardinal: Diary of a Foster Child* (1986), and *Mother of Many Children* (1977), which illustrate traditional teachings, the suicide of a neglected Cree child, and how women pass stories to their families, respectively. She believes that films can be "used as tools for social change, so that similar tragedies [such as the suicide of the Cree youth Richard Cardinal] do not continue to happen."[38]

Navajo Geraldine Keams is best known for her acting role in the movie *The Outlaw Josey Wales* (1983) and her work as consultant for the award-winning documentary about the Navajo-Hopi land issue, *Broken Rainbow* (1985), but she is also a poet, screenwriter, and co-founder of the Big Mountain Support Group of Los Angeles. Keams spent many of her formative years on the Navajo reservation, attending school and listening to her traditional grandmother tell tribal stories. Influenced by her grandmother, Keams believes that women are the tribal caretakers, and she feels a responsibility to maintain the cultural integrity of her tribe. Keams believes stereotypes of Indians can be corrected through films, theater, poetry, or novels. She produces her own films, she says, "out of a desperate cry to express some kind of truth."[39]

Valerie Red Horse, a businesswoman and actress, decided to write a screenplay that portrays Native women realistically instead of creating more images of "Indian Maidens." Her movie, *Naturally Native* (1998), opened at the Sundance Film Festival after an arduous production schedule, but this endeavor has led to numerous other projects such as a feature-length movie on Navajo code-talkers and an NBC movie of the week. The recipient of a B.A. in theatre arts at UCLA and now the head of her own production company, Red Horse Native Productions, Inc., she asserts that her "main purpose is to entertain and to create a good story. . . . we can also educate and enlighten simultaneously."[40]

Former newswoman Patty Talaongva, a Hopi, founded White Spider Communications in order to produce documentaries about tribal histories and cultures from the point of view of tribal members. "I think it's time Indian people start telling their own stories," says Talaongva. "We continue to be ignored by the local and national media, and one way [to get attention] would be to have our own TV and radio outlets." She produced a film about the Yavapai Nation in Prescott, serves on the boards of Atlatl (which promotes Native art) and the Native American Journalists Association, and helped the Inter-Tribal Council of Arizona to receive funding by documenting the needs of elders. Talaongva, whose Hopi name is Qotsakookyangw (White Spider), is currently preparing a documentary on World War II code talkers, including Hopis, Comanches, Choctaws, and Seminoles.[41]

## Dancing and Powwows as Empowerment

For many Natives dancing is not just an expression of identity; it is also a form of worship, healing, and celebration. Teaching one's children to dance assures the continuation of tribal culture and kinship ties, and attending powwows, stomps, and other dances is one way to socialize and celebrate community. The continuation of tribal dance steps and music allows a place for at least a modicum of tradition in the modern world.[42] The Nuvatukyaovi Hopi Youth Dance Group, for example, was formed by Hopis who desired to make certain that Hopi children retain their tribal culture. In the words of Delores Coochyamptewa, "The self esteem is for them to carry within themselves. It's like a light that should continue to burn. To be proud of themselves, to identify not just with what's modern but with that which is Hopi, and to carry it with them. They learn that nobody can take that away from them."[43]

Many Natives who dance at powwows do so for profit and for attention. Benjamin R. Kracht asserts that powwows are "sacred" to southern Plains tribes, at least, "because they are replete with set patterns of ceremonial song and dance that reflect an Indian identity."[44] R. D. Theisz explained in his essay "Song Texts and Their Performers" that singing and dancing among Lakotas are the "predominant symbols of being a Lakota." Powwows feature ever-changing dance and song styles, costumes, and participants and grew out of tribal religious and social ceremonies that have evolved over the years to "strengthen tribal traditions." Although Lakota powwowers attempt to keep "traditions," many of the songs are sung by those who have little knowledge of the Lakota language and who thus produce songs that elders say "don't make sense."[45]

Nevertheless, powwow dancing can be an expression of Native pride. Normally, costumes, hairstyles, songs, and so on stem from one's tribe. Powwows can also allow for expression of general Indianness by sporting outfits, dancing styles, and songs that originated from different geographical regions or integrate elements from many tribal groups. Boye Ladd, a Winnebago fancy dancer, believes that powwows help create a feeling of unity among tribes: "The modern-day pow wow has brought a lot of tribes together, its brought unity. We are saying 'we' now as opposed to saying only 'Sioux,' 'Cheyenne,' or 'Crow.'"[46]

Through these aspects and events that are common to most powwows, in addition to parades, rodeos, "Miss Powwow" pageants, sales of arts and crafts, fry bread, and other foods, the "49" after the dancing is over, camping out, looking forward to visiting with friends and family, and preparing for the dance (which for some dancers with intricate costumes and/or rigorous dance moves that require a fitness regimen is a daily process), specific tribal identity and often a pan-Indian identity is reinforced, celebrated, invigorated, and expressed. Sandro James Lovejoy, a fancy dancer, explains his love for dancing: "As I walk on the Sacred Mother Earth, I only consider myself or my status as a Native American Fancy Dancer. . . . My status as a Fancy Dancer has given me prestige and respect and has helped me find my identity. I could not imagine myself any other way. . . . If it were up to me, I would live my life as a Fancy Dancer over and over into a season of infinity."[47]

In his 1996 essay on the powwow as a public arena, Mark Mattern acknowledges the powwow as a "unifying force in Indian life" because of the dances' secular and religious traditions, which "emphasize unity and inclusiveness." The emcee, who is usually male, informs and reminds participants and spectators about the significance of the various dances, which usually tie into the tribe's history and culture. The music and dance, both of which are repetitive, "reinforce the commitment to unity represented by the circle in which they take place." "Honoring" includes the "grand entry" into the circle and the "giveaway," which honors specific people important to the organization of the powwow or to an event within the tribe. Such forces include the drum, which is heard by everyone on the powwow grounds and symbolizes the heartbeat of all living creatures (although research does indicate that drumbeats induce "deeper alpha waves" in the brain, which allow "profound thinking and learning").[48]

Powwows are opportunities for many Natives who work regular jobs during the weekdays to leave work behind and celebrate their Native identity with others. At powwows, children interact with their families and elders in a common setting that helps ensure the continuity of many tribal cultural aspects. Powwows are necessary for Henrietta Mann Morton, who states, "For a brief period of time we can put aside our professional non-Indian roles and come together from our diverse tribal backgrounds and with a unity of spirit enjoy the dance and celebrate life."[49]

Mattern also discusses aspects of the powwow that outsiders are usually not aware of: the inter- and intra-tribal social and political conflicts that surround the meaning of the powwow. While some Natives believe that powwows are dance contests that bestow trophies, ribbons, and prize money for the "best" dancers, some of whom can make up to fifty thousand dollars a year, others see the powwow arena as a place for political discussion.[50] The emcee might discuss political events throughout the powwow, and the dancers and singers may focus their attention on the politics, such as at a powwow sponsored by the American Indian Movement. Among Kiowas, many powwows are organized to raise money for needy tribal members.[51] Because these conflicts surface around most powwows (at least the ones Mattern discusses and the ones I have been involved with in Texas and Oklahoma), "Indians do not simply reaffirm and reinforce their mutual identity and commitments through powwow practices; they negotiate them." Mattern believes that the disagreements help form or create the tribe's "resiliency and flexibility."[52]

Kiowa women began participating in powwows in the late 1950s and are quick to point out their roles in the dances. The Kiowa War Mothers (mothers of war veterans) formed in 1944, when they began creating lyrics about soldiers to incorporate into the female Round Dance.[53] Although they must dance behind men in the Gourd Dance, one woman comments that "if it wasn't for women, a woman, there would be no men at this dance. . . . all the members know that they are incapacitated if they do not have a woman. . . . Who is the best person that they [the men dancers] would want to back them up. Who stands there behind them in that 104 degrees and gives out the most beautiful tremelos in honor of that man? No one else can do this but a woman."[54]

While powwows are usually viewed as a major unifying force of Native identity, the powwow is not viewed in the same light by all Natives. As with other forms of dancing, not every Native agrees on the meaning of the powwows and why they should be held, if at all. The annual "Red Earth" powwow held at Oklahoma City has recently garnered criticism from many Natives for being purely "a show" for non-Natives, too expensive for many Natives to attend. Russell Means's comment about powwowers exemplifies the anti-powwow opinion that many Natives have:

It is our songs, not our languages, that have always been the most important part of our cultural heritage. We have songs for everything. . . . We never should have allowed other Indians to learn our songs. After a generation of mixing them with those of other Indian cultures, the Plains songs have been corrupted. They are *our* songs, so I resent it. Starting in the 1950s, city-dwelling Indian have gone to powwows where they can dress up for a few hours a month to play Indian, as if that can somehow "justify" their Indian blood. The rest of the time, they are lost in the maze of white society. The powwows give them an excuse to sell out. At powwows, they dress in any style, borrowing from other Indian nations without understanding the meaning of the traditional garments, without knowing why they are worn. There is no discipline and therefore no pride. Since the powwows began, the Indian nations have become weaker year by year. They have become caricatures of their own traditions, unrecognizable as communities, as nations, almost unrecognizable as Indians.[55]

Means may not be correct about tribal nations becoming weaker by the year, but he is justifiably annoyed at powwows becoming pan-Indian events. Powwows in Arizona and New Mexico often feature dancers from Southwest tribes who dress in Plains tribes' outfits and dance to Plains tribes' songs. One Choctaw woman from Oklahoma of my acquaintance used to dance in her traditional calico dress, but because that outfit was not "flashy" enough, she switched to the Kiowa buckskin outfit (complete with Kiowa, not Choctaw, accessories) and has won dances ever since.

On the other hand, Boye Ladd defends the monetary incentive that drives some dancers: "Many champions are well respected in pow-wow circles, but come Monday they are a janitor for the white man. Outside of powwow circles they are looked down upon. If there is more money available this way of life becomes a respected profession. After all if the white man can go and hit a ball with a stick for a million dollars, why can't the Indian earn a living at his 'sport'?"[56]

Other Natives argue that powwows should be a religious event and the dancing should be focused on religious expression, not competition or politics. James Watt, a Blackfeet traditional dancer, says that when he is dancing, "It's me and the Creator. . . . He encourages me to dance good for Him all the time."[57] Such Natives also are against the use of eagle-bone whistles for mundane secular use such as signaling drummers, women drumming, and women performing the "fancy shawl dance," the rigorous female counterpart of the men's fancy dance.

For others, the powwow can be an expression of status. Some families host powwows on their property and retain full power over every aspect of the event, including who can participate and spectate, thus reinforcing their power within their community. Interestingly, some of these individuals I know have said that they dance for religious reasons, yet they cannot explain any aspect of their tribal religions and they also vigorously compete in contests, leaving the impression that their intentions for dancing are indeed political and social status.

Despite debates over the meaning of powwow dancing and the corruption in some powwow dances, the powwow has endured as a social gathering. Powwows give "emotional connection" for many Natives who need to feel Native. Dancers dance for themselves as a form of creative expression, for their tribe, for money, as an energetic expression of their pride in being Native, or perhaps for a combination of all these reasons. As Flathead traditional dancer Phillip Paul explains, powwows are "a time to celebrate our survival."[58]

# 12

## Feminists, Tribalists, or Activists?

Chandra Talpade Mohanty writes in the anthology she co-edited, *Third World Women and the Politics of Feminism*, that women of color, or "third world women," all have the "common context of struggle."[1] Indeed, women of color may still struggle against colonialism, racism, and stereotypes, but as multi-heritage progressive Indigenous women illustrate, these struggles have not always been the same nor are their strategies of resistance.

The reasons for differences among Native women are as varied as the tribes themselves. Each tribe's social, cultural, economic, religious, and political values will vary over time, but many cultural traditions do persist. Also, the racial heritage of women and their physical appearance have strong impacts on their identity development and political allegiances and how others perceive them. Racism within tribes often results in class systems, and so on. There are varieties of values within a single tribe as well. A mixed-heritage, educated Cherokee woman, for example, will have a markedly different worldview and values than an uneducated, full-blood, non-Christian one. An urban, educated Navajo with a terminal degree will likely have a strong Navajo identity yet different values than an uneducated reservation Navajo. Sometimes it appears that women of different tribes have more in common with each other than they do with women of their own tribe.

Because Native women vary in their cultural ideologies, appearance, and social and moral values, no one feminist theory totalizes Native women's thought, and there are differences of opinion among Native women over who among them are "feminists." How we as Native women define ourselves as female and how we relate to the concept of feminism, to feminists, and to each other, how we define colonialism, and how men and women should behave depend on our relation to our tribes, our class, appearance, life partners, education, and religion. For example, traditional Native women—those women who adhere as closely to their tribal traditions as possible and often are not formally educated—have been more concerned about tribal or community survival than either gender oppression or individual advancement in economic status, academia, or in other facets of society.

Not every Native woman has the same ideas about what feminism or activism means.[2] A Hopi student commented in my recent undergraduate American Indian Women in History class that she does not refer to herself as either a feminist or an activist. "I'm normal," she said. A white woman in the same class asserted, "I see activists as actually doing something and feminists as whiners." Another young woman, a "mixed-blood full-blood" from Arizona tribes, believes that feminists are "lesbians behind microphones." Indeed, not everyone is educated about feminist theory, and the wide variety of ideas among Native women about "feminism" further illustrates the variety of voices in Native America.

In *The Reader's Companion to U.S. Women's History*, Joy Harjo and Susan M. Williams define "tribal feminism" as a "multisphered concept with the family as the center, surrounded by clan identification, then tribe and tribal relationships, which can mean relationships with state and federal governments and those with other tribal and international governments."[3] Wilma Mankiller, Marysa Navarro, and Gloria Steinem write in the same volume that "feminism is also history and even memory."[4] These definitions imply that tribes are traditionally matriarchal, but not all tribes are. Many Native women agree with the concepts that Native women are influential and powerful tribal members, but they do not always assign labels to their positions.

Many traditional Native women—who might more accurately be called "tribalists"—are not concerned with definitions of feminism, because they are secure in their identities as tribal women; they do not need scholars to tell them of the importance of women to their tribes. They usually have no interest in white feminist theory, because they have witnessed white women enjoying the power privileges that come with being white at the expense of women of color. Some Native women see some biracial Native feminists (who often have little knowledge of their tribal traditions) in the same light. Some Native women argue that, while they might be oppressed because of their gender, they are primarily disempowered because of their race, and they believe that it is more important to eradicate racist oppression than sexist oppression.

Some Native females with little or no knowledge of their tribal past feel the effects of racial and gender oppression and believe that white feminist theory might offer them advice and encouragement.

Other Native women want to recreate themselves as modern Native females, and in order to understand their tribal past some of these women depend on scholarly interpretations of the feminine domain within their tribes.

Some of us are Native women scholars, and there is an assumption that because we are outspoken and interested in "women's studies" that we are "feminists." While some scholars do define themselves as "feminists," most Native women I know are strong, confident, and active in their quests to assist their tribes but do not always use the term "feminist" as a self-descriptor. In a personal discussion about feminism and writing, Elizabeth Cook-Lynn once commented that because the University of Wisconsin Press put her picture on the cover of her book *Why I Can't Read Wallace Stegner and Other Essays,* "most people think that I must be a feminist. I'm not. I'm tribal."

An alternative term to describe Native women may indeed be *tribalist.* But the majority of Native women go about their daily business with little appreciation for what scholars decide to label them. Indeed, as Hunkpapa Lakota Barbara Cameron says, "I don't like being put under a magnifying glass and having cute liberal terms describe who I am."[5] For the sake of scholarly discussion, however, it appears that those Native women most concerned with tribal issues would prefer *tribalist* or *activist.* "Womanist," a term coined by Alice Walker, is an option, but it still implies concern with females, not the tribal group as a whole.

In Bea Medicine's 1978 essay "The Native American Woman," one woman proudly calls herself a "militant," but that label seems too rigid and violent.[6] Native women do not want to be perceived as being angry all the time when we are not; nor do we want to be labeled complainers who offer no solutions to the problems we mention. We must learn how to bridge gaps between Native men and women, and among Native women, without being divisive and judgmental. We also must figure out how to address tribal concerns at the same time that we face important issues that concern Native women. This is not easy.

Often scholars use these debates over terminology for political and personal purposes. For example, some writers suggest that traditional-ist Native women are the authoritative voices on Native issues rather than those who are more assimilated. In the pages that M. Annette Jaimes and Theresa Halsey devote to feminism in their 1992 essay "American Indian Women at the Center of Indigenous Resistance in Contemporary North America," they criticize prominent Native writers such as Shirley Hill Witt and Suzan Shown Harjo because, in their opinion, these women are too assimilated and are more concerned about fighting for "civil rights" than about fighting for tribal sovereignty. These women, they contend, "have tended to be among the more assimilated of Indian women activists, generally accepting of the colonialist ideology that indigenous nations are now legitimate sub-parts of the U.S. geopolitical corpus rather than separate nations, that Indian people are now a minority within the overall population rather than the citizenry of their own distinctive nations. Such Indian women activists are therefore usually more devoted to 'civil rights' than to liberation per se."[7] Jaimes and Halsey's essay is problematic for a variety of reasons. A major one is that the women Jaimes and Halsey take to task actually are strong advocates for tribal rights. Witt, for example, is a highly educated Mohawk who helped form the National Indian Youth Council and is member of the U.S. Civil Rights Commission, while Harjo, a Muscogee, chairs the Morningstar Foundation, and is an outspoken critic of sports-team mascots that feature Natives.[8]

The reality is that most Native women—whether full-blood or mixed-blood, living on or off tribal lands, activist or indifferent—are concerned about both racial and gender oppression. Despite rhetoric about white feminism having no meaning for Native women, not all Native women reject every aspect of white feminism, and they are no less "Indian" for their beliefs. When they identify themselves as "feminists," they often mean they are "Native Activists," concerned with more than just female marginalization. Indeed, they fight for fishing, land, water, and treaty rights, and at the same time, they have no desire to be called inferior by anyone because they are women. They fight for racial liberation in order to transcend the effects of colonialism that may cause tribal men to behave abusively in the first place. There are, however, many Native women who identify themselves as "feminists." Some have no connection to their tribe and are essentially "white" in attitude, while others, such as Wilma Mankiller, interpret the term to mean that they use female power to aid their tribe.

Like other Native women did and still do, Anna Mae Pictou-Aquash had searched for ways to meet the demands of all her worlds: self, family, community, tribe, state, and country. Often Native women are pressured to keep and practice the old ways while at the same time learning non-Native ways to support their families. Native women inside and outside the academy speak of the interconnectedness of female, male, tribal, and racial oppression, and like Anna Mae, they strive for liberation of all. They may sometimes struggle for gender rights, but their gender is inexorably tied to their race and tribe.

## That Colonialism Excuse

> We are American Indian women, in that order. We are oppressed, first and foremost, as American Indians, as peoples colonized by the United States of America, not as women. . . . Decolonization is the agenda, the whole agenda, and until it is accomplished, it is the only agenda that counts for American Indians. – Lorelei DeCora, co-founder of WARN and nurse

Many Native women aspire to the historically, traditionally powerful social, political, economic, and religious roles they held in their tribes. They cannot reclaim their cultures by themselves, however. Women might be aware of their traditional and potential power, but men often try to ignore it. Most of the male leaders of the American Indian Movement (AIM) admit they knew little about their cultures until they joined AIM, and although they were taught about the traditional tribal roles of women, their behavior did not always reveal enthusiasm for tribal stories that featured powerful females. Inside the barricades at Wounded Knee, seemingly separated from the vocal, attention-getting males and away from the limelight of the overbearing press, women worked at washing and patching clothes, scrubbing dishes, and tending to the sick and injured. White women were aware of the Native females at Wounded Knee and were not pleased with them for accepting what they interpreted as inferior, subservient roles. While the Native women physically labored—certainly more than the male leaders—not all of the women expressed sentiments that their roles were less important than the men's. They justified their "invisible" work by stating that men and women have specific tasks to perform and all duties are essential to tribal survival. Many of these women were able to switch gears and work where needed; in essence, unlike most of the men, they were flexible in their activism. They tended to the sick and washed dirty laundry but also would step forward to speak publicly if given the opportunity.

Feminism of the 1970s, especially, dwelled upon women as victims of patriarchal control. Little thought was given to the heterogeneity among women, particularly to those of color who also had to contend with racial oppression and, in the case of many Native women, those who were concerned about community and tribal survival. In 1975 Seneca activist Laura Waterman Wittstock attempted to explain the Native perspective to feminists by stating, "No group can impart power on another group. Setting women aside as a group of under-privileged human beings and then trying to figure out ways to impart power to them ignores custom, culture, and in the instance of American Indians, national sovereignty."[9]

Native women at Wounded Knee acknowledged that the U.S. government and the press would listen to the men, not them, and they understood the practicality of allowing the men to speak and negotiate for the group. Women did indeed possess the emotional strength and knowledge to take matters into their own hands, but who outside the tribe would listen to them? Who would take them seriously? The women participants at Wounded Knee are similar to the women of the Iroquois and other tribes who, in colonial times, were aware that the male Euro-Americans did not want to deal with women during social, political, and economic negotiations, despite the reality that women of the Northeast had considerable power in all aspects of tribal life. At least five of the thirteen Oglalas involved in negotiations with the government after the Wounded Knee takeover were traditional women. While these women allowed the men to take center stage, they did not approve of Native men adopting the European ideology that females are subservient to males. Younger, less secure women, however, often acquiesced to the men's wishes.

"There is a curious contradiction in Sioux society," wrote Mary Crow Dog. "The men pay great lip service to the status women hold in the tribe. Their rhetoric on the subject is beautiful. . . . they always stood up for our rights—against outsiders!" But the reality within the compound at Wounded Knee differed: "We did the shit work, scrubbing dishes or making sleeping bags out of old jackets." Crow Dog also lamented the chauvinism among the ranks of Lakota AIM men, including her one-time husband, medicine man Leonard Crow Dog. She expressed irritation at the Native and white female "groupies" who were willing to serve as "wives" to the AIM leadership—that is, in addition to providing sex, they cooked, cleaned, sewed, and braided the men's hair.[10]

AIM male leaders of the 1970s and 1980s attempted to revive the Plains "warrior" role of the past by stepping forward as aggressive leaders, but they failed to advocate for a struggle against the bonds of colonial oppression and to embrace gender equality. Russell Means, in his lengthy autobiography, for example, commented on the women at Wounded Knee: "Taking the glory was not on their agenda. Understanding the female-male balance, they felt no need to be anointed publicly with leadership."[11] That may be true, but Means was not about to allow females publicity.[12] The few women Means wrote about were members of his family or women elders, and nowhere in his lengthy autobiography does he mention Anna Mae Pictou-Aquash, despite her leadership role in AIM. He has also revealed his feelings about women in a diatribe delivered to Peter Matthiessen over the exposed FBI informer Douglass Durham: "Durham was a gofer, a *nothing!* He was like a woman, *worse* than a woman; we used to give him pocket money, send him out for coffee!"[13] Means rationalizes his sexist attitude: "If our older women knew and respected their role, Indian men of my generation didn't. We had been robbed of our heritage through the brutality experienced by our parents and passed on to us all."[14]

Anna Mae Pictou-Aquash was not the only woman who dealt with misogyny among AIM men. In 1990 Laguna Pueblo writer Paula Gunn Allen revealed one reason why some Indian women preferred not to work closely with male AIM leaders:

They were out drinkin' all the time, they were fuckin' their way across the United States, they were leaving a lot of uncared for babies behind, not to mention young women. Dreadful things. Finally, these three women called them in and they said in no uncertain terms, "We'll show you who the real warriors are here. We are! You think you're so big. You haven't done nothing and you can't do nothing without us." Every Indian knows that. You want something done, call a woman. They all know that. The men know it, the women know it. But the situation is such that when the white world wants things Indian, a spiritual leader for example, you know who they call. They call the men.[15]

Many Native men did struggle for racial equality, but their aggressive behavior, often made worse by excessive drinking, destroyed the male-female balance essential to their cultures. In private correspondence with me, a critic of one prominent AIM leader (who lived in the leader's home for a while, where he observed firsthand his treatment of females) contended that the man defeated the purpose of fighting for tribal rights and sovereignty: "He is quick to intimidate the weak, especially females, and both verbally and physically abuses them." Indeed, other men are also cognizant of the AIM males behavior. Paul DeMain, a writer for *News from Indian Country*, has covered news regarding Anna Mae Pictou-Aquash for years, and he commented in July 2000 that the leadership of AIM finally needs to be "turned over, over to women like Wilma Mankiller, Lisa Bellanger, Janet McCloud, Maise Shenandoah, Winona LaDuke, Dorothy Davida, Dora Amman, Marge Powless, Susan Harjo and hundreds of others like them who would return the Movement to where it should have gone if it hadn't been hijacked by paranoia, egos and self-gratitude at the expense of Indian women."[16]

Another example of how the AIM male leadership took advantage of their notoriety with the press (who wanted to see aggressive Indian men in leadership roles) and of Native women's tolerance of their misogyny concerns Vernon Bellecourt. In the early 1970s, upon meeting AIM activist Francis Wise, who happened to be standing next to AIM member Carter Camp, Bellecourt commented, "Carter, have your woman [meaning Wise] braid my hair."[17] Granted, many modern Sioux women defend such comments because traditionally women did braid men's hair. But for modern Native men to expect women to be subservient to men in all spheres of tribal life is not traditional thinking or behavior. The comment did not sit well with Wise, one of the few women who rebelled against such social skills.

Women have also formed societies to deal with the problem of abuse, which is prevalent within tribes today. On the Lakota reservation at Rosebud, for example, there is the White Buffalo Calf Woman Society, and at Pine Ridge is the Sacred Shawl Society. Lakota activist Tillie Black Bear, founder of the White Buffalo Calf Women's Society, was presented by President Clinton with the Eleanor Roosevelt Award in 2000 for her tireless work on behalf of abused women and children. Formerly a victim of abuse herself, Black Bear also founded the National Coalition against Domestic Violence and Sexual Assault.[18]

In her review of Mary Crow Dog's *Lakota Woman*, Annette Jaimes stated: "The psychic need of American Indian men to reassert their identities as fully functioning and empowered human beings is thus both contaminated by the imposition of Eurocentric outlooks on the nature of their supposed inadequacies and rendered compulsive by the sheer extent of their real diminishment under the weight of colonial rule. Their attempts to compensate are essentially beyond their rational control. . . . In Fanonesque fashion, Crow Dog contends that such behaviors are an integral and probably unavoidable aspect of the early phases of any decolonization struggle."[19] These are interesting claims, considering that nowhere in *Lakota Woman* does Crow Dog evaluate colonialism, and in only one sentence does she even hint at excusing men's behavior. In response to a white nurse who "berated us for doing the heavy work while the men got all the glory," Crow Dog writes, "We told her that her kind of women's lib was a white, middle-class thing, and that at this critical stage we had other priorities. Once our men got their rights and their balls back, we might start arguing with them about who should do the dishes." She also hated this role, calling it "shit work."[20] Additionally, to take seriously what Jaimes has written means that we must accept the scenario of a male Native in the United States abusing his partner and then justifying his dysfunctional behavior with Jaimes's arguments. Furthermore, the most prominent AIM leaders were not raised in a traditional manner, they did not (and do not) speak their tribal languages, and they did not have knowledge of women's traditional tribal roles until they became active in AIM. In fact, few of the men to date have shown any indication that they wish to see a revitalization of traditional tribal egalitarian gender roles.

Women who are more connected to their tribes and who view themselves as oppressed often tend to try and "recapture its [the tribe's] collective past," in this case, return to tribalism and traditional gender roles.[21] While activists Lorelei Means, Janet McCloud, and others have advocated "decolonization," they have not defined the term, which can refer to a variety of ideologies, including the most radical: the complete return of traditions, which also means that whites will disappear, bison will return, dead Natives will arise, and the tribes will no longer use any material goods or political, religious, social, or economic ideas brought to the New World by foreigners. Perhaps this is more idealistic than realistic. As Roxanne Swentzell, a Santa Clara Pueblo, observes, "Some Native Americans have a lot of old ways of 'seeing' that are really good, but I don't think that most really understand what the 'old way' means anymore. They are just holding onto symbols and rituals because they know there was something there once. Hopefully, someday they will know what it means."[22]

A more practical, but still challenging, definition of decolonization is that tribes will become self-sufficient—decolonized tribal governments will make their own decisions without interference and will no longer depend on the U.S. government for assistance. This is also known as "self-determination." According to Mililani Trask, self-determination also includes "freedom from the internal controls and psychological obstacles that are the legacy of past colonization."[23] Onondaga Nancy Johnson concurs, stating, "At Onondaga, we have sovereignty and jurisdiction because we've maintained our cultural purity as far as religion and the government is concerned. Also, we don't take federal money from the U.S. government."[24]

Not all Natives aspire to "decolonization" because they are comfortable in their lifestyles. Terry Tafoya, a Taos/Salish psychotherapist, is aware that "some people are fearful of traditions being revived, created, celebrated. My family has been called, in a derogatory way, 'blanket Indians.'" Tafoya explains that decolonization is not possible: "But we've worked hard to maintain the traditions of responsibility and obligation. People might think that means doing everything the way it was done before contact, but that's never really been our teaching. Times change. The elements continue forward. You take foundations of understanding and apply them to new situations."[25]

Jaimes and Halsey mainly quote women who were active in the 1970s Red Power Movement. Like many women in the Black Power Movement, these women do not want their comments to cause further divisiveness between Native men and women and thus weaken their struggle for racial equality. Native women have much to lose by publicly discussing the dysfunctional gender roles within their tribes during the 1970s and today. Despite sexism that pervades their societies, American Indigenous women, like African American and Chicana women, keep their secrets close and often fight for group rights more aggressively than they fight for gender and individual rights. Wittstock explains, "Any who believe that giving up cultural and racial customs in exchange for enhanced individual rights and privileges play into the end-game—the dominant societies will increase in strength, the non-white communities will lose power increasingly."[26] Perhaps, but it is clear that while Native men and women can work together for tribal rights, they also must work together in order for true egalitarian societies to reemerge.

Native women concede that male AIM leaders were and are sexist, having learned misogynist ways of thinking in white society. They have no desire to denigrate Native men, believing that they, too, are powerless in white society. Thus, many of the women agree that combating racism against their tribes is more important than personal gain. One woman present during the Wounded Knee takeover sums up the differences between white and Indian ways of thinking about feminism this way: "In your [white] culture you have lots of problems with men. Maybe we do too, but we don't have time to worry about sexism. We worry about survival."[27] To feminists, domestic duties may seem less important than some men's roles, but these women argue that they felt empowered in their domestic sphere, and they defended their role.

On the other hand, during the 1970s at least, the domestic sphere was the only one the activist men allowed women to have. The men's goals were to survive, of course, but also to elevate themselves. Like some African American men who believe that black women hinder black struggles as a whole if they focus on feminist issues, Native men also chide Native women who focus on gender inequality rather than tribal issues. Many males involved in the Red Power Movement used Native women's wishes for racial equality in their rhetoric, in addition to using the press's desire to see modern male warriors (not women) for their personal advantage. Ironically, Native women were well aware of the motivations of the male leaders, and one reason they formed Women of All Red Nations (WARN) was because they were tired of their partners' infidelities and attention-seeking. They formed an organization of their own in order to deal with a variety of social issues that appear to be most important to Native females: education, health care, sterilization, treaty rights, and political incarceration of Native people.[28]

Jaimes's thoughts on what one of my Navajo students termed "that colonialism excuse" do not appear to be popular among many other Native women or men and students who have read her review of Mary Crow Dog's book in my classes. For example, a Navajo/Tohono O'Odham woman in one of my courses, who identifies as Navajo and is active in tribal politics, commented after reading the review of *Lakota Woman*, "The colonialism excuse may work for those women up there [north], but it doesn't fly for us down here [in the Southwest]." Others in the room applauded. In other classes, Native women and men comment that Jaimes's thesis is "ridiculous," "unrealistic," and, as one older Hopi woman said, "it's a good excuse for women to allow themselves to be victims."

Indeed, most Native women refuse to be victims of gender oppression, instead taking charge of their lives and reveling in their roles and status as women who hold their tribes together. They have little patience with identity politics and with those who accuse them of accepting "colonialist ideology" because they will not allow Native men to behave badly. To be sure, oppression against their tribes is a major concern, but they fully expect men to work with women in order to eradicate racial oppression. Many men agree with them.

Regardless of the authors' motivations for voicing their ideologies, Jaimes and Halsey make an important point in their essay. As I discuss in chapter 6, more than a few things have occurred to cause problems between genders. The "colonialism excuse" might ring more true among men and women who are well versed in tribal traditions and desire to regain those traditions but have great difficulty in living traditionally than among those far removed from tribal traditions. Many Native women are married to non-Native men who know nothing about their wives' tribal traditions. While some men attempt to learn and are respectful of their spouses, Native women with abusive husbands (like women of other races) have to look to themselves for answers to their dilemmas.

Many Navajos, for example, have close ties to their lands, are traditionalists residing on the reservation, and have a strong sense of Navajo identity. They also appear to be suffering from unprecedented violence, alcoholism, and gang violence on their reservation. Peggy Bird, the director of the Native American Family Violence Prevention Project in Shiprock, New Mexico, concurs that colonialism may have much to do with these issues: "I would say the violence in the native community is a reflection of what's been learned over the centuries of different oppression they experienced. . . . We are now oppressing ourselves." She adds, "There are still some people who have and maintain balance and connections with traditions and cultures. They are the strongholds in the community. They are the ones working hard to remind people about different values that we live—about living in harmony with each other."[29]

Feeling good about one's self and adhering to traditions are first steps not only in stopping abuse but also in stopping feelings of victimization. As Mililani Trask has stated, "As indigenous women, we have rich traditions upon which we can rely and from which we can and should draw our sustenance. Primary in all traditional societies were the religious practices that provided the foundations of our cultures and governments. Acknowledging our spiritual belief systems and incorporating them to the greatest extent possible in our daily lives are keys to self-empowerment and self-determination for indigenous peoples."[30] The Morningstar House, therefore, advocates educating clients about the traditional ways of most tribes: women were respected because they are "life bearers, life givers, and the heart of the community," while men were "protectors and providers and children are seen as gifts from the Creator."[31]

Peggy Sanday notes that rape-prone societies are identified by male dominance, interpersonal violence, and sexual separation and rape-free societies are marked by the high status of women who are continually honored through all conduits of society—social, political, religious, and economic. If she is correct, then it would seem that those Native societies that traditionally and currently revere women would not have abusive Native males.[32] Of course, in order for the Morningstar House strategy to work, both genders have to understand and acknowledge the traditional place of women. Over the course of time, traditions and individual tribal members' ties to those values and beliefs become more tenuous. Add in all the other negative forces of colonialism, as well as substance abuse, and the stress of everyday life may account for why many men take their frustrations out on women.

By no means have all Native men absorbed the patriarchal mindset that colonialism brought to the New World. Many Native men refuse to become victimized by the forces of colonialist psychology and do not approve of excusing bad behavior by blaming colonialism for dysfunctional gender roles. Women speak glowingly of some male AIM members who treated women with respect and honor. Many men who follow traditions by placing women in egalitarian roles display little ego and have no desire to place themselves in dominant positions. As Sam English, Turtle Mountain Chippewa artist and honorary board member of the Morningstar House, comments, "We American Indian men need to support American Indian women. We need to quit the snide remarks about having men involved with American Indian women's programs."[33]

Many of my Native male colleagues agree with the Navajo woman who rejects "that colonialism excuse" as a rationale for bad behavior. "That's a sorry argument," one male colleague said to me after a discussion about this essay. As his ancestors surely thought long ago, he argues that "we have to take responsibility for our own actions."

# Notes

## Introduction

1. Information on these statistics are found in numerous places: The 1990 Census; the Indian Health Service, *Trends in Indian Health*; Karen Gullo, "Violent Crime Rises for Natives," *News from Indian Country*, late March, 2001, 1A; Devon A. Mihesuah, "Indians in Arizona," in Smith, ed., *Politics and Public Policy in Arizona*; and Utter, *American Indians*, esp. 297–318.

2. In my book, *American Indians*, 97, 98, 101, the most common stereotypes of Natives include: Indians are all alike; Indians were conquered because they were weak and powerless; if Indians had banded together, they could have prevented the European invasion; Indians had no civilization until Europeans brought it to them; Indians arrived in this hemisphere via the Siberian land bridge; Indians were warlike and treacherous; Indians had nothing to contribute to Europeans or to the growth of America; Indians did not value or empower women; Indians have no religion; Indians welcome outsiders to study and participate in their religious ceremonies; Indians are a vanished race; Indians are confined to reservations, live in tipis, wear braids, and ride horses; Indians have no reason to be unpatriotic; Indians get a free ride from the government; Indians' affairs are managed for them by the BIA; Indians are not capable of completing school; Indians cannot vote or hold office; Indians have a tendency toward alcoholism; "my grandmother was an Indian"; Indians are all full-bloods; all Indians have an "Indian name"; Indians know the histories, languages, and cultural aspects of their own tribe and all other tribes; Indians are stoic and have no sense of humor; and Indians like having their picture taken.

See also Bataille and Silet, *The Pretend Indians*; Hanson and Rouse, "Dimensions of Native American Stereotyping"; Hanson and Rouse, "American Indian Stereotyping"; Hill, Solomon, Tiger, and Fortenberry, "Complexities of Ethnicity"; Hirschfelder, *American Indian Stereotypes*; Marsden and Nachbar, "The Indian in the Movies"; and Stedman, *Shadows of the Indians.*

3. Bieder, *Science Encounters the Indian,*; Hinsley, *The Smithsonian and the American Indian*; Mihesuah, ed., *Repatriation Reader.* See also Whitt, "Cultural Imperialism."

4. Sources of information on these issues include: *Akwesasne Notes,* which has chronicled uranium tailings pollution on tribal lands for twenty years; Grinde and Johansen, *Ecocide of Native America*; Jaimes, ed., *The State of Native America,* esp. chaps. 5–8; LaDuke, *All Our Relations*; and Weaver, ed., *Defending Mother Earth.*

5. In the 28 February 1993 issue of the *Chico (California) Enterprise Record* and in the 1 December 1993 commentary in the *Orion (California State University, Chico),* Joseph R. Conlin, a professor of history at CSU, Chico, stated that minority professors are incompetent and asserted that "little more is required of Affirmative Action faculty than to show evidence of a majority of the vital life signs." See also Mihesuah, ed., *Natives and Academics*; and Fixico, ed., *Rethinking American Indian History.*

6. Some scholars, like Marge Bruchac, argue that the term "squaw" is traditionally used in Abenaki as *nidobasqua* (a female friend), *manigebeskwa* (woman of the woods), and *squsachem* (female chief), and none are used with negative connotations. Further, Bruchac states that "I, for one, don't mind one bit being called a squaw, as long as the speaker understands that it originated not in some ignorant swear word, but in a marvelously descriptive indigenous language." From a dialogue on the use of the word "squaw," H-*AmIndian, (.msu.edu),* 31 August 1999.

Numerous other Natives took offense and responded with comments such as: "My tribe is in the West and we did not call our women squaw. And I don't like people referring to my wife or daughters as squaws even it if is not negative." Another: "Spare me. In my mind, no self-respecting Indian woman would ever agree to being called 'squaw.'"

7. A major problem is the creation of Hopi arts and crafts by non-Hopis, who are taking away the self-expression from Hopi artists. The Hopis of Arizona express their concern over the more than one hundred thousand imitation and fake Kachina dolls that are made and sold each year. Seventy percent of their tribespeople earn a part of their income from arts and crafts production. An excerpt from *Buyer Beware of Fake and Imitation Hopi Arts and Crafts,* a brochure published by the Hopi Foundation, reads: "The Hopi are the true owners of their cultural heritage. Only the Hopi and their pueblo

relatives have esoteric manifestations called Kachinas within their culture. . . . Fake and imitation crafts hurt the self-employment status of the Hopi. It literally erodes the economic self-determination and self reliance of the entire tribe."

The Zia sun symbol has been most prominently displayed on the New Mexico state flag for seventy-five years, but it is also emblazoned on car license plates and portable toilets. The tribe has recently voiced its objections to outsiders' using what they claim is their most sacred symbol—the sun sign. Their goal is to protect the symbol from use without their permission, and the tribe is asking one million dollars for every year the symbol has been used as the state's emblem. "The white man's world has misappropriated a symbol that is an integral part of the tribe's culture," said a Zia elder. California tribes have recently discussed how to protect their pictographs, dance and spiritual regalia, and tribal songs from being used as symbols by outsiders. See Rebecca Lopez, "Tribes Seek Trademark Protection for Symbols," *Arizona Daily Sun (Flagstaff)*, 9 July 1999, A2; Jennifer Auther, "Zia Pueblo Seeks Compensation for State Use of Its Sacred Symbol," *Amarillo Globe-News*, 3 February 1999.

The appropriation of a people's art is not limited to American Indians. Expressing outrage over the revelation that Elizabeth Durack, an eighty-two-year-old Irishwoman, had been creating "aboriginal art" under the name of Eddie Burrop, many Australian aborigines who stress the importance of personal identity as a part of the art simply stopped painting. See Peter James Spielmann, "Acclaimed Aboriginal Artist Turns Out to Be a White Woman," *Arizona Daily Sun*, 8 March 1997, 14.

8. See Mathes, "Nineteenth-Century Women and Reform."

9. Northern Arizona University, Office of Native American Student Services, "Native American Student Profile, Graduation, and Persistence Report," fall 2000. See also the Applied Indigenous Studies homepage at *http://ais.nau.edu* and Native American Student Services at *http://www2.nau.edu/nass*.

10. Numerous works discuss changes brought by colonialism. Although they do not focus on colonialism as a force that affected women directly, these solid works are among the best at documenting the effects of white-Indian contact in northern North America: Axtell, *Natives and Newcomers*; Axtell, *The Invasion Within*; Berkhofer, *The White Man's Indian*; T. H. Breen, "Creative Adaptations: Peoples and Cultures," in Greene and Pole, eds., *Colonial British America*, 195–232; Crosby, *The Columbian Exchange*; "Further Readings" in Hurtado and Iverson, eds., *Major Problems in American Indian History*; Jennings, *The Invasion of America*; Stannard, *American Holo-*

*caust*; Thornton, *American Indian Holocaust and Survival*; White, *Roots of Dependency*; and Wright, *The Only Land They Knew*.

11. Medicine, " Role and Function of Indian Women"; Allen, *The Sacred Hoop*; Anderson, *Chain Her by One Foot*; Bonvillian, "Gender Relations in Native North America"; Brown, *Strangers in Blood*; Brown, "Economic Organization"; Buffalohead, "Farmers, Warriors, and Traders"; Devens, *Countering Colonization*; Etienne and Leacock, eds., *Women and Colonization*; Foster, "Of Baggage and Bondage"; Gonzalez, "An Ethnohistorical Analysis"; Guemple, "Men and Women"; Braund, *Deerskins and Duffles*; Jacobs, *Engendered Encounters*; Klein, "The Plains Truth"; Landes, *Ojibwe Woman*; Leacock, "Women in an Egalitarian Society: The Montagnais-Naskapi of Canada" and "Women's Status in Egalitarian Society: Implications for Social Evolution," in *Myths of Male Dominance*; Powers, *Oglala Women*; Rosaldo and Lamphere, eds., *Women, Culture, and Society*; Shoemaker, " Rise or Fall of Iroquois Women"; Shoemaker, ed., *Negotiators of Change*; Van Kirk, *Many Tender Ties*; and Young, "Women, Colonization and the Indian Question."

12. See Spellman, *Inessential Woman*.

13. Calvin Martin discusses his idea of an Indian "worldview" in *American Indians and the Problem of History*. While Martin is correct in his assertion that traditional Indian thoughts are much different from Euro-American thoughts (whatever they are), the problem with his discussion is that there is no one "worldview" among tribes.

14. The term "traditional" changes over time. A Native who speaks her tribal language and participates in tribal religious ceremonies is often considered traditional, but she is traditional only for this decade because chances are that she wears jeans, drives a car, and watches television—very "untraditional" Native things to do. Plains Natives who rode horses in the 1860s are considered traditional today, but they were unlike their traditional ancestors of the early 1500s, who had never seen a horse. Here, "multi-heritage" Native refers to an individual who is of two or more races—one being Native—and who defines "Indian" as his or her primary reference group. A mixed-heritage person can also be racially full-blood but is knowledgeable of and can function in more than one culture (i.e., is "living in two worlds"). "Full-blood" here refers to blood quantum, although some Natives take it to mean a person who is traditional but not necessarily racially "full-blood"; many "mixed-bloods" are called "full-bloods" because of their knowledge of culture.

15. For discussions of identity and difference, see Phelan, *Getting Specific*. For discussions of racial and ethnic identity, see Isaacs, *Idols of the Tribe*; and Bandura and Huston, "Identification as a Process of

Incidental Learning." For theoretical foundations indispensable to the study of mixed-heritage peoples, see Brown and Root, *Complexity and Diversity*; Fontaine, ed., *Race, Class, and Power in Brazil*; Graham, ed., *The Idea of Race in Latin America*; Padilla, ed., *Acculturation*; Root, ed., *Racially Mixed People in America*: Root, *Multiracial Experience*; Scheick, *Half-Blood*; and Spickard, *Mixed Blood*.

16. In "The 150 Percent Man," Malcolm McFee proposes that the "levels of acculturation" concept may be an inaccurate form of categorization because, in his view, "new ways can be learned without abandoning the old." This statement is indeed true, but because some Natives did abandon their "old ways" in attempts to become more like the dominant society (for a variety of reasons), I find the phrase "level of acculturation" appropriate in many instances.

17. Rose, "*Iyeska Win.*" "Racial identity" is the biological race one claims. A "multi-heritage" person might claim all of his or her racial heritages or only one; he or she can be biologically "mixed-blood" or "full-blood" and have no exposure to the cultural mores of an American Indian tribe, connected to his or her group only by virtue of genetics.

"Cultural identity" reflects the cultural standards of a society to which one subscribes. Michael Green describes cultural identity as an identity that "gives the individual a sense of a common past and of a shared destiny." Tribes have the commonalties of having to deal with the effects of colonialism (racism, prejudice, and loss of culture, land, and population) and originally having members who were exclusively indigenous peoples. Natives who only recognize this general definition of Indians' "common past" and who utilize a spectrum of tribal symbols and cultural mores to construct their version of a Native subscribe to a "pan-Indian cultural identity." Green also asserts that culture "unifies and integrates the individuals, gives them a sense of belonging, and a sense of their own uniqueness as a people. Further, a culture provides the individuals within that culture a way of life that is constitutive of what it means to be a human being." Using this definition of culture, Natives who practice their specific tribal traditions and are profoundly affected socially, religiously, and politically by those traditions are often referred to as "culturally Indian." See Green, *Issues in Native American Identity*.

"Ethnic" or "group" identity is a term that is often interchangeable with "cultural identity." Borrowing from Peter Rose, "ethnicity" is a "group classification in which the members share a unique social and cultural heritage passed on from one generation to the next." Ethnicity does not have a biological basis. Native ethnic or cultural identities have a variety of meanings attached to them by Native and non-Native societies and by individuals who claim them; they are salient terms that change with the economic, political, and social tides. "Traditional" Natives adhere to the culture of their tribe by speaking the language, practicing religious ceremonies, and living among their tribespeople; they might use the term "ethnic" to mean that both their racial background *and* their cultural adherence are Native. Other individuals who claim to be Native but who have no cultural connection to their tribe may also refer to themselves as ethnically Native. Native ethnic or cultural identities have a variety of meanings attached to them by Native and non-Native societies and by individuals who claim them: they are salient terms that change with the economic, political, and social tides. See Rose, *They and We.*

For detailed discussion about terminology, see Cornell and Hartmann, *Ethnicity and Race,* esp. 15–38.

18. Stonequist, *Marginal Man.* Stonequist's view of marginality is negative. He described the "marginal man" as one who lives in "psychological uncertainty" between two worlds, one of which is dominant over the other. Although his theory is flawed in a variety of ways, it nevertheless provokes numerous questions, such as: Cannot a person actually "live in two worlds"? Are all marginal persons "pathological personalities," as he implies? Most important: What are the positive aspects of being marginal? McFee, "The 150 Percent Man."

19. Collins, *Fighting Words,* xvii.

20. See Yellow Bird, "What We Want to Be Called."

## 1. Merging Feminist Studies with Indigenous Women's Studies

1. Kramarae and Spender, eds., *The Knowledge Explosion.*

2. Deloria, "Commentary."

3. Linda Smith, *Decolonizing Methodologies,* 3.

4. See, for example, Anzaldúa, ed., *Making Face, Making Soul;* Brooks-Higgenbothan, "The Problem of Race"; hooks, *Ain't I a Woman!* and *Feminist Theory;* Hull, Scott, and Smith, eds., *All the Women Are White;* Moraga and Anzuldúa, eds., *This Bridge Called My Back;* Lerner, *Black Women in White America,* chaps. 5–7, and "Reconceptualizing Differences among Women"; Mohanty, Russo, and Torres, eds., *Third World Women;* and Russo, "We Cannot Live without Our Lives: White Women, Antiracism, and Feminism," in Mohanty, Russo, and Torres, eds., *Third World Women,* 297–313.

5. See, for example, Green, *Native American Women;* Prucha, *Bibliographical Guide;* and Bataille and Sands, eds., *American Indian*

*Women: A Guide to Research* and *American Indian Women: Telling Their Lives.*

The Living Legends Oral History Collection at the Oklahoma Historical Society in Oklahoma City contains dozens of taped interviews with male and female Oklahoma tribal members that were conducted in the 1970s. These interviews reveal interesting details regarding the informants' lives and their views on Indian identity and tribal politics. The Indian and Pioneer Histories, edited by Grant Foreman, also at the Oklahoma Historical Society, contains thousands of interviews of Oklahomans made as part of the Works Projects Administration. Although poorly indexed and of uneven quality, the collection is nevertheless useful for researchers with patience It includes short autobiographies, interviews (usually conducted by individuals with absolutely no knowledge about Natives), and genealogies of Native women who were born in the mid-nineteenth century. Natives who attended boarding schools left behind diaries, letters, newspaper editorials, and alumni association newsletters.

6. N. Scott Momaday, "Oral Traditions of the American Indian," speech given at Brigham Young University, Provo, Utah, 1975.

7. Quintana, "Women."

8. See, for example, Jaimes, ed., *State of Native America*, 311–44.

9. Mihesuah, ed., *Natives and Academics*, 37–54.

10. Andrews is the author of, most notably, *Medicine Woman, Jaguar Woman, Star Woman,*and *Crystal Woman*, all published by Harper and Row.

11. See Wendy Rose, "The Great Pretenders"; and Andrea Smith, "For All Those Who Were Indian" and "Opinion." See also Donaldson, "On Medicine Women"; Gniewek, "The Silent Genocide"; "Plastic Indians," *Indian Country Today*, 26 August–2 September 1996, A3, A6; and *White Shamans and Plastic Medicine Men.*

12. See Mihesuah, "Suggested Research Guidelines."

## 2. Writing about Anna Mae Pictou-Aquash

This chapter is based on my presentation at the American Society for Ethnohistory meeting, 2000.

## 3. Review of Frazier's *On the Rez*

This chapter originally appeared as "Infatuation Is Not Enough," in the section "Reviews of Ian Frazier's *On the Rez*," *American Indian Quarterly* 24:2 (Spring 2000): 279–306.

1. *Arizona Republic (Phoenix)*, 5 December 1992, E3.

2. Oscar C. Villalon, "Outside on the Rez: Frazier Took Some Heat for His Account on Indian Life," *San Francisco Chronicle*, 28 February 2000.

## 4. Comments on McCarriston's "Indian Girls"

This chapter originally appeared in a forum, "Responses to 'Indian Girls,'" *HEArt* 5:1 (fall 2001): 18–19.

 1. McCarriston's poem was published in *Ice-Floe* 1:2 (December 2000).

## 5. In the Trenches of Academia

This chapter meshes my presentations given at the University of Utah's Native American Heritage Week Celebration, 2000, and at the First Annual Graduate Student Conference on American Indian Research, Arizona State University, 2000.

 1. Elizabeth Cook-Lynn discusses Indian intellectuals in "American Indian Intellectualism and the New Indian Story."

 2. Minh-La, *Woman, Native, Other*, 6.

 3. Quoted in Bruchac, ed., *Survival This Way*, 113.

 4. Several recent popular books that focus on other topics also reflect the effort to find truth. In 1996, Mary Lefkowitz's *Not Out of Africa: How Afrocentrism Became an Excuse to Teach Myth as History* was published in response to Afrocentrists' unfounded claims that, among other myths, Beethoven was Afro-European, Socrates was African, and Greek civilization was stolen from Africa.

Another historian, Deborah Lipsault, wrote *Denying the Holocaust: The Growing Assault on Truth and Memory*, which focuses primarily on the Institute for Historical Review in California. This institute regularly publishes information that fuels Holocaust deniers' argument that the event did not happen. Lipsault utilizes facts, not emotionalism, to discredit these deniers. Ironically, she receives letters from Holocaust survivors who express their disappointment over such things as her discounting the rumor that Nazis converted Jews into soap. Her correction of these claims, they believe, diminish their case against Nazis.

More recently, Lerone Bennett Jr.'s *Forced into Glory: Abraham Lincoln's White Dream* examines Lincoln's bigotry toward blacks, his support of the "Black Laws" and the Fugitive Slave Act, and his plans to ship African-Americans back to Africa. To be sure, the themes of the book are controversial and compelling, but the irony is that according to *Time*, Bennett's well-researched book has been all but ignored by all the major newspapers. Lincoln is a hero to many blacks and whites, and the image of a tired, besieged president who "freed the slaves" prior to being assassinated is too strong to deconstruct. Clearly America is not ready to look at history through a clearer lens and to reassess one of its heroes. See White, "Was Lincoln a Racist?"

5. Debo, "To Establish Justice," 405.

6. Chambers, "Migrancy, Culture, and Identity," 78–79.

7. Christian, "The Race for Theory," 335.

8. Himmelfarb, "Telling It as You Like It."

9. Norris, "Postmodernizing History."

10. Collins, *Black Feminist Thought*, 251.

11. Shoemaker, ed., *Negotiators of Change*, 20.

12. Suleri, "Woman Skin Deep," 752.

13. Bird and Harjo, eds., *Reinventing the Enemy's Language*.

14. DeSalvo, *Writing as a Way of Healing*, 11.

15. Clifford and Marcus, eds., *Writing Culture*, 20.

16. Behar, "Introduction"; Abu-Lughod, "Can There Be a Feminist Ethnography?"; and Stacey, "Can There Be a Feminist Ethnography?"

17. MacKinnon, *Feminism Unmodified*, 50.

18. Anna Quindlen, "Journalism 101: Human Nature," *Newsweek*, 15 November 1999, 104.

19. See, for example, Clifton, *The Invented Indian*.

20. Wilson, "American Indian History," 23.

21. Linda Tuhiwai Smith, *Decolonizing Methodologies*, 19.

22. For information on NAU's program, see *http://www.ais.nau.edu*.

23. Rich, *On Lies, Secrets and Silence*, 232.

24. Gutierrez's work has been analyzed in numerous places, including "Commentaries," *American Indian Culture and Research Journal* 17:3 (1993): 121–78; and Miller, "Licensed Trafficking and Ethnogenetic Engineering," in Mihesuah, ed., *Natives and Academics*, 100–110.

Recently, Malotki proposed to give a talk titled "Hopi Cannibalism" and was censured by NAU's president, causing an outcry among faculty and students, who believed that his "academic freedom" had been violated. See "NAU Censors Prof's Title of Hopi Lecture," and "NAU Censors Professor," *Lumberjack* (NAU), 21–27 February 2001, 1, 2; "Professor's Actions Undermine Freedom" [the president's response], *Lumberjack*, 28 February–13 March 2001; and "Letters: Professor's Reputation Speaks for Itself," *Lumberjack*, 14–20 March 2001, 9.

25. For information regarding the Salt Trail incident, see "Hopis Want to Block Historian's Book," *Arizona Republic*, 19 August 1990, D8; "Hopis Against Book's Printing," *Arizona Daily Sun*, 16 Septem-

ber 1990, 1, 4; "Dispute between Scholar, Tribe Leaders over Book on Hopi Ritual Raises Concerns about Censorship of Studies of American Indians," *Chronicle of Higher Education*, 17 October 1990, A6, 8, 9. See also Mihesuah, "Suggested Research Guidelines," which includes the following:

In April 1991, Northern Arizona University President Eugene Hughes, upon recognizing the need for guidelines directed towards administrators, staff, faculty, and students who conduct research on American Indians, formed a five-member committee comprised of representatives from history, anthropology, modern language, and religious studies. Our group was thus named the Native American Research Guidelines Advisory Committee (N.A.R.G.A.C.). The guidelines we established are intended to supplement the university's guidelines (such as the I.R.B. guidelines) by addressing religious, social, political, and other cultural aspects. However, they have not been formally approved and they may never be.

Some of the ideas I mention here may infuriate those researchers who are ardent subscribers to the imperialistic tenets of academic freedom. But considering the long history of exploitation of Indians at the hands of some non-Indians, it is only appropriate that the research of American Indians be monitored by universities and by tribes.

1. Only the tribes' elected political and religious leadership should review and approve the research proposal. It is not uncommmon for a researcher to obtain permission to study a tribe from one or two individuals, or from one tribal faction, and then claim that he or she has "tribal consent." The problem with this strategy (besides being unethical) is that the tribe may be divided along political, social, religious, geographic, or class lines. Progressive and traditional elements exist in almost every tribe. Not all members of the same tribe subscribe to the same values, support the same tribal politicians, or live in the same area. Many Indians know nothing about their cultures.

Because of the socio-economic differences between members of the same tribe, a variety of situations may arise to complicate the researcher's study. For example, some tribal members may not be initiated into certain religious societies and do not know enough to tell researchers factual information. On the other hand, maverick tribal members may be inclined to reveal secretive tribal religious knowledge for monetary gain, and some individuals may reveal private information under the assumption that the researcher will not make public the information. It is important that researchers deal with the tribes' leadership and not take advantage of intra-tribal differences.

2. Researchers should remain sensitive to the economic, social, physical, psychological, religious, and general welfare of the individuals and cultures being studied. When individuals of different cultures interact, misunderstandings often result. What may be "ethical" and "respectful" to one group may be seen as "unethical" and "disrespectful" to another. Behaviors can be interpreted differently. The well-published, grant-winning, aggressive researcher seeking knowledge may be admired among academics,

but among other peoples he or she may appear to be nosey, pushy, and therefore offensive. The researcher may not understand the tribes' cultural mores, and indeed, he or she may believe that the Indians' cultures are inferior to his or her own (conversely, potential subjects may feel the same way about the researcher and his or her culture), but that should not deter the investigator from acting with the greatest sensitivity.

Peoples of non-Euro-American traditions may not share prevailing academic views on the gathering, distribution, and or publication of cultural information. They may not understand the need a person from one culture has to collect data from a person of another culture for curiosity's sake. For example, many non-Indians are fixated on Indian religions and they intrude on ceremonies and dances with tape recorder and camera in hand with the belief that Indians' religions are open to scrutiny by anyone. Some intruders want to participate in ceremonies and many imitate them. Witness the number of bogus medicine men and women in our country today. Many are frauds that conduct seminars with the intention of duping the ignorant public. Numerous books on Indian religions have been criticized by tribes because of the unscrupulous ways information was obtained.

It also must be kept in mind that many tribes will not object too strenuously to a topic because it might reveal facts. A potential publisher of the aforementioned religious book was confused when tribal members argued that many parts of the book were inaccurate, but would not tell editors why because religious leaders did not want the correct information revealed.

3. Researchers who are preparing grant applications that deal with Indians should be prepared to spend months, if not a year, to allow the subjects to thoroughly understand every aspect of the study. The Hopis, for example, take a least a year to approve research projects, and there is a good chance that they may disapprove of your study. It is not wise to write a grant application under the assumption that the tribe will cooperate.

4. Use caution when using cameras and tape-recorders. Make certain that informants understand what you will do with the pictures or tapes. Many people do not take kindly to having their picture published without permission and they may not want their recorded voice deposited in an archive. Tribes can confiscate recording devises if they are used improperly.

5. Informants should be given fair and appropriate return. This can be in the form of money, a copy of the book, or an acknowledgment, depending on the agreement between the investigator and the informant. Some researchers balk at this, but considering that the writer/researcher is the one who usually benefits from the study, fair return is just that—fair. Otherwise, the researcher has used the informant for his or her own gain. Informants have a right to remain anonymous, but proper credit must be given to informants who do wish to be acknowledged.

6. The anticipated consequences of the research should be communicated to individuals and groups that will be affected. What is likely to happen? Potential informants may not want to be involved after hearing about the

entire process and the researcher will end up with half a study—so do not be secretive. The researchers should inform the tribe of publishing houses or journals that may print results of the study.

7. Every attempt should be made to cooperate with the current host society. An unfortunate scenario for some scholars could be that one political party will be in power when the research proposal is approved, but another political entity unsupportive of the project may come to power before the project is completed. Bob Trotter, Chair of the Department of Anthropology at NAU and a member of N.A.R.G.A.C., tells a story of a student who was almost finished with her dissertation on a tribe in South America when a new political party—different from the one who had given her permission to study the tribe—took command and made her leave. She also had to surrender ten years worth of notes and what she had written of her dissertation behind.

Obviously, problems must be anticipated. Written agreements may not have the same meaning and legal exigency for all peoples. Some may agree to the project then they may turn around later and become uncooperative. Researchers at NAU are encouraged not to take on a project with a group that is politically unstable, because the researcher may have to abandon the project.

8. Physical anthropologists, archaeologists, and other researchers wishing to desecrate Indian burials in order to study Indian remains and funerary objects should obtain permission to do so from tribes. The issues of desecration of Indian burials and sacred objects, the study of the remains and objects, and the repatriation of these items to tribes is quite volatile and multi-faceted. Researchers should realize that the study of the past does impact on the present, and they need to understand that activities that some scholars see as academic study is viewed by Indians as grave robbing.

Those who study Indian remains should respect the dignity of living Indians by not plundering graves without permission from the descendants of the deceased. Researchers should be aware of the Native American Graves Protection and Repatriation Act (N.A.G.P.R.A.) that restricts the desecration of Indian graves, and they should check state laws that have enacted criminal prosecution for trafficking human remains.

9. Results of the study should be reviewed by the tribes' elected representatives and religious leaders. Many researchers object to having non-scholars critique their writings. But this step is vital. It ensures that sensitive information remains secret and that the researcher presents acceptable information correctly. A Ph.D. should not be viewed as a license to obtain everything about tribal histories and culture, nor should a researcher with a terminal degree consider himself or herself an "expert" on Indian matters. In actuality, many Indians do know more about the topic than the researcher, although the former may not have completed high school. Not enough researchers ask for Indians' input anyway and their studies could be improved if they did.

10. The researcher must follow the guidelines for each new project. Some

tribes as a whole have no problems or objections to academic research and publication of data about their cultural heritage—but many do. Just because a researcher had a fruitful experience with one tribe does not mean the next tribe will welcome him or her with open arms. All tribes are different. Where some welcome research, others view it as violating their privacy and the sanctity of their traditions. Many tribes have indeed been exploited. Failure to respect Indians' wishes concerning research could hamper the plans of future researchers.

## 6. Colonialism and Disempowerment

1. Mankiller quoted in Griffin, "Relearning to Trust Ourselves," 73.

2. Basso, "The Gift of Changing Woman"; Downs, *The Navajo*; Frisbie, *Kinaalda*; Ce'cile R. Ganteaume, "White Mountain Apache Dance: Expressions of Spirituality," in Heth, ed., *Native American Dance*, 65–76, 79–81; and Quintero, "Coming of Age the Apache Way."

3. Allen, *Sacred Hoop*, 13–29; Niethammer, *Daughters of the Earth*, 243–46, Cate Montana, "News Close to Heritage of Okanagan Nation," *Indian Country Today*, special edition, "Hitting the Pow Wow Circuit," 22–29 March 1999, 57.

4. Many tribes are matrilineal (descent is traced through the females) and/or matrilocal (residence after marriage is near the wife's family), but there is no evidence to support the assertion that some tribes were at one time purely matriarchal, that is, having all policy and economics controlled by females. Some scholars use matriarchy to refer to female ideologies, as opposed to patriarchy, which is a culture or society founded on male ideals.

Sources on matrilineal/matriarchal tribal roles include: Holland-Braund, "Guardians of Tradition"; Bonvillain, "Gender Relations"; Brown, "Economic Organization"; Fred Eggan, "The Choctaw and Their Neighbors in the Southeast: Acculturation under Pressure," in Eggan, *The American Indian*; Fenton, "Structure, Continuity, and Change"; Guemple, "Men and Women"; Jacobs, *Engendered Encounters*; Harry A. Kersey Jr. and Helen M. Bannan, "Patchwork and Politics: The Evolving Roles of Florida Seminole Women in the Twentieth Century," in Shoemaker, ed., *Negotiators of Change*, 193–212; Clara Sue Kidwell, "Choctaw Women and Cultural Persistence in Mississippi," in Shoemaker, ed., *Negotiators of Change*, 115–34; Eleanor Burke Leacock, "Montagnais Women and the Jesuit Program for Colonization," in Etienne and Leacock, eds., *Women and Colonization*, 25–42; Leacock, "Women in an Egalitarian Society: The Montagnais-Naskapi of Canada," and "Women's Status in Egalitarian Society:

Implications for Social Evolution," in Leacock, *Myths of Male Dominance*; Katherine M. B. Osburn, "'Dear Friend and Ex-Husband': Marriage, Divorce, and Women's Property Rights on the Southern Ute Reservation, 1887–1930," in Shoemaker, ed., *Negotiators of Change*, 157–75; and Young, "Women, Colonization, and the Indian Question."

5. Allen, *Sacred Hoop*, 2, 256. See also Williams, *Spirit and the Flesh*.

6. "Seeking the Balance," 17.

7. Allen, *Sacred Hoop*, 30–42; Fenton, "Structure, Continuity and Change"; Fiske, "Colonization"; Sierra Adare, "Maisie Shenandoah, Oneida Wolf Clan Mother," *News from Indian Country*, late June 2000, 12–13A; Kidwell, "Power of Women"; Niethammer, *Daughters of the Earth*, 139–46; Shoemaker, ed., *Negotiators of Change*, 72–89.

8. Robert Anderson, "Northern Cheyenne War Mothers"; Klein, "Plains Truth"; Buffalohead, "Farmers, Warriors, and Traders"; Gridley, *American Indian Women*, 18; Landes, *Ojibwe Woman*; McClary, "Nancy Ward"; Powers, *Oglala Women*; Tucker, "Nancy Ward."

9. Buchanan, *Apache Women Warriors*; Ewers, "Deadlier Than the Male"; Fowler, *Shared Symbols* and *Arapahoe Politics*; Hungry Wolf, *Ways of My Grandmothers*; Jones, *Sanapia*; Landes, *Ojibwe Woman*; Lewis, "Manly-Hearted Women"; Lurie, ed., *Sister of Crashing Thunder*; and Powers, *Oglala Women*.

Charlotte Seymour-Smith's *Dictionary of Anthropology* states that, in some patriarchal societies, women possess some domestic authority and autonomy, although the political systems are dominated by men. Many Indian societies that are considered to be patriarchal apparently were more egalitarian than purely male-dominated. Even matriarchal and matrilineal societies have political spheres headed by men, who are usually advised by women.

10. Allen, *Sacred Hoop*, 36. A perceptive take on the idea that Euro-Americans used imagination than more fact in chronicling Indian history and culture is historian Curtis M. Hinsley's description of nineteenth-century digging, excavation, and collecting of Indian remains and cultural objects as deeply psychological and patriotic. Hinsley writes that scholars, young men, and politicians were all contributors in "creating" the new American nation by imposing their versions of Indian history and cultures into American history. They even created their own identities by "absorbing and domesticating their predecessors . . . into themselves. . . . Digging in the prehistoric dirt and constructing heroic tales on what they found, these men . . . faced the challenge of replacing a heritage of heroism built on classical literature with an identity constructed of shards and bones and

preliterate silence. No wonder they kept digging." Hinsley, "Digging for Identity," 47.

In *The View From Officer's Row: Army Perceptions of Western Indians*, Sherry Smith utilizes letters, diaries, and government reports to inform us what non-Indians believed to be true about Indian women. In 1876, Richard Irving Dodge, a career military man, wrote *The Plains of North America and Their Inhabitants*, a book replete with patriarchal discussion of Indian females that tells us more about the Eurocentric author than it does about his subjects. For discussion of how Euro-Americans viewed Indians, see Doggett, ed., *New World of Wonders*; Green, "Pocahontas Perplex"; and Honour, *European Vision of America*. Today, the reality of Indian women is altered in romance novels, movies, and the multi-million-dollar industry of "Indian Maiden Art."

11. See Morrison, *Chief Sarah*; and Hopkins, *Life among the Paiutes*.

12. On E. Pauline Johnson, see Strong-Boag and Gerson, *Paddling Her Own Canoe*.

13. On the LaFlesche sisters, see Clarke and Webb, "Susette and Susan LaFlesche"; Norma Kidd Green, *Iron Eye's Family*; and Wilson, *Bright Eyes*.

14. For information on Mourning Dove, see Brown, "Mourning Dove's Canadian Recovery Years"; Brown, "Mourning Dove's Voice in Co-Ge-We-A"; and Miller, ed., *Mourning Dove*.

15. For discussion on this theme see Pearce, *Savagism and Civilization*.

16. Anderson, *Chain Her by One Foot*; Blackburn, *Harvest of Souls*; Devens, *Countering Colonization*; Prucha, *The Churches and the Indian Schools*; Prucha, *American Indian Policy in Crisis*; and Tinker, *Missionary Conquest*.

17. Hackett, ed., *Revolt of the Pueblo Indians*; Johns, *Storms Brewed in Other Men's Worlds*; Jones, *Pueblo Warriors and Spanish Conquest*; and Spicer, *Cycles of Conquest*.

18. See "American Indian Prophets"; Edmunds, *Shawnee Prophet*; Herring, *Kenekuk*; Miller, *Prophetic Worlds*; Mooney, *Ghost-Dance Religion*.

19. See Courts of Indian Offenses, 1 November 1883, *Annual Report of the Secretary of the Interior*, House Executive Document no. 1, 48th Cong., 1st sess., serial 2190, pp. x–xiii, in Prucha, ed., *Documents of U.S. Indian Policy*, 160–62.

20. For information on Indians and HIV/AIDS, see Vernon, *Killing Us Quietly*.

21. The best source of information on the changing social and

political Cherokee systems is Perdue, *Cherokee Women*. See also Mankiller and Wallis, *Mankiller*, 15–29; and Strickland, *Fire and the Spirits*.

22. Ackerman, "The Effect of Missionary Ideals."

23. These changes are major themes in Perdue, *Cherokee Women*. See also McLoughlin, *Cherokees and Missionaries*; McLoughlin, *Cherokee Renascence*.

24. Shoemaker, "Rise or Fall of Iroquois Women," 41. Shoemaker brings to our attention the different interpretations of Iroquois women's economic position within the tribes. In "Economic Organization and the Position of Women," Judith K. Brown states, "It is concluded that the high status of Iroquois women reflected their control of their tribe's economic organization" (151), while Tooker, in "Women in Iroquois Society," believes that Iroquois women did not dominate tribal economics; rather, men and women conducted "economic exchange," resulting in women's power coming from a matrilineal instead of a matriarchal organization. Shoemaker asserts that "Throughout the nineteenth century, the Senecas accommodated Euroamerican culture but never accepted it entirely" (52). Actually, numerous Senecas lived in Indian Territory during that time, and some attended the Cherokee Female Seminary, a tribally backed boarding school; the institution's ideology was "anything white was best."

25. Shoemaker, "Rise or Fall of Iroquois Women," 52.

26. Green, "Mary Musgrove."

27. Caldwell, *Thoughts on the Original Unity of the Human Race*; Morton, *Crania Americana*; and Nott, "Unity of the Human Race." See also Bieder, *Science Encounters the Indian*; and Hinsley, *The Smithsonian and the American Indian*.

28. Wilson, "Blood Quantum."

29. Rose, "*Iyeska Win*," 69. See also Isaacs, *Idols of the Tribe*, 93–114, for discussion about feelings of inadequacy in use of language. For a comparative voice, see Min, "Language Lessons."

30. For information on Gertrude Bonnin (Zitkala-Scarona), see Fisher, "Zitkala-Scarona"; Johnson and Wilson, "Gertrude Simmons Bonnin"; and Welch, "Zitkala-Scarona."

31. Engels, *Origin of the Family*; Holmstrom, "Marxist Theory"; and Jaggar, *Feminist Politics*.

32. Brown, *Strangers in Blood*; and Van Kirk, *Many Tender Ties*.

33. Van Kirk, "Role of Native Women."

34. Hamamsky, "Role of Women"; Lamphere, "Historical and Regional Variability"; and McPherson, "From Dezba to 'John.'"

35. Comer, "Hokahe!" 197.

36. *Santa Clara v. Martinez*, 436 U.S. 49 (1978); Indian Act, Can. Rev. Stat., 1970, c. 1–6, s. 12 (1)(b).

37. *Sandra Lovelace v. Canada.* See also Bayefsky, "Human Rights Committee"; and Berry, "Contextualising International Women's Rights."

38. MacKinnon, "Whose Culture? A Case Note on *Martinez v. Santa Clara Pueblo* (1983)," in *Feminism Unmodified*, 63–69. See also Harris, "Race and Essentialism"; and Judith Resnik, "Dependent Sovereigns: Indian Tribes, States and the Federal Courts," available online at *http://www.tribal-institute.org/articles/resnik1.html*.

39. Swentzell's quote is from Crozier-Hogle and Wilson, comps., *Surviving in Two Worlds*, 217.

40. For information on federal boarding schools, see Adams, *Education for Extinction*; Coleman,*American Indian Children at School*; Ellis, *To Change Them Forever*; Lomawaima, *They Called It Prairie Light*; McBeth, *Ethnic Identity*; *In the White Man's Image*; and Trennert, *Phoenix Indian School*, 34.

41. The Meriam Report led to the passage of the Indian Reorganization Act and to the reorganization of the Bureau of Indian Affairs under John Collier. See Brookings Institution, *Problem of Indian Administration*.

42. *Indian Reorganization Act*; House Concurrent Resolution 108.

43. *Arizona Republic*, 11 October 1987, A20–21, 23; 3 October 1990, B2; *Arizona Daily Sun*, 26 September 1990; 3 February 1991, 23.

44. Mihesuah, *American Indians*.

45. Dillingham, "Indian Women"; England, "Look at the Indian Health Service Policy"; Larson, "And Then There Were None"; Lawrence, "Indian Health Service"; Torpy, "Native American Women"; "Killing Our Future: Sterilization and Experiments," *Akwesasne Notes* 9 (early spring, 1977): 4; "Marie Sanchez: For the Women," *Akwesasne Notes* 9 (December 1977): 14–15; James Robison, "US Sterilizes 25 Percent of Indian Women: Study," *Chicago Tribune*, 22 May 1977, sec. 1, p. 36.

46. Bachman, *Death and Violence*, 91.

47. Fairchild, Fairchild, and Stoner, "Prevalence of Adult Domestic Violence."

48. Bhuyan, "Talking about Sexual Assault"; Karen L. Testerman, "High Domestic Violence Rates Shows Need for Shelter," *Indian Country Today*, 15–22 September 1997, B7; Paula Arrillaga, "Rez Teens Fight Violence, Despair," *Arizona Daily Sun*, 15 April 2001, 1, 11A.

49. "Special Report: The Lost Generation, Conflict, Culture, and

Family Change on the Rez," *Arizona Daily Sun,* 11 and 13 October 1998, A1, 5.

50. Wise and Wise, "Conversation with Mary Brave Bird."

51. For discussion and debate on the concept of black "self hatred," see Baldwin, "Theory and Research"; Penn, Gaines, and Phillips, "Desirability of Own-Group Preference" and " Hermeneutic Rejoinder"; Helms, "More Psychologists"; Sellers, "Call to Arms"; Taylor, "Reaction to Penn"; Parham, "Own Group Preferences"; and Kambon and Hopkins, "African-Centered Analysis."

52. Maracle, *I Am Woman,* 123.

53. Durham, "Those Dead Guys." See also Churchill, "Nobody's Pet Poodle," for a discussion of Durham's identity claims.

54. Robert A. Williams Jr., "Gendered Checks and Balances." See also Patricia Penn Hilden's nonsensical attack on Sherman Alexie in "Ritchie Valens Is Dead," 236, 252 n.44.

55. This discussion is not meant to imply that Natives should not criticize each other when the situation is warranted. Rather, its purpose is to bring to light the reality that jealousy, insecurity, and fear all play major roles in intertribal and intratribal relationships.

56. Anzaldúa, *Borderlands/La Frontera,* 38.

57. Axtell, *Invasion Within;* Berkhofer, *White Man's Indian;* Berkhofer, "White Conceptions of Indians"; Bieder, *Science Encounters the Indian;* Dilworth, *Imagining Indians;* Fiedler, "Indian in Literature"; Green, "Pocahontas Perplex"; Green, "Indian in Popular American Culture"; Horsman, "Scientific Racism"; Jennings, *Invasion of America;* Nash, "Image of the Indian"; Pearce, *Savagism and Civilization;* Pearce, *Savages of America;* Riley, "Some European (Mis)Perceptions"; Sheehan, *Savagism and Civility;* Smith-Rosenberg, "Captured Subjects/Savage Others"; Smits, "The 'Squaw Drudge'"; and Vaughan, "From White Man to Red Skin."

58. Roger Bastide, "Color, Racism and Christianity," in Franklin, ed., *Color and Race,* 36–37.

59. Egan, "BYU Gene Data May Shed Light on Origin of Book of Mormon's Lamanites," *Salt Lake Tribune,* 30 November 2000, B1.

60. Danticat, "Local Color." Other books by Danticat include *Breath, Eyes, Memory, Krik! Krak!* and *Farming of Bones.*

61. Szaba, "Morphing Pot."

62. For discussion about the effects of Barbie, see Edut, ed., *Adios Barbie.* Disney's *Pocahontas* has also caused distress to many Indian women, mainly because the story presented in the movie is not true but also because of the character's perfect face and body, images impossible for young women to emulate. See " 'Pocahontas': One of the Best or Worst Films about American Indians?" *Indian Country*

*Today*, 1 June 1995, C3, 6; and "Pocahontas Rates an F in Indian Country," *Indian Country Today*, 6 July 1995, D1.

63. Roberts, "Native Beauty."

64. Crow Dog and Erdoes, *Lakota Woman*, 9.

65. Silko, *Yellow Woman*, 108.


### 7. Culturalism and Racism at the Cherokee Female Seminary

1. See Mihesuah, *Cultivating the Rosebuds*. The total enrollment is estimated, because ten years of seminary rolls are missing. Although thirty years of rolls are available, my estimate of the enrollment is lower than the apparent totals on the rolls, because many girls attended the seminary for more than one year. For this study, each name was counted only once, for a total of almost three thousand different names.

2. "An Act in Relation to the Male and Female Seminaries, and Establishing Primary Departments Therein for the Education of Indigent Children," 28 November 1873, *Constitutions and Laws of the American Indian Tribes*, 7:267–69.

3. Not all full-bloods were traditional and/or poor, nor were all mixed-bloods progressive and/or wealthy.

4. Thomas Lee Ballenger, "Names of Students of Cherokee Male and Female Seminaries," Tahlequah, Oklahoma, 1876–1904, Thomas Lee Ballanger Collection, Northeastern State University, Archives and Special Collections, John Vaughn Library, Tahlequah, Oklahoma (hereafter NSU).

5. "Ann Florence Wilson's Grade Book" or "Cherokee Female Seminary Records of Grades, 1876–1909," in Northeastern State University's Office of Admissions and Records, Administration Building, Tahlequah, Oklahoma (hereafter "Wilson's Grade Book").

6. Letter dated 10 September 1889, in Cherokee Female Seminary Miscellaneous Box, NSU.

7. I compiled the information on the students' socioeconomic backgrounds using the Index to the Five Civilized Tribes, Final Dawes Roll, M1186, roll 1, and the Enrollment Cards for the Five Civilized Tribes, 1898–1914, rolls 2–15, cards 1–11132, at the National Archives in Fort Worth, Texas.

8. Index to the Five Civilized Tribes; Enrollment Cards for the Five Civilized Tribes; and Starr, *History of the Cherokee Indians*, 489–680.

9. Pearl Mayes Langston, interview with author, 6 June 1989, Fort Gibson, Oklahoma.

10. Albert Sydney Wyly to John D. Benedict, 1908 Cherokee Female Seminary Miscellaneous Box, NSU.

11. For information on Ann Florence Wilson, see Abbott, "Ann Florence Wilson."

12. Fry, comp., *Cherokee Female Seminary Years*, 83.

13. Kate O'Donald Ringland to Abraham Knepler, 21 April 1938, in Knepler, "Digest of the Education of the Cherokee Indians," 323; and Rick Corley, interview with author, 27 December 1988, Arlington, Texas.

14. *Cherokee Advocate*, 23 August 1873, 2.

15. "Wilson's Grade Book."

16. Charlotte Mayes Sanders, interview with author, 20 October 1988, Tahlequah, Oklahoma.

17. "Wilson's Grade Book."

18. *Cherokee Advocate*, 2 May 1884.

19. Sanders interview.

20. *Cherokee Rose Buds*, 2 August 1854, 2.

21. Fry, comp., *Cherokee Female Seminary Years*, 104–5.

22. *Twin Territories*, June 1899.

23. *Wreath of Cherokee Rose Buds*, 14 February 1855, 2, at Anthropological Archives, Smithsonian Institution, Washington DC.

24. *Wreath of Cherokee Rose Buds*, 14 February 1855, 5; 2 August 1854, 6, NSU.

25. *Wreath of Cherokee Rose Buds*, 14 February 1855, 5.

26. *Wreath of Cherokee Rose Buds*, 14 February 1855, 4, 6.

27. Ballenger, "Colored High School."

28. I derived the students' blood quantums from census records; Index to the Five Civilized Tribes; and Enrollment Cards for the Five Civilized Tribes. The Final Dawes Roll has many errors in regard to the Cherokees' blood quantums, so I cross-referenced with other family members. If the student died prior to the opening of the rolls, I found the quantum via either siblings, children, or parents. I located married names on the census records, in newspapers, and in Starr, *History of the Cherokees*. A few of the early students, graduates, and their husbands had died, leaving no progeny and thus no clue as to their degree of Cherokee blood, but only two were reported to be fullbloods. Some of the students during the later years (1903–9) were not enrolled because they were recent arrivals to Indian Territory.

29. *Kansas City Times*, 29 July 1889, 2. Stephens's comment almost echoes Thomas Jefferson's speech to Indians visiting Washington DC in 1808: "You will unite yourselves with us, join in our great councils and form one people with us, and we shall all be Americans; you will mix with us by marriage, your blood will run in our veins, and will spread with us over this great continent." Saul K. Padover, *Thomas Jefferson on Democracy* (New York: Mentor, New American Library,

Appleton-Century, 1939), 106–7, quoted in McLoughlin, *Cherokee Renascence*, 37.

30. *Cherokee Advocate*, 4 February 1851, 2.
31. *Sequoyah Memorial*, 2 August 1855, NSU.
32. *Wreath of Cherokee Rose Buds*, 14 February 1855, 3.
33. *The Journal*, 17 May 1877, 1.
34. Cited in Travis, "Life in the Cherokee Nation," 30.
35. *Cherokee Rose Buds*, 2 August 1854, 3.
36. *Wreath of Cherokee Rose Buds*, 1 August 1855, 1–2.
37. *Wreath of Cherokee Rose Buds*, 1 August 1855, 1–2.
38. *Wreath of Cherokee Rose Buds*, 1 August 1855, 2.
39. *Wreath of Cherokee Rose Buds*, 14 February 1855, 8.
40. Mihesuah, *Cultivating the Rosebuds*, 95–112.
41. *Cherokee Rose Buds*, 2 August 1854, 3.
42. *Wreath of Cherokee Rose Buds*, 1 August 1855, 4.
43. Statement by Professor Rudi Halliburton at the Seventeenth Annual Symposium on the American Indian, 3–8 April 1989, Northeastern State University, Tahlequah, Oklahoma.
44. See Mihesuah, *Cultivating the Rosebuds*, 100–104, for some of the non-seminary graduates and the colleges and universities they enrolled in.
45. "Wilson's Grade Book."
46. See N. B. Johnson, "The Cherokee Orphan Asylum."
47. The students' home districts were compiled from the 1880 Cherokee Census and Index and the 1890 Cherokee Census (no index), National Archives; "Wilson's Grade Book"; "Mary Stapler's Class Book," NSU; Catalog of the C.N.F.S., 2896 and Announcements for 1897 and 1898, 3–6, NSU; Souvenir Catalog: 1850–1905, NSU; "Register and Accounts of Female Seminary Primary and Boarding School Students," bound ledger, NSU.
48. At least one hundred families sent three or more children, including sisters and cousins, to attend the seminary at the same time.
49. The parents' literacy rates were compiled from the 1880 Cherokee Census and Index and the 1890 Cherokee Census (no index), National Archives.
50. Catherine Hastings Maxfield, 1855, and Martha Whiting Fox, 1856. 1880 Cherokee Census and Index, National Archives.
51. *Cherokee Advocate*, 9 September 1893, 2; 16 September 1893, 2; 30 September 1893, 2; 7 October 1893, 2; 14 October 1893, 2; Coppock to Benedict, 11 July 1901, *Report of the Commissioner of Indian Affairs (rcia)*, 57th Cong., 1st sess., H. Doc. 5 (serial 4291), 318–19; Cherokee National Records, Oklahoma Historical Society, Indian

Archives Division, Oklahoma City, Oklahoma (hereafter Oklahoma Historical Society).

52. *Cherokee Advocate*, 31 August 1881, 1.

53. Hewes, *Occupying the Cherokee Country*, 39.

54. Ard Hoyt to Jeremiah Evarts, 14 August 1823, American Board of Commissioners of Foreign Missions, letter 104, ABC, 18.3.1, vol. 3, in McLoughlin, *Cherokee Ghost Dance*, 494.

55. Report of W. Duncan, 25 September 1856, *rcia* for 1853, 34th Cong., 3rd sess., 1857, serial 893, 692.

56. "An Act Relating to Education," *Compiled Laws of the Cherokee Nation* (Tahlequah, Indian Territory: National Advocate Print, 1881), sec. 20, in *Constitutions and Laws of the American Indian Tribes*, 9:236.

57. "Fourth Annual Message of Chief Dennis W. Bushyhead," in Annual Messages of Hon. Chief D. W. Bushyhead, 33, Special Collections, NSU; *Cherokee Advocate*, 17 November 1889, 1; message of Chief Joel B. Mayes to National Council, 17 November 1889, in *Cherokee Letter Book*, 14:4, and J. B. Mayes to T. J. Morgan, 18 October 1890, in *Cherokee Letter Book*, 3:11, Phillips Collection, Western History Collection, University of Oklahoma, Norman.

58. RCIA for 1899, 56th Cong., 2d sess., 1899–1901, H. Doc. 5, serial 3915, 92.

59. *Cherokee Female Seminary Souvenir Catalog: 1850–1906*, NSU.

60. See Mihesuah, *Cultivating the Rosebuds*, 95–112, for information about graduates' professions; 125–31 for the girls' husbands; and appendix F for seminarians who married each other.

61. These assertions are based on findings in the 1880 and 1890 Cherokee Census Records and the Dawes Rolls and Enrollment Cards. Additionally, in almost every interview I conducted during my study of the history of the female seminary, the subjects asserted that they were indeed more Cherokee than they appeared, because "the Dawes Roll is wrong." My comment regarding Americans' affinity toward the Cherokee tribe is based on the startling number of students, colleagues, and acquaintances who have told me that they have a "full-blood Cherokee" mother or grandmother. Few of these individuals can substantiate their claims; they are not enrolled members of the Cherokee Nation because, they assert, their ancestors were "out of town" during the enrollment.

62. The female seminary was open for business for forty academic years.

63. Statistics compiled from the 1880 Cherokee Census and Index and the 1890 Cherokee Census (no index), National Archives.

64. Fry, comp., *Cherokee Female Seminary Years*, 157.

65. Interview with author, Tahlequah, Oklahoma, 18 October 1988.

## 8. Finding a Modern American Indigenous Female Identity

1. Allen, "Who Is Your Mother?" 14.
2. Allen, "Who Is Your Mother?" 14.
3. Griffin, "Relearning to Trust Ourselves," 73; Mankiller and Wallis, *Mankiller*, 256.
4. Cross, *Shades of Black*; Kim, "Processes of Asian American Identity Development"; and Hayes-Bautista, "Becoming Chicano." See also Atkinson, Morten, and Sue, "Minority Development Model."
5. Cross, *Shades of Black*, 189–223; and Parham, "Cycles of Psychological Nigrescence."
6. Kim, "Processes of Asian American Identity Development," ix.
7. See, for example, the works of Erik Erikson.
8. Maria P. P. Root, "Resolving 'Other' Status: Identity Development of Biracial Individuals," in Brown and Root, *Complexity and Diversity*, 188. Moore expounds upon the idea that "race is socially and economically constructed to serve the interests of the privileged" in "Check the Box That Best Describes You."
9. Cross, *Shades of Black*, 190–98.
10. Cross, *Shades of Black*, 198–201. Throughout this chapter I will use the gender-specific, feminine form of singular pronouns ("her," "she") to avoid fracturing the text with repeated use of "his or her," "she or he," or similar structures.
11. Cross, *Shades of Black*, 201–9.
12. Cross, "The Thomas and Cross Models," 18; and Cross, *Shades of Black*, 209–16.
13. In this essay "worldview" refers to a person's value system and how he or she interprets events and history. There is, of course, no one "Indian worldview."
14. See Kerwin and Ponterotto, "Biracial Identity Development."
15. I base the assertion that some who desire to become Indian also progress through stages in part on personal observation of numerous non-Natives posing as Natives in Arizona, Texas, and Oklahoma. Some have grown from showing interest in Indians to becoming "medicine people" of tribes they at one time knew nothing about. One, a white man now deceased, married a Creek woman, shaved his arms ("Indians have no body hair, you know"), and proceeded to hold sweats and ceremonies that he claimed were Lakota. Another, a Hispanic man, followed the same routine. I met his mother at a Grand Prairie powwow, where she admitted that the family was not Native,

yet her son is now a "spiritual leader of the Mescalero Apache tribe" who utilizes Lakota religious traditions. Others pose in academia.

16. Parham, "Cycles of Psychological Nigrescence," 199.

17. There are two major developmental stages of the identity process. The basic one is a simplistic, category-style identity process that generally occurs in preschool. The second stage is more complex because as children develop, their cognitive capacity becomes more developed. Any comprehensive psychological study of indigenous American identity must include discussion of the works of developmental psychologists. See also Bruner, "Primary Group Experience."

18. Quoted in Carroll, "Values and Vision," 66.

19. Parham, "Cycles of Psychological Nigrescence," 195.

20. Donna Kato, "Study: Kids Tuned in to Ethnic Stereotyping," *Arizona Republic*, 8 May 1998, A11.

21. The decision to identify one's self with an ancestor's race or culture when one does not subscribe to that culture is what Howard Stein and Robert Hill term "dime store" ethnicity or "unreal" ethnicity, because one shops for an identity as one would for items at a dime store. See Stein and Hill, *Ethnic Imperative*, 22.

22. For information about relocation, see Burt, "Roots of the Native American Urban Experience"; Fixico, *Termination and Relocation*; and Joe, "Forced Relocation and Assimilation."

23. Quoted in Griffin, "Relearning to Trust Ourselves," 38.

24. Mankiller and Wallis, *Mankiller*, 71.

25. Quoted in Griffin, "Relearning to Trust Ourselves," 38.

26. Manitowabo, "An Ojibwa Girl in the City."

27. Tolan, "Love Doesn't Stop for Race," *Arizona Daily Sun*, 2 June 1996, 1, 8.

28. Russell, Wilson, and Hall, *Color Complex*, 96.

29. Root, "Resolving 'Other' Status," 191–93.

30. Brave Bird with Erdoes, *Ohitika Woman*, 9, 31.

31. Root, "Resolving 'Other' Status," 190–92.

32. For discussion on urban identities, see Steele, "Urban Identity in Kansas."

33. Cross, *Shades of Black*, 119.

34. Mankiller and Wallis, *Mankiller*, 103.

35. Damion Rios, "We Are Family: Cobra Gang as Tough, and Loyal, as They Come," *Arizona Daily Sun*, 12 October 1998, A1, 7.

36. Letter to the editor from Orlando Tom in *Indian Country Today*, 1–8 December 1998, A5. For information on Indian-black relations, see Vernon Bellecourt, "The Glorification of Buffalo Soldiers Raises Racial Divisions between Blacks, Indians," *Indian Country Today*, 4 May 1994, A5; Katz, *Black Indians*; McLoughlin, "Red Indians, Black

Slavery"; Perdue, *Slavery and the Evolution of Cherokee Society*; and "Confounding the Color Line," the *American Indian Quarterly's* special segment on Indian-black relations.

37. Parham, "Cycles of Psychological Nigrescence," 199.

38. See Snipp, "Who Are the American Indians?"

39. Goodman, *Race Awareness*, 19.

40. Isaacs, *Idols of the Tribe*, 76; see also 71–92 for a longer discussion on the importance of names; and Root, "Resolving 'Other' Status," 189–90.

If Isaacs is referring to white society, however, the "dominant group" is not the society with which some individuals identity. Therefore, numerous non-Natives change their names in order to sound "more Indian." Jamake Highwater has been proven to be J. Marks, and "medicine woman" Oh Shinnah Fast Wolf was originally christened Penny McKelvey. The late Sun Bear was actually Vincent LaDuke, a Native and the father of political activist Winona LaDuke. See *Lakota Times*, 7 August 1991, A1, 2. Non-Natives with no tribal connections who re-christen themselves are, as Gerald Vizenor writes, "mere simulations with no active memories or stories." Vizenor, "Native American Indian Identities," 119.

41. Root, "Resolving 'Other' Status," 189.

42. McRoy and Freeman, "Racial Identity Issues."

43. Cross, *Shades of Black*, 199.

44. Green, *Issues in Native American Cultural Identity*, 7.

45. Carter, "Wantabes and Outalucks"; and Andrade, "Are Tribes Too Exclusive?"

46. See Gans, "Symbolic Ethnicity"; and Smith, "For All Those Who Were Indian."

47. Brave Bird with Erdoes, *Ohitika Woman*, 19, 23.

48. Buffy Ste. Marie, "Victims No More," *Akwesasne Notes* (early winter 1976): 29.

49. Bonney, " Role of AIM Leaders"; Bellecourt interview; Means interview; Matthiessen, *Spirit of Crazy Horse*; Means, *Where White Men Fear to Tread*; Stumbo, "A World Apart"; and Vizenor, "Dennis of Wounded Knee."

50. Quoted in Leibold, *Surviving in Two Worlds*, 4.

51. Mankiller and Wallis, *Mankiller*, 163.

52. *Arizona Daily Sun*, 2 June 1995, 1, 8.

53. Fanon, *Black Skin, White Masks*, 63.

54. McPherson, "From Dezba to 'John.'"

55. Root, "Resolving 'Other' Status," 197–201.

56. Root, "Resolving 'Other' Status," 199–200.

57. Rose, "*Iyeska Win*," 100.

58. Berry, *Almost White*, 160.

59. Root, "Resolving 'Other' Status," 200.

60. McFee, "The 150 Percent Man."

61. Quoted in Crozier-Hogle and Wilson, comps., *Surviving in Two Worlds*, 20–29.

62. Ester Belin, "In the Cycle of the Whirl," in Ortiz, ed., *Speaking for the Generations*, 56.

63. Root, "Resolving 'Other' Status," 196.

64. Williams, "Theatre of Identity." Gerald Vizenor gracefully discusses some questionable connections to Indianness in the chapter "Wistful Envies" in his *Fugitive Poses*, 61–118.

65. Quoted in Abbott, ed., *I Stand in the Center of the Good*, 52.

66. Elkin, "Family, Socialization," 147.

67. "New Sensitive Census"; "Census Changes to Recognize Mixed Races," *Arizona Republic*, 30 October 1997, A1, 11; Yamamoto, "Interracial Marriage in Hawaii." Among the best works on the Métis are Cox, ed., *Native People, Native Lands*; Dickason, *Canada's First Nations*; Peterson and Brown, *New Peoples*; and Royal Commission on Aboriginal Peoples, *Looking Forward, Looking Back*.

68. Itabari Njeri, "Call for Census Category Creates Interracial Debate," *Los Angeles Times*, 13 January 1991, E1, 9–11; and Leland and Beals, "In Living Colors."

69. Root, "Resolving 'Other' Status," 200–201.

70. Bataille and Silet, *Pretend Indians*; Hill, Solomon, Tiger, and Fortenberry, "Complexities of Ethnicity"; Hirschfelder, *American Indian Stereotypes*; Marsden and Nachbar, "Indian in the Movies"; Mihesuah, *American Indians*; and Stedman, *Shadows of the Indians*.

71. Spickard, *Mixed Blood*; and Berzon, *Neither White nor Black*.

72. Quoted in Berta Delgado, "Native Voices: American Indian Students Help Others Learn of Culture," *Dallas Morning News*, 26 November 1996, A24, 25.

73. Quoted in Croonenberghs, "Metis Women."

74. See " 'Pocahontas': One of the Best or Worst Films about American Indians?" *Indian Country Today*, 1 June 1995, C3, 6; and "Pocahontas Rates an F in Indian Country," *Indian Country Today*, 6 July 1995, D1.

75. Green, " Pocahontas Perplex."

76. Quoted in Griffin, "Relearning to Trust Ourselves," 39.

77. Hagan, "Full Blood, Mixed Blood."

78. Gaynor, *I Will Survive*.

79. Hanson and Rouse, "Dimensions of Native American Stereotyping."

80. Hanson and Rouse, "American Indian Stereotyping."

81. Code of Federal Regulations (CFR), Title 25, Part 83, "Procedures for Establishing That an American Indian Group Exists as an Indian Tribe." See also McCullough and Wilkins, "'Constructing' Nations."

82. "Act to Promote Development of Indian Arts and Crafts," Public Law (PL) 101–644, 104 Stat. 4662.

83. "A Saint of South Texas: Retired Peyote Dealer Remains a Symbol of Hope for a Misunderstood Faith," *Dallas Morning News*, 15 March 1997, 1, 3G; and "Congress Considers Native American Church Pleas on Peyote Use," *Dallas Morning News*, 20 June 1994, 1, 8A.

84. Root, "Resolving 'Other' Status," 203.

85. *Indian and Pioneer Histories*, 9:373 (microfilm), Oklahoma Historical Society, Oklahoma City, Oklahoma.

86. Crow Dog with Erdoes, *Lakota Woman*, 176, 184–85.

87. Brenda Norrell, "Native American Women, Singular Voices," *Indian Country Today*, 30 March–16 April 1998, C1.

88. See, for example, Anderson, "Waldron-Black Tomahawk Controversy."

89. Franklin, ed., *Color and Race*, ix.

90. Bradshaw, "Beauty and the Beast"; Danticat, "Local Color"; Itabari Njeri, "Colorism: In American Society Are Lighter-Skinned Blacks Better Off?" *Los Angeles Times*, 24 April 1988, FI, 10, 12–13; Stone, "Appearance and the Self"; and Szaba, "Morphing Pot."

91. Okazawa-Rey, Robinson, and Ward, "Black Women."

92. Interview #84.028, 8 March 1984, Mrs. Allie Mae Statham, Living Legends Collection, Oklahoma Historical Society, Indian Archives Division, Oklahoma City.

93. Quoted in Bruchac, ed., *Survival This Way*, 122–23; see also Miller, "The Story Is Brimming Around," 9.

94. See Benson, Hampsten, and Sweney, eds., *Day In, Day Out*, 23–27.

95. Quoted in Crozier-Hogle and Wilson, comps., *Surviving in Two Worlds*, 4.

96. Cross, *Shades of Black*, 202.

97. Frazier, *Black Bourgeoisie*.

98. Russell, Wilson, and Hall, *Color Complex*, 56–57.

99. Parham, "Cycles of Psychological Nigrescence," 201 (emphasis mine).

100. Quoted in Bruchac, ed., *Survival This Way*, 79.

101. Brave Bird with Erdoes, *Ohikita Woman*, 10.

102. Stonequist, *Marginal Man*. See also Green, "A Re-examination"; Goldberg, "A Qualification"; and Wright and Wright, "A Plea."

103. Allen, "A Stranger in My Own Life."

104. Root, "Resolving 'Other' Status," 193.

105. Root, "Resolving 'Other' Status," 201–2; and Root, "A Bill of Rights for Racially Mixed People," in *The Multiracial Experience,* 3–14.

106. The debate over criteria for tribal enrollment and for identifying as a Native is intensifying. In regard to extending tribal membership to individuals who are culturally ignorant, Jerry Bread, director of the American Indian Teacher Corps at the University of Oklahoma, commented that "It's a dilution of our identity. Many people who are culturally non-Indian will be classified as a member of that tribe, and they'll bring with them values that are not the same values that formulated the spirit of the tribe." "Oklahomans Rush to Join Tribal Rolls," *Dallas Morning News,* 12 June 1995, 7A. See also John Leville, review of *Indians Are Us? Culture and Genocide in Native North America,* by Ward Churchill, *American Indian Quarterly* 20 (winter 1996): 109–18, which addresses Churchill's notable essay "Nobody's Pet Poodle: Jimmie Durham, an Artist for Native North America"; Clifton, ed., *Being and Becoming Indian;* Clifton, *Invented Indian;* Tim Giago, "It's Time to Establish Guidelines for Tribal Enrollment Criteria," *Indian Country Today,* 10–17 March 1997, A4; Quinn, "Southeast Syndrome"; Starna, "Southeast Syndrome"; and Jaimes, "Federal Indian Identification Policy: An Usurpation of Indigenous Sovereignty in North America," in Jaimes, ed., *State of Native America,* 123–38.

107. Quoted in Bruchac, ed., *Survival This Way,* 34.

### 9. 1970s Activist Anna Mae Pictou-Aquash

1. This essay should be considered merely a brief overview of an extremely complicated topic. Information was gathered from numerous sources, only some of which are listed here. It is difficult, however, to ascertain with certainty the origin of some statements and events because often the only sources available are journalistic and do not provide references. I primarily have cited only those statements that appear to be unique to this essay. For information on Anna Mae specifically, see Brand, *Life and Death;* Weir and Bergman, "The Killing of Anna Mae Aquash," 51–55; and Witt, "The Brave Hearted Woman."

Several Web sites are devoted to Aquash's life and the intrigue surrounding her death. See *www.dickshovel.com/annalay.html* and *www.dickshovel.com/annaarch.html* as well as the numerous interconnected pages that feature original material and reprinted excerpts from previously published material on Anna Mae. The most comprehensive and the tribally endorsed volume on Mi'kmaqs is Prins, *The Mi'kmaq*.

2. Numerous books chronicle the activities of AIM and the events leading up to and following the occupation of Wounded Knee. Among the most notable: Matthiessen, *In the Spirit of Crazy Horse*; Warrior and Smith, *Like a Hurricane*; Wyler, *Blood of the Land*. Most of these works, however, focus on AIM men and do not discuss women's roles within the movement to any notable extent.

Anderson, Brown, Lerner, and Shafer, *Voices from Wounded Knee*; Brave Bird with Erdoes, *Ohitika Woman*; and Crow Dog and Erdoes, *Lakota Woman*, provide female voices. Care must be taken in reading the Crow Dog and Brave Bird books, as many scholars and activists have argued that both were heavily edited by the white male coauthor, Erdoes.

See also Stumbo, "A World Apart"; Vizenor, "Dennis of Wounded Knee"; Means interview; and Bellecourt interview.

3. Deloria, *Behind the Trail of Broken Treaties*.

4. Mihesuah, "American Indian Identities"; Nagel, *American Indian Ethnic Renewal*; and Bonney, "Role of AIM Leaders."

5. For opposing viewpoints on Wilson's tenure as chairman, see *Indian Country Today*'s issue "Looking Back at Wounded Knee," 25 February 1993.

6. Quoted in Brand, *Life and Death*, 117.

7. Personal correspondence, from entry in diary dated 29 January 1986.

8. Sayer, *Ghost Dancing the Law*.

9. Trudell quoted in *Incident at Oglala*; Yellow Hair quoted in *In the Spirit of Crazy Horse* (video).

10. "Anatomy of an Informer," parts 1 and 2, *Akwesasne Notes* 7:2 (early summer 1975): 14–16, 7:5 (early winter 1975): 10–13.

11. Banks, " *Black Scholar* Interviews."

12. To illustrate the intrigue surrounding some aspects of this case, a Web site offering a reprint of the "Anna Mae Aquash Time Line" compiled by *News from Indian Country*, 18 March 1998, states that the "Pie Patrol" comprised women active in AIM: Madonna Gilbert, Thelma Rios-Conroy, and Lorelei Decora Means. In *Lakota Woman*, Mary Crow Dog describes the patrol as "loud-mouth city women, very media conscious, hugging the limelight" (138); yet, curiously, in her second book, *Ohikita Woman*, she describes these same women as those she felt "particularly close to" at "the Knee" (194, 200–201 ).

13. See *http://www.dickshovel.com/bra2.html*.

14. Matthiessen, *In the Spirit of Crazy Horse*, 147.

15. Brand, *Life and Death*, 133, 136; and Weir and Bergman, "Killing of Anna Mae Aquash," 54.

16. See *Incident at Oglala* for a chronicle of events. See also Peltier and Arden, *Prison Writings*.

17. Letter from Shirley Hill Witt, regional director, and William F. Muldrow, equal opportunity specialist, U.S. Commission on Civil Rights, to John A. Buggs, 31 March 1976.

18. Quoted in Antell, "American Indian Women Activists," 158. Consider also the statement by Mililani B. Trask (the elected prime minister [kia-aina] of the Sovereign Native Nation of Ka Lahui Hawai'i) that "And many times when you are fighting for human rights, when you are fighting against historic injustices, there are not a lot of people with the integrity, the willingness, or the fortitude to stand with you. When you have a strong religious and spiritual foundation, you will find, in those times of despair, that you are not walking alone." "Decolonizing Hearts and Minds," 33.

19. Quoted in *Brave Hearted Woman*.

20. Matthiessen, *In the Spirit of Crazy Horse*, 270.

21. Quoted in Weir and Bergman, "Killing of Anna Mae Aquash," 54.

22. See *http://www.dickshovel.com/bra2.html*.

23. *Indian Country Today*, 29 March–5 April 1999, A4; "Justice at Last for Anna Mae?" *Toronto Sun*, 13 June 1999, C6.

24. Jamie Monastyrski, "Aquash Family Accuses AIM of Her Murder," *Indian Country Today*, 4–11 October 1999; personal communication with Shannon M. Collins, 3 November 1999. The news conference was also reported by the Associated Press and at *http://members.aol.com/Apictou/pictou-branscombe.html*. Subsequent information about the murder is contained in the "Richard Two Elk Interview," 16 June 2000, in *News from Indian Country*, Aquash Special Edition II, 2000.

25. Quoted in *Brave Hearted Woman*.

26. The ANNA Foundation, Inc.'s Web address is *http://members.aol.com/ANNAinc/Foundation.html*.

27. Quoted in Weir and Bergman, "Killing of Anna Mae Aquash," 53.

## 10. Interview with Denise and Deborah Maloney-Pictou

1. For information about Leonard Peltier, see Peltier and Arden, *Prison Writings*; *Incident at Oglala*; *In the Spirit of Crazy Horse* (video); and Matthiessen, *In the Spirit of Crazy Horse*.

2. Robert A. Pictou-Branscombe is a member of the Mi'kmaq Nation and is second cousin to Anna Mae Pictou-Aquash. He is cofounder of the ANNA (Assembly for Northern Native Americans) Foundation. He served as staff sergeant in the Marine Corps, did five tours in Vietnam, and was awarded the Silver Star, two Purple Hearts, and twenty-one other decorations. The most complete documentation of the Denver press conference in which Robert A. Pictou-Branscombe and Russell Means named Anna Mae's killers is in *News from Indian Country*, "Aquash Special Edition 1999" (see also *www.Indiancountrynews.com*).

3. See, for example, *Indian Country Today*, 4–11 October 1999; 24 November 1999; 5 January 2000; 12 January 2000 (Denise and Deborah are misidentified in the cover photo; Denise is on the left); and *News from Indian Country*, "Aquash Special Edition 1999" (see also *www.Indiancountrynews.com*).

4. Shannon M. Collins is co-founder and executive director of the ANNA Foundation and manages the ANNA Foundation headquarters in Rimrock, Arizona. Formerly, she was the executive director of the Leonard Peltier Charitable Foundation, conducted personal research analysis of issues of impoverishment on Native reservations, performed volunteer work for charitable organizations, and for thirty years was a professional singer, writer, public relations consultant, model, and press agent.

5. In September 1999 Robert A. Pictou-Branscombe held a press conference in Ottawa (in front of Parliament) and announced who he believed murdered Anna Mae. One source of information about the conference is *Indian Country Today*, 4–11 October 1999 (Denise and Deborah are again misidentified).

6. *Brave Hearted Woman*.


## 11. Activism and Expression as Empowerment

1. Melanie McCoy briefly discusses the relationship between gender and politics in "Gender or Ethnicity." A lack of data hindered her study, however: only nineteen female tribal leaders out of fifty-three (or 36 percent) responded to McCoy's questionnaire. Nevertheless, McCoy has brought to light interesting issues about Indian women leaders, and her work calls for a larger study.

2. McCoy, "Gender or Ethnicity."

3. Trask, "Decolonizing Hearts and Minds," 35.

4. McCoy, "Gender or Ethnicity."

5. See Hauptman, "Alice Jemison."

6. See Hauptman, "Designing Woman."

7. Roberta Avery, "One of the First Indian Land Claim Advocates," *News from Indian Country,* mid-January 2001, 8B.

8. For information on Wilma Mankiller, see Mankiller and Wallis, *Mankiller;* and Bataille, *American Indian Women: Telling Their Lives,* 161–62.

9. For information on LaDonna Harris, see Stockel, ed., *LaDonna Harris;* and Bataille, *American Indian Women: Telling Their Lives,* 107–8.

10. For information on Ada Deer, see Fanlund, "Indians in Wisconsin"; Peroff, *Menominee Drums;* Deer, "How the Good Guys Won"; and Bataille, *American Indian Women: Telling Their Lives,* 76–78.

11. Damian Aros, "Tribal Women Can Be Leaders, Too," *Arizona Daily Sun,* 14 November 1997, A1, 11.

12. Bataille, *American Indian Women: Telling Their Lives,* 274–75; and Witt, "An Interview with Dr. Annie Dodge Wauneka."

13. For information on Winona LaDuke, see *http://voices.cla.umn.edu/authors/WinonaLaDuke.html;* and *http://www.adot.com/WinonaLaDuke.html.* See also LaDuke's works listed in the bibliography. Vincent LaDuke/Sun Bear's home page is at *http://www.liteweb.org/wildfire/.*

14. For information on White Earth see Meyer, *The White Earth Tragedy.*

15. In a statement issued in 1995, "The Indigenous Women's Network: Our Future, Our Responsibility," LaDuke outlined the beliefs of the group:

(1) women should not have to trade their ecosystem for running water, basic housing, health care, and basic human rights; (2) development projects . . . often replicate patriarchy and sexism, and by and large cause the destruction of matrilineal governance structure, land tenure, and cause a decline in the status of women. . . . Indigenous women are frequently moved from a central role in their societies to the margins and refugee status of industrial society; (3) the intellectual knowledge systems today often negate, or deny the existence, of inherent property rights of indigenous people to our cultural and intellectual knowledge, calling us "primitive." . . . This situation affects Indigenous women, as a part of our communities, but in a larger scale, has affected most women; (4) Subsequently, our women find that the basic rights to control our bodies are impacted by all of the above, through developmental policies aimed at non-consensual or forced sterilization, medical testing, invasive genetic sampling, and absence of basic facilities and services.

See *http://www.igc.apc.org/beijing/plenary/laduke.html* and *http://www.womenspress.com/newspaper/2000/15-24indigenous.html.*

16. Trosper, "Traditional American Indian Economic Policy."

17. For information on Grace Thorpe, see Bataille, *American Indian Women: Telling Their Lives*, 259–60. On Alcatraz, see Fortunate Eagle, *Alcatraz! Alcatraz!*; Johnson, Champagne, and Nagel, "American Indian Activism and Transformation"; and *American Indian Culture and Research Journal*'s special issue "Alcatraz Revisited."

18. "Small Wonder in Montana" and "Conceived in Sin?" at *http://www.indians.org/library/nate.html*.

19. Witt, "Women Fighting the Tide." See also Bataille, *American Indian Women: Telling Their Lives*, 167–68.

20. Isaacs, *Idols of the Tribe*, 94–95.

21. Quoted in "Tribes Seek to Preserve Languages," *Arizona Republic*, 15 June 1998, B3.

22. Quoted in Leibold, *Surviving in Two Worlds*, 105.

23. "Tribes Seek to Preserve Languages."

24. "Native Tongue: Oklahoma School Trying to Revive Cherokee, Creek through Classes," *Dallas Morning News*, 26 January 1997, 37, 43A.

25. *Arizona Daily Sun*, 10 November 1998, A1–11.

26. "Teaching Their Heritage," *Dallas Morning News*, 10 May 1998, 39, 41A; Brenda Norrell, "Language—The Root of Being," *Indian Country Today*, 9–16 March 1997, B7.

27. Norrell, "Language."

28. Buffy Ste. Marie, "Victims No More," *Akwesasne Notes* (early winter 1976): 29.

29. Feder, *American Indian Art*.

30. For discussion about how art empowers children, see Ina L. Silverman, "Coping with Stress through Art: A Program for Urban Minority Children," in Harris, Blue, and Griffith, *Racial and Ethnic Identity*, 115–35.

Two examples point to the reality that minority writers are pigeonholed:

Chickasaw writer Linda Hogan states in regard to the difficulties in teaching Indian literature that the non-Indians in the class are "so unreasonable, they're so needy in what they want from an Indian person. . . . And I don't want to be in that role." See Miller, "Story Is Brimming Around," 7.

A former NAU colleague, Puerto Rican Victor Villanueva, writes about himself in *Bootstraps*: "A manuscript in the mail. 'Would you please review this bibliography of Mexican-American literature?' He enjoys the literature well enough, Galarza and Anaya and others. But he knows more of Chaucer and Milton and Yeats than of Puerto Rican writers like Piri Thomas or Tato Laviera or Nicolasa Mohr. He knows Mexicans less. He has been stereotyped again: Hispanic, a monolith." (xiii).

31. Underhill *Navajos*, 186. See also Dedera, *Navajo Rugs*; Amaden, *Navajo Weaving*; and Hatcher, *Visual Metaphors*.

32. Quoted in "Surviving as a Native Woman Artist," in McKague, *Racism in Canada*, 7–10.

33. Quoted in Abbott, ed., *I Stand in the Center of the Good*, 13, 24.

34. Quoted in Knapp, "Circle of Unity," 53.

35. Debra Moon, "Hopi Recruit Local Artisans to Tie Language, Culture and Community Together," *News from Indian Country*, mid-January 2001, 9B; Hopi Pu'tavi Project, Inc., P.O. Box 466, Second Mesa AZ 86043; Sydney, "Hopi Women." Sydney is briefly profiled in Stan Bindell, "Hopi Student Returns to Teach," *News from Indian Country*, late February 2001, 8B.

36. See Green, *Native American Women*, 165–66.

37. Greer, "Three Native Women," 27.

38. Greer, "Three Native Women," 27.

39. Bataille, "An Interview with Geraldine Keams."

40. *www.naturallynative.com/prodtn/anout.html*; and Daune Stinson, "Moving and Shaking with Valerie Red-Horse," *News from Indian Country*, mid-January 2001, 10B.

41. Dawn Thomas, "Weaving a Web of Communication," *News from Indian Country*, late May 2000, 11B.

42. Heth, ed., *Native American Dance*; and Eschbach and Applbaum, "Who Goes to Powwows?"

43. Hank Simpson, "Nuvatukyaovi Hopi Youth Dancers: Water Maidens, Warriors, and Self-Worth," *Flagstaff Live!* 4–10 June 1998, 13–14.

44. Kracht, "Kiowa Powwows," 322.

45. Theisz, "Song Texts," 119.

46. Roberts, *Powwow Country*, 22.

47. *Indian Country Today* supplement, "Hitting the Pow Wow Circuit," 24 March 1997, 23, 45.

48. Mattern, "Powwow as a Public Arena," 183–201; Frank Clarke, "Modern Medicine Learns from Traditional Indian Ways," *Lakota Times*, 23 January 1998, 10.

49. Quoted in Roberts, *Powwow Country*, 25.

50. Parfit, "Powwow," 94.

51. Lassiter, *Power of Kiowa Song*, 245 n.8.

52. Mattern, "Powwow as a Public Arena," 192.

53. Mattern, "Powwow as a Public Arena," 127.

54. Mattern, "Powwow as a Public Arena," 86, 241 n.4.
55. Means, *Where White Men Fear to Tread*, 69.
56. Quoted in Roberts, *Powwow Country*, 34.
57. Quoted in Roberts, *Powwow Country*, 120.
58. Quoted in Roberts, *Powwow Country*, 36.

## 12. Feminists, Tribalists, or Activists?

1. Mohanty, Russo, and Torres, introduction to *Third World Women*, 7.
2. Neither do many black women. bell hooks discusses black women's opposition to white feminist ideologies in "Black Students Who Reject Feminism," *Chronicle of Higher Education*, 13 July 1994, A44.
3. Susan M. Williams and Joy Harjo, "American Indian Feminism," in Mankiller, Mink, Navarro, Smith, and Steinem, *Reader's Companion*, 198.
4. Wilma Mankiller, Marysa Navarro, and Gloria Steinem, "Feminism," in Mankiller, Mink, Navarro, Smith, and Steinem, *Reader's Companion*, 187.
5. Quoted in Medicine, *Native American Woman*, 93. This idea is also explored in Lam, "Feeling Foreign in Feminism"; and Lugones and Spelman, "Have We Got a Theory for You!"
6. Medicine, *Native American Woman*, 93.
7. Jaimes and Halsey, "American Indian Women," 331–32. Although Jaimes and Halsey are attempting to make a point, this is not the only incorrect piece of information in the essay, which leaves many of their other conclusions in doubt. For example, on page 323 the authors write, "The capstone of this drive to utilize law as 'the perfect instrument of empire' came during the 1950s when the government set out to drive native people from the land altogether."
The phrase they put in quotes—"the perfect instrument of empire"—is taken from Rafael's *Contracting Colonization* (23), in which Vicente quotes the Spanish humanist Antonio de Nebrija, through the bishop of Avila: "Your majesty, language is the perfect instrument of empire." This was in regard to the Spanish empire's attempt to make Castilian the dominant language of Spain in the late fifteenth century. Law and language, as they are used in these two works, are not the same thing.
8. For information on Witt, see Bataille, *Native American Women*, 282–83. Further, women who Jaimes and Halsey claim are more traditional have, in numerous cases, proven to be less than supportive of their activist sisters. For example, several anonymous sources close to the Anna Mae Pictou-Aquash murder investigation allege that nu-

merous AIM women had knowledge of the circumstances surrounding Anna Mae's death at the time it occurred.

9. "On Women's Rights for Native Peoples," *Akwesasne Notes* 7:4 (early autumn 1975): 39. See also Mililani B. Trask's comment about feminism in the 1960s: "I read all the appropriate materials, but for some reason it did not strike a chord in me as an indigenous woman. I found that much of the analysis of sexism was applicable to me, but I did not find any decent analysis of racism, ethnicity, and cultural difference. In these very significant areas, the white feminist literature fell far short of what I was looking for" ("Decolonizing Hearts and Minds," 36).

10. Crow Dog and Erdoes, *Lakota Woman*, 65–66, 69, 78, 138.

11. Means, *Where White Men Fear to Tread*, 265.

12. Indeed, he said during his 1974 trial that one way to express manhood was through activism. See Sayer, *Ghost Dancing the Law*, 91.

13. Matthiessen, *In the Spirit of Crazy Horse*, 125.

14. Means, *Where White Men Fear to Tread*, 265.

15. Quoted in Antell, "American Indian Woman Activists," 170–71.

16. Paul Demain, *News from Indian Country*, 14 July 2000; see also *http://www.press-on.net/Commentaries/071400_Aim_steps_down. html*.

17. Anonymous communication with the author, 2000.

18. Kay Humphrey, "Tillie Black Bear, Rosebud Activist, Honored by President Clinton," *Indian Country Today*, 20 December 2000, D1.

19. Jaimes, Review of *Lakota Woman* (emphasis mine).

20. Crow Dog and Erdoes, *Lakota Woman*, 131, 138.

21. Quoted from Englander, "Through Their Words." Thanks to Melissa Dyea for bringing this to my attention.

22. Quoted in Crozier-Hogle and Wilson, comps., *Surviving in Two Worlds*, 217.

23. Trask, "Decolonizing Hearts and Minds," 35.

24. Knapp, "Circle of Unity."

25. Quoted in Leibold, *Surviving in Two Worlds*, 140.

26. "On Women's Rights," 39. See also Aída Hurtado, "An Introduction to Power: The Restructuring of Gender in the Political Movements of the 60s," in Hurtado, *Color of Privilege*, 91–122.

27. Madonna Gilbert, quoted in Braudy, "We Will Remember," 94.

28. WARN is also discussed by Seneca social worker Agnes Williams in Knapp, "Circle of Unity," 32–35. See also Powers, *Oglala Women*, 126, 150; Winona LaDuke, "Words from Indigenous Women's Net-

work Meeting," *Akwesasne Notes* 17:6 (early winter 1985): 8–9; and "Women of All Red Nations (WARN)" *Akwesasne Notes* 10:5 (winter 1978): 15.

29. Quoted in Mary Tolan, "Oppressed as Oppressor?" *Arizona Daily Sun*, 13 October 1998, 6.

30. Trask, "Decolonizing Hearts and Minds," 34.

31. Karen L. Testerman, "High Domestic Violence Rates Shows Need for Shelter," *Indian Country Today*, 15–22 September 1997, B7.

32. Sanday, *Female Power and Male Dominance*, 19.

33. Quoted in Testerman, "High Domestic Violence Rates."

# Bibliography

**Manuscript Materials**

National Archives, Fort Worth, Texas.
    MI186. Roll 1. Index to the Five Civilized Tribes. Final Dawes Roll.
    MI186. Enrollment Cards for the Five Civilized Tribes, 1898–1914,
    Rolls 2–15, Cherokees by Blood, cards 1–11132.
    7RA07-1. Cherokee Census of 1880, schedules 1–6, rolls 1–4.
    7RA08-1. Cherokee Census of 1890, schedules 1–4, rolls 1–4.
Northeastern State University, Archives and Special Collections,
    John Vaughn Library, Tahlequah, Oklahoma.
    Annual Messages of Hon. Chief D. W. Bushyhead.
    Catalog of the C.N.F.S. and Announcements for 1897 and 1898
    Cherokee Female Seminary Miscellaneous Box.
    Mary Stapler's Class Book.
    Register and Accounts of Female Seminary Primary and Boarding
    School Students.
    Souvenir Catalogs.
    Thomas Lee Ballenger Collection.
Northeastern State University, Office of Admissions and Records,
    Administration Building, Tahlequah, Oklahoma. "Ann Florence
    Wilson's Grade Book."
Oklahoma Historical Society, Indian Archives Division, Oklahoma
    City, Oklahoma.
    Cherokee National Records. CHN 97. "Cherokee Schools: Female
    Seminary," Documents 2735–77, 11 May 1887–December 1902.
    Indian and Pioneer Histories.
    Living Legends Collection.
University of Oklahoma, Norman, Western History Collection.
    Cherokee Letter Book.

**Published Materials**

Abbott (Mihesuah), Devon A. "Ann Florence Wilson, Matriarch of the Cherokee Female Seminary." *Chronicles of Oklahoma* 67 (winter 1989–90): 426–37.

Abbott, Lawrence, ed. *I Stand in the Center of the Good: Interviews with Contemporary Native American Artists.* Lincoln: University of Nebraska Press, 1994.

Abu-Lughod, Lila. "Can There Be a Feminist Ethnography?" *Women and Performance: A Journal of Feminist Theory* 5:1 (1990): 7–27.

Ackerman, Lillian A. "The Effect of Missionary Ideals on Family Structure and Women's Roles in Plateau Indian Culture." *Idaho Yesterdays* (spring/summer 1987): 64–73.

Adams, David Wallace. *Education for Extinction: American Indians and the Boarding School Experience, 1875–1928.* Lawrence: University Press of Kansas, 1995.

"Alcatraz Revisited: The Twenty-fifty Anniversary of the Occupation, 1969–1971." Special issue of *American Indian Culture and Research Journal* 18:4 (1994).

Allen, Paula Gunn. *The Sacred Hoop: Recovering the Feminine in American Indian Traditions.* Boston: Beacon Press, 1986.

——. "A Stranger in My Own Life: Alienation in Contemporary American Indian Prose and Poetry." *melus* 7:3 (fall 1980): 4.

——. "Who Is Your Mother? Red Roots of White Feminism." In *The Graywolf Annual Five: Multicultural Literacy,* ed. Rick Simonson and Scott Walker, 13–27. St. Paul MN: Graywolf Press, 1988.

Amaden, Charles A. *Navajo Weaving.* Salt Lake City UT: Peregrine Smith, 1975.

"American Indian Prophets: Religious Leaders and Revitalization Movements." Special issue of *American Indian Quarterly* 9:3 (summer 1985).

Anderson, Harry H. "The Waldron-Black Tomahawk Controversy and the Status of Mixed Bloods among the Teton Sioux." *South Dakota History* 21:1 (spring 1991): 69–83.

Anderson, Karen. *Chain Her by One Foot: The Subjugation of Women in Seventeenth-Century New France.* New York: Routledge, 1991.

Anderson, Robert. "The Northern Cheyenne War Mothers." *Anthropological Quarterly* 29:3 (1956): 82–90.

Anderson, Robert, Joanna Brown, Jonny Lerner, and Barbara Lou Shafer. *Voices from Wounded Knee, 1973: In the Words of the Participants.* New York: Akwesasne Notes, 1974.

Andrade, Ron. "Are Tribes Too Exclusive?" *American Indian Journal* (July 1980): 12–13.

Antell, Judith Anne. "American Indian Women Activists." Ph.D. diss., University of California, Berkeley, 1990.

Anzaldúa, Gloria. *Borderlands/La Frontera: The New Mestiza.* San Francisco: Aunt Lute, 1987.

Anzaldúa, Gloria, ed. *Making Face, Making Soul/Hacienda caras: Creative and Critical Perspectives by Women of Color.* San Francisco: Aunt Lute Books, 1990.

Atkinson, Donald R., George Morten, and Derald Wing Sue. "Minority Development Model." In *Counseling American Minorities: A Cross-Cultural Perspective,* 191–200. Dubuque IA: Wm. C. Brown, 1989.

Axtell, James. *The Invasion Within: The Contest of Cultures in Colonial North America.* New York: Oxford University Press, 1985.

———. *Natives and Newcomers: The Cultural Origins of Native America.* New York: Oxford University Press, 2001.

———. *The Pleasures of Academe: A Celebration and Defense of Higher Education.* Lincoln: University of Nebraska Press, 1999.

Bachman, Ronet. *Death and Violence on the Reservation: Homicide, Family Violence, and Suicide in American Indian Populations.* New York: Auburn House, 1992.

Baldwin, Joseph A. "Theory and Research Concerning the Notion of Black Self-Hatred: A Review and Reinterpretation." *The Journal of Black Psychology* 5:2 (February 1979): 51–77.

Ballenger, Thomas L. "The Colored High School of the Cherokee Nation." *Chronicles of Oklahoma* 30 (winter 1952–53): 454–62.

Bandura, A., and A. Huston. "Identification as a Process of Incidental Learning." *Aboriginal Social Psychology* 63 (1961): 311–18.

Banks, Dennis. "The *Black Scholar* Interviews: Dennis Banks." *Black Scholar* (June 1976): 28–36.

Basso, Keith H. *The Gift of Changing Woman.* Anthropological Papers no. 76, Smithsonian Institution, Bureau of American Ethnology Bulletin no. 196. Washington DC, 1966. 113–73.

Bataille, Gretchen. "An Interview with Geraldine Keams." *Explorations in Ethnic Studies* 10:1 (January 1987): 1–8.

———. *Native American Women: A Biographical Dictionary.* New York: Garland Publishing, 1993.

Bataille, Gretchen, and Kathleen M. Sands, eds., *American Indian Women: A Guide to Research* New York: Garland Publishing, 1991.

———. *American Indian Women: Telling Their Lives.* Lincoln: University of Nebraska Press, 1984.

Bataille, Gretchen, and Charles P. Silet. *The Pretend Indians: Images of Native Americans in the Movies.* Ames: Iowa State University Press, 1980.

Bayefsky, Anne F. "The Human Rights Committee and the Case of Sandra Lovelace." *Canadian Yearbook of International Law* 20 (1982): 244–66.

Behar, Ruth. "Introduction: Women Writing culture: Another Telling of the Story of American Anthropology." *Critique of Anthropology* 13:4 (1993): 307–25.

Bellecourt, Vernon. Interview, "He Is the Symbol of the Most Militant Indian Group Since Geronimo." *Penthouse*, July 1973, 58–60, 62–64, 122–32.

Bennett, Lerone, Jr. *Forced Into Glory: Abraham Lincoln's White Dream.* Chicago: Johnson Publishing, 2000.

Benson, Bjorn, Elizabeth Hampsten, and Kathryn Sweney, eds. *Day In, Day Out: Women's Lives in North Dakota.* Grand Forks: University of North Dakota Press, 1988.

Berkhofer, Robert F., Jr. "White Conceptions of Indians." In *Handbook of North American Indians*, 4:522–47. Washington DC: Smithsonian Institution, 1988.

———. *The White Man's Indian.* New York: Vintage, 1978.

Berry, Brewton. *Almost White.* Toronto: Collier-Macmillan, 1963.

Berry, David S. "Contextualising International Women's Rights: Canadian Feminism, Race and Culture." In *Legal Feminisms: Theory and Practice*, 119–34. Aldershot, U.K.: Dartmouth Publishing, Ashgate Publishing, 1998.

Berzon, J. *Neither White nor Black: The Mulatto Character in American Fiction.* New York: New York University Press, 1978.

Bhuyan, Rupaleem. "Talking about Sexual Assault on a Native American Reservation." Unpublished paper, May 2000.

Bieder, Robert E. *Science Encounters the Indian, 1820–1880: The Early Years of American Ethnology.* Norman: University of Oklahoma Press, 1986.

Bird, Gloria, and Joy Harjo, eds. *Reinventing the Enemy's Language: Contemporary Native Women's Writing of North America.* New York: W.W. Norton, 1997.

Blackburn, Carole. *Harvest of Souls: The Jesuit Missions and Colonialism in North America, 1632–1650.* Montreal: McGill-Queen's University Press, 2000.

Bonney, Rachel A. "The Role of AIM Leaders in Indian Nationalism." *American Indian Quarterly* 3:3 (1977): 209–24.

Bonvillian, Nancy. "Gender Relations in Native North America." *American Indian Culture and Research Journal* 13:2 (1989): 1–28.

Bradshaw, Carla K. "Beauty and the Beast: On Racial Ambiguity in Racially Mixed People." In *Racially Mixed People in America*, ed. Maria P. P. Root, 77–90. Newbury Park CA: Sage, 1992.

Brand, Joanna. *The Life and Death of Anna Mae Aquash.* 2d ed. Toronto: Lorimer, 1993.

Braudy, Susan. "We Will Remember Survival School: The Women and Children of the American Indian Movement." *Ms.,* July 1976, 94.

Braund, Kathryn E. Holland. *Deerskins and Duffles: Creek Indian Trade with Anglo-Americans, 1685–1815.* Lincoln: University of Nebraska Press, 1993.

Brave Bird, Mary, with Richard Erdoes. *Ohitika Woman.* New York: Harper Collins, 1992.

*Brave Hearted Woman.* Prod. Lan Brookes Ritz. 1979. Videocassette.

Brookings Institution, Institute for Government Research. *The Problem of Indian Administration: Summary of Findings and Recommendations* Washington DC: Institute for Government Research, 1928.

Brooks-Higgenbothan, Evelyn. "The Problem of Race in Women's History." In *Coming to Terms: Feminism, Theory, Politics,* ed. Elizabeth Weed, 122–33. New York: Routledge, 1989.

Brown, Alanna Kathleen. "Mourning Dove's Canadian Recovery Years, 1917–1919." *Canadian Literature* 124–25 (spring/summer 1990): 113–23.

———. "Mourning Dove's Voice in Co-Ge-We-A." *Wicazo Sa Review* 4 (1988): 2–15.

Brown, Dee. *Bury My Heart at Wounded Knee: An Indian History of the American West.* New York: Holt, Rinehart, and Winston, 1971.

Brown, Jennifer S. H. *Strangers in Blood: Fur Trade Company Families in Indian Country.* Vancouver: University of British Columbia Press, 1980.

Brown, Judith K. "Economic Organization and the Position of Women among the Iroquois." *Ethnohistory* 17 (summer–fall 1970): 151–67.

Brown, L., and Maria P. P. Root. *Complexity and Diversity in Feminist Theory and Therapy.* New York: Haworth, 1990.

Bruchac, Joseph, ed., *Survival This Way: Interviews with American Indian Poets.* Tucson: University of Arizona Press, 1987.

Bruner, Edward M. "Primary Group Experience and the Process of Acculturation." *American Anthropologist* 58:4 (August 1956): 605–23.

Buchanan, Kimberly Moore. *Apache Women Warriors.* El Paso: Texas Western Press, 1986.

Buffalohead, Priscilla. "Farmers, Warriors and Traders: A Fresh Look at Ojibwe Women." *Minnesota History* 48 (1983): 236–44.

Burt, Larry W. "Roots of the Native American Urban Experience: Relocation Policy in the 1950s." *American Indian Quarterly* 10 (1986): 85–99.

*Buyer Beware of Fake and Imitation Hopi Arts and Crafts.* Brochure published by The Hopi Foundation (P.O. Box 705, Hotevilla AZ 86030). 1995.

Caldwell, Charles. *Thoughts on the Original Unity of the Human Race.* Cincinnati: J. A. and V. P. James, 1852.

Carroll, Rhoda. "The Values and Vision of a Collective Past: An Interview with Anna Lee Walters." *American Indian Quarterly* 16.1 (winter 1992): 63–73.

Carter, Kent. "Wantabes and Outalucks: Searching for Indian Ancestors in Federal Records." *Chronicles of Oklahoma* 56 (spring 1988): 94–104.

Chambers, Iain. "Migrancy, Culture, and Identity." In *The Postmodern History Reader,* ed. Keith James, 77–81. New York: Routledge, 1997.

Christian, Barbara. "The Race for Theory." In Anzaldúa, ed., *Making Face, Making Soul,* 335–45.

Churchill, Ward. "Nobody's Pet Poodle: Jimmie Durham, an Artist for Native North America." In *Indians Are Us? Culture and Genocide in Native North America,* 89–114. Monroe ME: Common Courage Press, 1994.

Clarke, Jerry E., and Martha Ellen Webb. "Susette and Susan La-Flesche: Reformer and Missionary." In Clifton, ed., *Being and Becoming Indian,* 137–59.

Clifton, James. *The Invented Indian: Cultural Fictions and Government Policies.* New Brunswick NJ: Transaction, 1990.

Clifton, James, ed. *Being and Becoming Indian: Biographical Studies of North American Frontiers.* Chicago: Dorsey Press, 1989.

Clifford, James, and George Marcus, eds. *Writing Culture: The Poetics and Politics of Ethnography.* Berkeley: University of California Press, 1986.

Coleman, Michael C. *American Indian Children at School, 1850–1930.* Jackson: University Press of Mississippi, 1993.

Collins, Patricia Hill. *Fighting Words: Black Women and the Search for Justice.* Minneapolis: University of Minnesota Press, 1998.

———. *Black Feminist Thought: Knowledge, Consciousness and the Politics of Empowerment.* 2d ed. New York: Routledge, 2000.

Comer, Nancy A. "Hokahe! A Look at the Younger Indian Women." *Mademoiselle,* October 1970, 158–59, 195–98.

"Confounding the Color Line: Indian-Black Relations in Historical and Anthropological Perspective." *American Indian Quarterly* 22:1 &2 (winter/spring 1998).

*The Constitutions and Laws of the American Indian Tribes.* Vols. 1–10. Wilmington DE: Scholarly Resources, 1973, 1975.

Cook-Lynn, Elizabeth. "American Indian Intellectualism and the New Indian Story." In Mihesuah, ed., *Natives and Academics*, 110–38.

Cornell, Stephen, and Douglass Hartmann. *Ethnicity and Race: Making Identities in a Changing World*. Thousand Oaks CA: Pine Forge Press, 1998.

Cox, Bruce A,. ed., *Native People, Native Lands: Canadian Indians, Inuit, and Metis*. Ottawa: Carleton University Press, 1988.

Croonenberghs, Lise. "Metis Women at Turtle Mountain." In Benson, Hampsten, and Sweney, eds., *Day In, Day Out*, 78–79.

Crosby, Alfred. *The Columbian Exchange: Biological and Cultural Consequences of 1492*. Westport CT: Greenwood Press, 1972.

Cross, William E., Jr. *Shades of Black: Diversity in African-American Identity*. Philadelphia: Temple University Press, 1991.

——. "The Thomas and Cross Models on Psychological Nigrescence: A Literature Review." *Journal of Black Psychology* 4 (1978): 18.

Crow Dog, Mary, and Richard Erdoes. *Lakota Woman*. New York: Harper Collins, 1990.

Crozier-Hogle, Lois, and Darryl Babe Wilson, comps. *Surviving in Two Worlds: Contemporary Native American Voices*. Austin: University of Texas Press, 1997.

Danticat, Edwidge. *Breath, Eyes, Memory*. New York: Soho Press, 1994.

——. *Farming of Bones*. New York: Soho Press, 1998.

——. *Krik! Krak!* New York: Soho Press, 1995.

——. "Local Color: In Haiti, the Color of a Person's Skin Often Determines Whether She Is Considered Beautiful—or Not." *Allure*, September 1995, 124, 139.

Debo, Angie. "To Establish Justice." *Western History Quarterly* 7:4 (October 1976): 405–12.

Dedera, Don. *Navajo Rugs: How to Find, Evaluate, Buy and Care for Them*. Flagstaff AZ: Northland Press, 1975.

Deer, Ada. "How the Good Guys Won." *Journal of Intergroup Relations* 3 (1974): 41–50.

Deloria, Vine, Jr. *Behind the Trail of Broken Treaties: An Indian Declaration of Independence*. Austin: University of Texas Press, 1985.

——. "Commentary: Redskins, Research, and Reality," *American Indian Quarterly* 15 (fall 1991): 461.

DeSalvo, Louise. *Writing as a Way of Healing: How Telling Our Stories Transforms Our Lives*. New York: HarperCollins, 1999.

Devens, Carol. *Countering Colonization: Anthropological Perspectives*. New York: Praeger, 1980.

Dickason, Olive Patricia. *Canada's First Nations.* Norman: University of Oklahoma Press, 1992.

Dillingham, Brent. "Indian Women and Indian Health Services Sterilization Practices." *American Indian Journal* 3 (January 1977): 27–28.

Dilworth, Leah. *Imagining Indians in the Southwest: Persistent Visions of a Primitive Past.* Washington DC: Smithsonian Institution Press, 1996.

Dodge, Richard Irving. *Our Wild Indians: Thirty-three Years' Personal Experience among the Red Men of the Great West.* Chicago: A. G. Nettleton, 1882.

———. *The Plains of North America and Their Inhabitants.* 1876. Reprint, Newark: University of Delaware Press, 1989.

Doggett, Rachel, ed. *New World of Wonders: European Images of the Americas, 1492–1700.* Washington DC: Folger Shakespeare Library, 1992.

Donaldson, Laura E. "On Medicine Women and White Shame-ans: New Age Native Americanism and Commodity Fetishism as Pop Culture Feminism." *Signs* 24:3 (spring 1999): 677–96.

Downs, James. *The Navajo.* New York: Holt, Rinehart and Winston, 1972.

Durham, Jimmie. "Those Dead Guys for a Hundred Years." In *I Tell You Now: Autobiographical Essays by Native American Writers,* ed. Brian Swann and Arnold Krupat, 163–64. Lincoln: University of Nebraska Press, 1987.

Edmunds, R. David. *The Shawnee Prophet.* Lincoln: University of Nebraska Press, 1983.

Edut, Ophira, ed. *Adios Barbie: Young Women Write about Body Image and Identity.* Seattle: Seal Press, 1998.

Eggan, Fred. *The American Indian: Perspectives for the Study of Social Change.* Chicago: Aldine, 1966.

Elkin, Frederick. "Family, Socialization, and Ethnic Identity." In *The Canadian Family,* ed. K. Ishwaran, 147–58. Toronto: Gage, 1983.

Ellis, Clyde. *To Change Them Forever: Indian Education at the Rainy Mountain Boarding School, 1893–1920.* Norman: University of Oklahoma Press, 1996.

Engels, Fredrich. *The Origin of the Family: Private Property and the States.* New York: International Publishers, 1972.

England, Charles R. "A Look at the Indian Health Service Policy of Sterilization, 1972–76." *Red Ink* 3 (spring 1994): 17–21.

Englander, Marilyn Jean. "Through Their Words: Urban Indian Women and Traditional Continuity." Ph.D. diss., University of California, Santa Barbara, 1985.

Eschbach, Karl, and Kalman Applbaum. "Who Goes to Powwows? Evidence from the Survey of American Indians and Alaska Natives." *American Indian Culture and Research Journal* 24:2 (2000): 65–83.

Etienne, Mona, and Eleanor Leacock, eds. *Women and Colonization: Anthropological Perspectives.* New York: Praeger, 1980.

Ewers, John C. "Deadlier Than the Male." *American Heritage* 16 (1965): 10–13.

Fairchild, David G., Molly Wilson Fairchild, and Shirley Stoner. "Prevalence of Adult Domestic Violence among Women Seeking Routine Care in a Native American Health Care Facility." *American Journal of Public Health* 88:10 (1998): 1515–17.

Fanlund, Lari. "Indians in Wisconsin: A Conversation with Ada Deer." *Wisconsin Trails: The Magazine Life of Wisconsin* 24 (March/April 1983): 8–21.

Fanon, Frantz. *Black Skin, White Masks.* New York: Grove Press, 1967.

Feder, Norman. *American Indian Art.* New York: Harry N. Abrams, 1973.

Fenton, William N. "Structure, Continuity and Change in the Process of Iroquois Treaty-Making." In *The History and Culture of Iroquois Diplomacy: An Interdisciplinary Guide to the Treaties of Six Nations and Their League,* ed. Francis Jennings, William N. Fenton, Mary A. Druke, and David R. Miller, 9–10. Syracuse NY: Syracuse University Press, 1985.

Fiedler, Leslie A. "The Indian in Literature in English." In *Handbook of North American Indians,* 4: 573–81. Washington DC: Smithsonian Institution, 1988.

Fisher, Dexter. "Zitkala Scarona: The Evolution of a Writer." *American Indian Quarterly* 5 (August 1979): 229–38.

Fiske, Jo-Anne. "Colonization and the Decline of Women's Status: The Tsimshian Case." *Feminist Studies* 17:3 (fall 1991): 509–35

Fixico, Donald L., ed. *Rethinking American Indian History.* Albuquerque: University of New Mexico Press, 1997.

———. *Termination and Relocation: Federal Indian Policy, 1945–1960.* Albuquerque: University of New Mexico Press, 1986.

Fontaine, Pierre-Michel, ed. *Race, Class and Power in Brazil.* Los Angeles: Center for Afro-American Studies, University of California, 1985.

Fortunate Eagle, Adam. *Alcatraz! Alcatraz! The Indian Occupation of 1969–71.* Berkeley CA: Heyday Books, 1992.

Foster, Martha Harroun. "Of Baggage and Bondage: Gender and Status among Hidatsa and Crow Women." *American Indian Culture and Research Journal* 17:2 (1993): 121–52.

Fowler, Loretta. *Arapahoe Politics, 1851–1978: Symbols in Crises of Authority*. Lincoln: University of Nebraska Press, 1982.

———. *Shared Symbols, Contested Meanings: Gros Ventre Culture and History, 1778–1984*. New York: Cornell University Press, 1987.

Franklin, John Hope, ed. *Color and Race*. Boston: Houghton Mifflin, 1968.

Fraser, Walter J., Jr., R. Frank Saunders Jr., and Jon L. Waklyn Jr. *Web of Southern Social Relations: Essays on Family Life, Education and Women*. Athens: University of Georgia Press, 1985.

Frazier, Ian. *On the Rez*. New York, Farrar, Straus, and Giroux, 2000.

Frazier, E. Franklin. *Black Bourgeoisie*. New York: Free Press, 1957.

Frisbie, Charlotte Johnson. *Kinaalda': A Study of the Navajo Girl's Puberty Ceremony*. Salt Lake City: University of Utah Press, 1993.

Fry, Maggie Culver, comp. *Cherokee Female Seminary Years: A Cherokee National Anthology by Many Tribal Authors*. Claremore OK: Rogers State College Press, 1988.

Gans, Herbert. "Symbolic Ethnicity: The Future of Ethnic Groups and Cultures in America." *Ethnic and Racial Studies* 2 (January 1979): 1–20.

Gaynor, Gloria. *I Will Survive*. New York: St. Martin's Press, 1997.

Gniewek, Kara. "The Silent Genocide." *Red Ink* 5:1 (fall 1996): 60–71.

Goldberg, Milton M. "A Qualification of the Marginal Man Theory." *American Sociological Review* 6 (1941): 52–58.

Gonzalez, Ellice B. "An Ethnohistorical Analysis of Micmac Male and Female Economic Roles." *Ethnohistory* 29 (1982): 117–29.

Goodman, M. E. *Race Awareness in Young Children*. New York: Collier Press, 1968.

Graham, Richard, ed. *The Idea of Race in Latin America, 1870–1940*. Austin: University of Texas Press, 1990.

Green, Arnold W. "A Re-examination of the Marginal Man Concept." *Social Forces* 26 (1947): 167–71.

Green, Michael D. "Mary Musgrove: Creating a New World." In Perdue, ed., *Sifters: Native Women's Lives*, 29–47.

Green, Michael K. *Issues in Native American Identity*. New York: Peter Lang, 1995.

Green, Norma Kidd. *Iron Eye's Family: The Children of Joseph La-Flesche*. Lincoln NE: Johnson Publishing, 1969.

Green, Rayna. "The Indian in Popular American Culture." In *Handbook of North American Indians*, 4:587–606. Washington DC: Smithsonian Institution, 1988.

———. *Native American Women: A Contextual Bibliography*. Bloomington: Indiana University Press, 1983.

———. "The Pocahontas Perplex: The Image of Indian Women in

American Culture." *The Massachusetts Review* 16:4 (autumn 1975): 698–714.

Greene, Jack P., and J. R. Pole, eds. *Colonial British America: Essays in the New History of the Early Modern Era.* Baltimore MD: Johns Hopkins University Press, 1984.

Greer, Sandy. "Three Native Women (Alanis Obomsawin, Margo Kane, Maria Campbell)" *Turtle Quarterly* 4 (spring–summer 1991): 24–33.

Gridley, Marion. *American Indian Women.* New York: Hawthorn Books, 1974.

Griffin, Connie. "Relearning to Trust Ourselves: Interview with Chief Wilma Mankiller." *Women of Power* 7 (summer 1987): 38–40, 72–74.

Grinde, Donald A., and Bruce E. Johansen. *Ecocide of Native America: Environmental Destruction of Indian Lands and People.* Santa Fe NM: Clear Light Publishers, 1995.

Guemple, Lee. "Men and Women: Husbands and Wives: The Role of Gender in Traditional Inuit Societies." *Etudes/Inuit/Studies* 10:1–2 (1986): 9–24.

Hackett, Charles Wilson, ed. *Revolt of the Pueblo Indians of New Mexico and Otermin's Attempted Reconquest, 1680–1682.* 2 vols. Coronado Historical Series, vols. 8 and 9. Albuquerque: University of New Mexico Press, 1942.

Hagan, William T. "Full Blood, Mixed Blood, Generic, and Ersatz: The Problem of Indian Identity." *Arizona and the West* (winter 1985): 317–18.

Hamamsky, Laila Shukry. "The Role of Women in a Changing Navajo Society." *American Anthropologist* 59 (1957): 101–11.

Hanson, Jeffrey R., and Linda P. Rouse. "Dimensions of Native American Stereotyping." *American Indian Culture and Research Journal* 11:4 (1987): 33–58.

———. "American Indian Stereotyping, Resource Competition, and Status-Based Prejudice." *American Indian Culture and Research Journal* 15:3 (1991): 1–18.

Harris, Angela P. "Race and Essentialism in Feminist Legal Theory." *Stanford Law Review* 42 (1990): 581–616.

Harris, Herbert W., Howard C. Blue, and Ezra E. H. Griffith. *Racial and Ethnic Identity: Psychological Development and Creative Expression.* New York: Routledge, 1995.

Hatcher, Evelyn Payne. *Visual Metaphors: A Formal Analysis of Navajo Art.* New York: West Publishing Company, 1974.

Hauptman, Laurence M. "Alice Jemison: Seneca Political Activist, 1901–1964." *The Indian Historian* 12:2 (summer 1979): 15–62.

———. "Designing Woman: Minnie Kellogg, Iroquois Leader." In *Indian Lives: Essays on Nineteenth- and Twentieth-Century Native American Leaders*, ed. L. G. Moses and Raymond Wilson, 159–88. Albuquerque: University of New Mexico Press, 1993.

Hayes-Bautista, David E. "Becoming Chicano: A Disassimilation Theory of Transformation of Ethnic Identity." Ph.D. diss., University of California at Santa Barbara, 1974.

Helms, Janet E. "More Psychologists Discover the Wheel: A Reaction to Views by Penn, et al., on Ethnic Preference." *The Journal of Black Psychology* 19:3 (1993): 322–26.

Herring, Joseph. *Kenekuk: The Kickapoo Prophet.* Lawrence: University Press of Kansas, 1988.

Heth, Charlotte, ed. *Native American Dance: Ceremonies and Social Traditions.* Washington DC: National Museum of the American Indian, Smithsonian Institution, 1992.

Hewes, Leslie. *Occupying the Cherokee Country of Oklahoma.* Lincoln: University of Nebraska Press, 1978.

Hilden, Patricia Penn. "Ritchie Valens Is Dead: E. Pluribus Unum." In *As We Are Now: Mixblood Essays on Race and Identity*, ed. William S. Penn, 219–52. Berkeley: University of California Press, 1997.

Hill, Robert F., Glenn W. Solomon, Jane K. Tiger, and J. Dennis Fortenberry. "Complexities of Ethnicity among Oklahoma Native Americans: Health Behaviors of Rural Adolescents." In *The Culture of Oklahoma*, 84–100. Norman: University of Oklahoma Press, 1993.

Himmelfarb, Gertrude. "Telling It as You Like It: Postmodernist History and the Flight from Fact." *tls* 16 (October 1992).

Hinsley, Curtis M. "Digging for Identity: Reflections on the American Cultural Background of Repatriation." In Mihesuah, *Repatriation Reader*, 2–58.

———. *The Smithsonian and the American Indian: Making A Moral Anthropology in Victorian America.* Washington DC: Smithsonian Institution Press, 1994. Originally published as *Savages and Scientists: The Smithsonian Institution and the Development of American Anthropology, 1846–1910*, 1981.

Hirschfelder, Aelene. *American Indian Stereotypes in the World of Children.* Metuchen NJ: Scarecrow Press, 1982.

———. "Guardians of Tradition and Handmaidens to Change: Women's Roles in Creek Economic and Social Life during the Eighteenth Century." *American Indian Quarterly* (1990): 239–58.

Holmstrom, Nancy. "A Marxist Theory of Women's Nature." *Ethics* 94 (April 1984): 186–21.

Honour, Hugh. *The European Vision of America.* Cleveland OH: Cleveland Museum of Art, 1975.

hooks, bell. *Ain't I a Woman?* Boston: South End Press, 1981.

———. *Feminist Theory: From Margin to Center.* Boston: South End Press, 1984.

Hopkins, Sarah Winnemucca. *Life among the Paiutes: Their Wrongs and Claims,* ed. Mrs. Horace Mann. Reprint, Bishop CA: Chalfant Press, 1985.

Horsman, Reginald. "Scientific Racism and the American Indian in the Mid-Nineteenth Century." *American Quarterly* 27:2 (May 1975): 152–68.

House Concurrent Resolution 108, 83d Cong., 1st sess., 1 August 1953.

Hull, Gloria T., Patricia Bell Scott, and Barbara Smith, eds. *All the Women Are White, All the Blacks Are Men, but Some of Us Are Brave.* Old Westbury NY: Feminist Press, 1981.

Hungry Wolf, Beverly. *The Ways of My Grandmothers.* New York: William Morrow, 1980.

Hurtado, Aída. *The Color of Privilege: Three Blasphemies on Race and Feminism.* Ann Arbor: University of Michigan Press, 1996.

Hurtado, Albert J., and Peter Iverson, eds. *Major Problems in American Indian History.* Boston: Houghton Mifflin, 2001.

*Incident at Oglala: The Leonard Peltier Story.* Dir. Michael Apted. 1991. Videocassette.

Indian Act. Can. Rev. Stat., 1970, c. 1–6, s. 12(1)(b).

Indian Health Service. *Trends in Indian Health.* Washington DC: U.S. Dept. of Health and Human Services, Public Health Service, Indian Health Service, Office of Planning, Evaluation and Legislation, Division of Program Statistics, 1991.

*Indian Reorganization Act.* 48 Stat. 984, 25 USC 461 et seq. (1934).

*In the Spirit of Crazy Horse.* PBS video. 1990. ISBN 0-7936-0396-X. Videocassette.

*In the White Man's Image.* The American Experience, PBS. ISBN 0-7936-0635-7. 1991. Videocassette.

Isaacs, Harold R. *Idols of the Tribe: Group Identity and Political Change.* New York: Harper and Row, 1975.

Jacobs, Margaret D. *Engendered Encounters: Feminism and Pueblo Cultures, 1879–1934.* Lincoln: University of Nebraska Press, 1999.

Jaggar, Alison M. *Feminist Politics and Human Nature.* Totowa NJ: Rowman and Allanheld, 1983.

Jaimes, M. Annette. Review of *Lakota Woman,* by Mary Brave Bird. *American Indian Culture and Research Journal* 15:1 (1991): 110–11.

Jaimes, M. Annette, ed. *The State of Native America: Genocide, Colonization and Resistance*. Boston: South End Press, 1992.

Jaimes, M. Annette, and Theresa Halsey. "American Indian Women: At the Center of Indigenous Resistance in North America." In Jaimes, ed., *The State of Native America*, 311–44.

Jennings, Francis. *The Invasion of America: Indians, Colonialism, and the Cant of Conquest*. Chapel Hill: University of North Carolina Press, 1975.

Joe, Jennie R. "Forced Relocation and Assimilation: Dillon Myer and the Native American." *Amerasia Journal* 13:2 (1986–87): 161–65.

Johns, Elizabeth A. H. *Storms Brewed in Other Men's Worlds: The Confrontation of Indians, Spanish and French in the Southwest, 1540–1795*. College Station TX: Texas A&M University Press, 1975.

Johnson, David L., and Raymond Wilson. "Gertrude Simmons Bonnin, 1876–1938: 'Americanize the First Americans.'" *American Indian Quarterly* 12 (winter 1988): 27–40.

Johnson, N. B. "The Cherokee Orphan Asylum." *Chronicles of Oklahoma* 34 (summer 1956): 159–82.

Johnson, Troy, Duane Champagne, and Joanne Nagel. "American Indian Activism and Transformation: Lessons from Alcatraz." In *American Indian Activism: Alcatraz to the Longest Walk*. Urbana: University of Illinois Press, 1997.

Johnston, Basil H. *Indian School Days*. Norman: University of Oklahoma Press, 1989.

Jones, David E. *Sanapia: Comanche Medicine Woman*. New York: Holt, Rinehart and Winston, 1972.

Jones, Oakah L., Jr. *Pueblo Warriors and Spanish Conquest*. Norman: University of Oklahoma Press, 1966.

Kambon, Kobi K. K., and Reginal Hopkins, "An African-Centered Analysis of Penn et al.'s Critique of the Own-Race Preference Assumption Underlying Africentric Models of Personality." *The Journal of Black Psychology* 19:3 (1993): 342–49.

Katz, William Loren. *Black Indians: A Hidden Heritage*. New York: Atheneum, 1986.

Kerwin, Christine, and Joseph G. Ponterotto. "Biracial Identity Development: Theory and Research." In *Handbook of Multicultural Counseling*, ed. Joseph G. Ponterotto, J. Manuel Casas, Lisa A. Suzuki, and Charlene M. Alexander, 199–217. Thousand Oaks CA: Sage Publications, 1995.

Kidwell, Clara Sue. "The Power of Women in Three American Indian Societies." *The Journal of Ethnic Studies* 6:3 (winter 1979): 113–21.

Kim, Jean. "Processes of Asian American Identity Development: A Study of Japanese American Women's Perceptions of Their Struggle to Achieve Positive Identities as Americans of Asian Ancestry." Ed.D. diss., University of Massachusetts, 1981.

Klein, Alan M. "The Plains Truth: The Impact of Colonialism on Indian Women." *Dialectical Anthropology* 7 (1983): 299–313.

Knapp, Mille. "Circle of Unity: Portraits and Voices of Native Women." *Turtle Quarterly* 4 (spring/summer 1992): 29–53.

Knepler, Abraham. "Digest of the Education of Cherokee Indians." Ph.D. diss., Yale University, 1939.

Kracht, Benjamin R. "Kiowa Powwows: Continuity in Ritual Practice." *American Indian Quarterly* 18:3 (summer 1994): 312–28.

Kramarae, Cheris, and Dale Spender, eds. *The Knowledge Explosion: Generations of Feminist Scholarship.* New York: Altheas Series, 1992.

LaDuke, Winona. *All Our Relations: Native Struggles for Land and Life.* Cambridge MA: South End Press, 1999.

———. *Last Standing Woman.* Stillwater MN: Voyageur Press, 1997.

———. "The Morality of Wealth: Native America and the Frontier Mentality." *Radical America* 17 (1983): 69–79.

———. "Native America: The Economics of Radioactive Colonization." *Review of Radical Political Economy* 15 (1983): 9–19.

LaDuke, Winona, and Ward Churchill. "Native North America: The Political Economy of Radioactive Colonialism." In Jaimes, ed., *The State of Native America,* 241–66.

Lam, Maivan Clech. "Feeling Foreign in Feminism." *signs* 19:4 (1994): 865–96.

Lamphere, Louise. "Historical and Regional Variability in Navajo Women's Roles." *Journal of Anthropological Research* 45 (1989): 431–56.

Landes, Ruth. *The Ojibwe Woman.* New York: Norton, 1971.

Larson, Janet Karston. "And Then There Were None: Is Federal Policy Endangering the American Indian Species?" *Christian Century* 26 (January 1977): 62–63.

Lassiter, Erik Luke. *The Power of Kiowa Song: A Collaborative Ethnography.* Tucson: University of Arizona Press, 1998.

Lawrence, Jane. "The Indian Health Service and the Sterilization of Native American Women." *American Indian Quarterly* 24:3 (summer 2000): 400–19.

Leacock, Eleanor B. *Myths of Male Dominance: Collected Articles on Women Cross-Culturally.* New York: Monthly Review Press, 1981.

Lefkowitz, Mary. *Not Out of Africa: How Afrocentrism Became an Excuse to Teach Myth as History.* New York: Basic Books, 1996.

Leibold, Jay. *Surviving in Two Worlds: Contemporary Native American Voices.* Austin: University of Texas Press, 1997.

Leland, John, and Gregory Beals. "In Living Colors." *Newsweek*, May 5, 1997.

Lerner, Gerda. *Black Women in White America: A Documentary History*. New York: Pantheon, 1972.

———. "Reconceptualizing Differences among Women." *Journal of Women's History* (1990): 106–22.

LeVelle, John. Review of *Indians Are Us? Culture and Genocide in Native North America*, by Ward Churchill. *American Indian Quarterly* 20:1 (winter 1996): 109–18.

Lewis, Oscar. "Manly-Hearted Women among the Northern Piegan." *American Anthropologist* 43 (1947): 173–87.

Lipsault, Deborah. *Denying the Holocaust: The Growing Assault on Truth and Memory*. New York: Free Press, 1993.

Lomawaima, K. Tsianina. *They Called It Prairie Light: The Story of Chilocco Indian School*. Lincoln: University of Nebraska Press, 1994.

*Sandra Lovelace v. Canada*. Communication No. 24/1977 (14 August 1979), U.N. Doc. CCPR/C/OP/1 at 10.

Lugones, Maria C., and Elizabeth V. Spelman. "Have We Got a Theory for You! Feminist Theory, Cultural Imperialism and the Demand for 'The Woman's Voice.'" *Women's Studies International Forum* 6:6 (1983): 573–81.

Lurie, Nancy Oestreich, ed. *Sister of Crashing Thunder: The Autobiography of a Winnebago Indian*. Ann Arbor: University of Michigan Press, 1961.

MacKinnon, Catharine A. *Feminism Unmodified: Discourses on Life and Law*. Cambridge: Harvard University Press, 1987.

Manitowabo, Edna. "An Ojibwa Girl in the City." *This Magazine Is about Schools*. 4:4 (1970): 8–24.

Mankiller, Wilma, Gwendolyn Mink, Marysa Navarro, Barbara Smith, and Gloria Steinem. *The Reader's Companion to U.S. Women's History*. Boston: Houghton Mifflin, 1998.

Mankiller, Wilma, and Michael Wallis. *Mankiller: A Chief and Her People*. New York: St. Martin's Press, 1993.

Maracle, Lee. *I Am Woman: A Native Perspective on Sociology and Feminism*. Vancouver BC: Press Gang Publishers, 1996.

Marsden, Michael T., and Jack G. Nachbar. "The Indian in the Movies." In *Handbook of North American Indians*, 4:607–16. Washington DC: Smithsonian Institution, 1988.

Martin, Calvin. *American Indians and the Problem of History*. New York: Oxford University Press, 1986. Matthiessen, Peter. *In the Spirit of Crazy Horse*. New York: Viking Press, 1983.

Mattern, Mark. "The Powwow as a Public Arena for Negotiating

Unity and Diversity in American Indian Life." *American Indian Culture and Research Journal* 20:4 (1996): 183–201.

Mathes, Valerie Sherer. "Nineteenth-Century Women and Reform: The Women's National Indian Association." *American Indian Quarterly* 14:1 (winter 1990): 1–18.

McBeth, Sally J. *Ethnic Identity and the Boarding School Experience of West-Central Oklahoma American Indians.* Washington DC: University Press of America, 1983.

McCarriston, Linda. "Indian Girls." *Ice-Floe* 1:2 (December 2000).

McClary, Ben. "Nancy Ward: The Last Beloved Woman of the Cherokees." *Tennessee Historical Quarterly* 21 (December 1962): 352–64.

McCoy, Melanie. "Gender or Ethnicity: What Makes a Difference? A Study of Women Tribal Leaders." *Women and Politics* 12:3 (1992): 57–68.

McCullough, Anne Merline, and David E. Wilkins. " 'Constructing' Nations within States: The Quest for Federal Recognition by the Catawba and Lumbee Tribes." *American Indian Quarterly* 19:3 (summer 1995): 361–88.

McFee, Malcolm. "The 150 Percent Man: A Product of Blackfeet Acculturation." *American Anthropologist* 70 (1968): 1096–103.

McKague, Ormond, ed. *Racism in Canada.* Saskatoon SK: Fifth House Publishers, 1991.

McLoughlin, William G. *The Cherokee Ghost Dance.* Macon GA: Mercer University Press, 1984.

———. "Red Indians, Black Slavery and White Racism: America's Slaveholding Indians." *American Quarterly* 26 (October 1974): 367–85.

———. *Cherokee Renascence in the New Republic.* Princeton NJ: Princeton University Press, 1986.

———. *Cherokees and Missionaries: 1789–1839.* New Haven CT: Yale University Press, 1984.

McPherson, Robert. "From Dezba to 'John': The Changing Role of Navajo Women in Southeastern Utah." *American Indian Culture and Research Journal* 18:3 (1994): 202.

McRoy, Ruth G., and Edith Freeman. "Racial Identity Issues among Mixed Race Children." *Social Work in Education* 8 (1986): 164–74.

Means, Russell. Interview. *Penthouse*, April 1981, 136–38, 188–91, 194.

———. *Where White Men Fear to Tread: Autobiography of Russell Means.* New York: St. Martin's Press, 1995.

Medicine, Bea. *The Native American Woman: A Perspective.* Austin TX: National Education Laboratory, 1978.

———. "The Role and Function of Indian Women." *Indian Education* 7 (January 1977): 4–5.

Meyer, Melissa L. *The White Earth Tragedy: Ethnicity and Dispossession at a Minnesota Anishinaabe Reservation.* Lincoln: University of Nebraska Press, 1994.

Mihesuah, Devon A. "American Indian Identities: Issues of Individual Choices and Development." *American Indian Culture and Research Journal* 22:2 (1998): 193–226.

———. *American Indians: Stereotypes and Realities.* Atlanta GA: Clarity International, 1996.

———. "Anna Mae Pictou-Aquash." In Perdue, ed., *Sifters: Native Women's Lives*, 204–22.

———. "Comment on 'Indian Girls.'" *HEArt* 5:1 (fall 2000): 18–20.

———. *Cultivating the Rosebuds: The Education of Women at the Cherokee Female Seminary, 1951–1909.* Urbana: University of Illinois Press, 1993.

———. "Infatuation Is Not Enough." Review of *On the Rez*, by Ian Frazier." *American Indian Quarterly* 24:2 (spring 2000): 283–86.

———. "Suggested Research Guidelines for Institutions With Scholars Who Study American Indians." *American Indian Culture and Research Journal* 17 (fall 1993): 131–39.

———. *Roads of My Relations: Stories.* Tucson: University of Arizona Press, 1999.

Mihesuah, Devon A., ed. *Natives and Academics: Researching and Writing about American Indians.* Lincoln: University of Nebraska Press, 1998.

———. *Repatriation Reader: Who Owns Indian Remains?* Lincoln: University of Nebraska Press, 2000.

Miller, Carol. "The Story Is Brimming Around: Interview with Linda Hogan." *Studies in American Indian Literatures* 2:4 (winter 1990): 1–9.

Miller, Christopher. *Prophetic Worlds: Indians and Whites on the Columbia Plateau.* New Brunswick NJ: Rutgers University Press, 1985.

Miller, Jay, ed. *Mourning Dove: A Salishan Autobiography.* Lincoln: University of Nebraska Press, 1990.

Min, Sarah. "Language Lessons: Once I Learned to Speak Korean, I Could Finally Hear My Real Voice." *Glamour*, November 1997, 106.

Minh-La, Trinh T. *Woman, Native, Other.* Bloomington: Indiana University Press, 1989.

Mohanty, Chandra Talpade, Ann Russo, and Lourdes Torres, eds.

*Third World Women and the Politics of Feminism.* Bloomington: Indiana University Press, 1991.

Mooney, James. *The Ghost-Dance Religion and Wounded Knee.* Reprint, New York: Dover, 1973.

Moore, Zena. "Check the Box That Best Describes You." In *American Mixed Race: The Culture of Microdiversity,* ed. Naomi Zack, 39–51. Lanham: MD: Rowman and Littlefield, 1995.

Moraga, Cherríe, and Gloria Anzuldúa, eds. *This Bridge Called My Back: Writings by Radical Women of Color.* New York: Kitchen Table, Women of Color Press, 1983.

Morrison, Dorothy. *Chief Sarah: Sarah Winnemucca's Fight for Indian Rights.* Portland: Oregon Historical Society Press, 1991.

Morton, Samuel George. *Crania Americana; or, A Comparative View of the Skulls of Various Aboriginal Nations of North and South America.* Philadelphia: J. Dobson; London: Simpkin, Marshall, 1839.

Nagel, Joanne. *American Indian Ethnic Renewal: Red Power and the Resurgence of Identity and Culture.* New York: Oxford University Press, 1996.

Nash, Gary B. "The Image of the Indian in the Southern Colonial Mind." *The William and Mary Quarterly* 29:2 (April 1972): 197–230.

"The New Sensitive Census." *American Indian Report* 8:12 (December 1997): 8.

Niethammer, Carolyn. *Daughters of the Earth.* New York: Macmillan, 1977.

Norris, Christopher. "Postmodernizing History: Right-Wing Revisionism and the Uses of Theory." *Southern Review* (1988): 89–102.

Nott, Josiah C. "Unity of the Human Race." *Southern Quarterly Review* 9 (1846): 1–56.

Okazawa-Rey, Margo, Tracy Robinson, and Janie Victoria Ward. "Black Women and the Politics of Skin Color and Hair." *Women's Studies Quarterly* 14:1 & 2 (spring/summer 1986): 13–14.

Ortiz, Simon J., ed. *Speaking for the Generations: Native Writers on Writing.* Tucson: University of Arizona Press, 1998.

Padilla, A. M., ed. *Acculturation: Theory Models and Some New Findings.* Boulder CO: Westview, 1980.

Parfit, Michael. "Powwow: A Gathering of Tribes." *National Geographic,* June 1994, 88–113.

Parham, Thomas A. "Cycles of Psychological Nigrescence." *The Counseling Psychologist* 17:2 (April 1989): 187–226.

———."Own Group Preferences as a Function of Self-Affirmation:

A Reaction to Penn, et al." *The Journal of Black Psychology* 19:3 (1993): 337–41.

Pearce, Roy Harvey. *Savagism and Civilization: A Study of the Indian and the American Mind.* Baltimore MD: John Hopkins Press, 1953.

———. *The Savages of America: A Study of the Indian and the Idea of Civilization.* Baltimore MD: John Hopkins Press, 1965.

Peltier, Leonard, U.S. Prisoner 89637–132, and Harvey Arden. *Prison Writings: My Life Is My Sun Dance.* New York: St. Martin's Press, 1999.

Penn, Michael, Stanley Gaines, and Layli Phillips. "A Hermeneutic Rejoinder to Ourselves and Our Critics." *The Journal of Black Psychology* 19:3 (August 1993): 350–57.

———. "On the Desirability of Own-Group Preference." *The Journal of Black Psychology* 19:3 (August 1993): 303–21.

Perdue, Theda. *Cherokee Women: Gender and Culture Change, 1700–1835.* Lincoln: University of Nebraska Press, 1998.

———. *Slavery and the Evolution of Cherokee Society.* Knoxville: University of Tennessee Press, 1979.

Perdue, Theda, ed. *Sifters: Native Women's Lives.* New York: Oxford University Press, 2001.

Peroff, Nicholas C. *Menominee Drums: Tribal Termination and Restoration, 1954–1974.* Norman: University of Oklahoma Press, 1982.

Peterson, Jacqueline, and Jennifer S. H. Brown. *The New Peoples: Being and Becoming Metis in North America.* Lincoln: University of Nebraska Press, 1985.

Phelan, Shane. *Getting Specific: Postmodern Lesbian Politics.* Minneapolis: University of Minnesota Press, 1994.

Powers, Marla. *Oglala Women: Myth, Ritual, and Reality.* Chicago: University of Chicago Press, 1986.

Prins, Harald E. L. *The Mi'kmaq: Resistance, Accommodation, and Cultural Survival.* Fort Worth TX: Harcourt Brace College Publishers, 1996.

Prucha, Francis Paul. *American Indian Policy in Crisis: Christian Reformers and the Indian, 1865–1900.* Norman: University of Oklahoma Press, 1975.

———. *A Bibliographical Guide to the History of Indian-White Relations in the United States.* Chicago: University of Chicago Press, 1977.

———. *The Churches and the Indian Schools, 1888–1912.* Lincoln: University of Nebraska Press, 1979.

Prucha, Francis Paul, ed. *Documents of U.S. Indian Policy.* Lincoln: University of Nebraska Press, 2000.

Quinn, William W., Jr. "The Southeast Syndrome: Notes on Indian Descendant Recruitment Organizations and Their Perceptions of Native American Culture." *American Indian Quarterly* 14:2 (spring 1990) 147–54.

Quintana, Alvina E. "Women: Prisoners of the Word." In *Chicana Voices: Intersections of Race, Class, and Gender*, 208–19. Colorado Springs: National Association for Chicano Studies, Colorado College, 1990.

Quintero, Nita. "Coming of Age the Apache Way." *National Geographic* 157:2 (1980): 262–71.

Rafael, Vicente L. *Contracting Colonization: Translation and Christian Conversion in Tagalog Society under Early Spanish Rule.* Ithaca NY: Cornell University Press, 1988.

Rich, Adrienne. *On Lies, Secrets and Silence.* New York: W. W. Norton, 1979.

Riley, Glenda. "Some European (Mis)Perceptions of American Indian Women." *New Mexico Historical Review* 59:3 (July 1984): 237–66.

Roberts, Chris. *Powwow Country.* Helena MT: American and World Geographic Publishing, 1992.

Roberts, Nancy L. "Native Beauty: The Dignity and Grace of Indian Women." Annual Supplement. *US Art* (August 1994): 38–45.

Robertson, William. *History of America.* London: W. Strahan, 1777.

Roosevelt, Theodore Roosevelt. *The Winning of the West.* 4 vols. New York: Review of Reviews, 1904.

Root, Maria P. P. *The Multiracial Experience: Racial Borders as the New Frontier.* Newberry Park CA: Sage, 1996.

Root, Maria P. P., ed., *Racially Mixed People in America.* Newberry Park CA: Sage, 1992.

Rosaldo, Michelle Zimbalist, and Louise Lamphere, eds. *Women, Culture, and Society.* Stanford CA: Stanford University Press, 1974.

Rose, LaVera. "*Iyeska Win:* Intermarriage and Ethnicity among the Lakota in the Nineteenth and Twentieth Centuries." M.A. thesis, Northern Arizona University, 1994.

Rose, Peter I. *They and We: Racial and Ethnic Relations in the United States.* New York: Random House, 1964.

Rose, Wendy. "The Great Pretenders: Further Reflections on White-shamanism." In Jaimes, ed., *The State of Native America*, 403–21.

Royal Commission on Aboriginal Peoples. Report. *Looking Forward, Looking Back.* Vols. 1–5. Minister of Supply and Services Canada, 1996.

Russell, Kathy, Midge Wilson, and Ronald Hall. *The Color Complex: The Politics of Skin Color among African Americans.* New York: Harcourt Brace Jovanovich, 1992.

Sanday, Peggy R. *Female Power and Male Dominance: On the Origins of Sexual Inequality.* Cambridge: Cambridge University Press, 1981.

*Santa Clara v. Martinez,* 436 U.S. 49 (1978).

Sayer, John William. *Ghost Dancing the Law: The Wounded Knee Trials.* Cambridge: Harvard University Press, 1997.

Scheick, W. J. *The Half-Blood: A Cultural Symbol in Nineteenth-Century American Fiction.* Lexington: University of Kentucky Press, 1989.

"Seeking the Balance: A Native Women's Dialogue." *Akwe:won Journal* 10 (summer 1993): 16–29.

Sellers, Robert M. "A Call to Arms for Researchers Studying Racial Identity." *The Journal of Black Psychology* 19:3 (1993): 327–32.

Seymour-Smith, Charlotte. *The Dictionary of Anthropology.* Boston: G. K. Hall, 1986.

Sheehan, Bernard. *Savagism and Civility: Indians and Englishmen in Colonial Virginia.* Cambridge: Cambridge University Press, 1980.

Shoemaker, Nancy. "The Rise or Fall of Iroquois Women." *Journal of Women's History* 2 (1991): 39–57.

Shoemaker, Nancy, ed. *Negotiators of Change: Historical Perspectives on Native American Women.* New York: Routledge, 1995.

Silko, Leslie Marmon. *Yellow Woman and a Beauty of the Spirit.* New York: Touchstone, 1997.

Smith, Andrea. "Opinion: The New Age Movement and Native Spirituality." *Indigenous Woman* (spring 1991): 17–18.

———. "For All Those Who Were Indian in a Former Life." *Ms.,* November/December 1991, 44–45.

Smith, Linda Tuhiwai. *Decolonizing Methodologies: Research and Indigenous Peoples.* New York: St. Martin's Press, 1999.

Smith, Sherry. *The View From Officer's Row: Army Perceptions of Western Indians.* Tucson: University of Arizona Press, 1990.

Smith, Zach, ed. *Politics and Public Policy in Arizona.* Westport CT: Praeger, 1996.

Smith-Rosenberg, Carroll. "Captured Subjects/Savage Others: Violently Engendering the New American." *Gender and History* 5:2 (summer 1993): 177–95.

Smits, David D. "The 'Squaw Drudge': A Prime Index of Savagism." *Ethnohistory* 29:4 (1982): 281–386.

Snipp, Matthew. "Who Are the American Indians? Some Observations about the Perils and Pitfalls of Data for Race and Ethnicity." *Population Research and Policy Review* 5 (1986): 237–52.

Spellman, Elizabeth. *Inessential Woman: Problems of Exclusion in Feminist Thought.* Boston: Beacon Press, 1988.

Spicer, Edward H. *Cycles of Conquest: The Impact of Spain, Mexico, and the U.S. on the Indians of the Southwest, 1533–1960.* Tucson: University of Arizona Press, 1962.

Spickard, Paul R. *Mixed Blood: Intermarriage and Ethnic Identity in Twentieth-Century America.* Madison: University of Wisconsin Press, 1989.

Stacey, Judith. "Can There Be a Feminist Ethnography?" *Women's Studies International Forum* 11:1 (1988): 21–27.

Stannard, David E. *American Holocaust: The Conquest of the New World.* New York: Oxford University Press, 1992.

Starna, William A. "The Southeast Syndrome: The Prior Restraint of a Non-Event." *American Indian Quarterly* 15:4 (fall 1991): 493–502.

Starr, Emmett. *History of the Cherokee Indians, Their Legends and Folklore.* Muskogee OK: Hoffman Printing, 1984.

Stedman, Raymond William. *Shadows of the Indians: Stereotypes in American Culture.* Norman: University of Oklahoma Press, 1982.

Steele, C. Roy. "Urban Identity in Kansas: Some Implications for Research." In *The New Ethnicity: Perspectives from Ethnology,* ed. John W. Bennett, 167–78. St. Paul MN: West, 1975.

Stein, Howard, and Robert Hill. *The Ethnic Imperative: Examining the New White Ethnic Movement.* University Park: Pennsylvania State University Press, 1977.

Stockel, Henrietta, ed. *LaDonna Harris: A Comanche Life.* Lincoln: University of Nebraska Press, 2000.

Stone, Gregory P. "Appearance and the Self." In *Human Behavior and Social Processes,* ed. Arnold Rose, 86–118. Boston: Houghton Mifflin, 1962.

Stonequist, Everett. *The Marginal Man: A Study in Personality and Culture Conflict.* New York: Russell and Russell, 1937.

Strickland, Rennard. *Fire and the Spirits: Cherokee Law from Clan to Court.* Norman: University of Oklahoma Press, 1975.

Strong-Boag, Veronica Jane, and Carole Gerson. *Paddling Her Own Canoe: The Times and Texts of E. Pauline Johnson (Tekahionwake).* Toronto: University of Toronto Press, 2000.

Stumbo, Bella. "A World Apart." *Los Angeles Times Magazine,* June 15, 1986, 10–21.

Suleri, Sara. "Woman Skin Deep: Feminism and the Post-Colonial Condition." *Critical Inquiry* 18 (summer 1992): 756–69.

Sydney, Lucille. "Hopi Women in an Era of Change." Unpublished paper, 1998.

Szaba, Julia. "The Morphing Pot." *New Woman* (January 1995): 94–95, 114, 166.

Taylor, Jerome. "Reaction to Penn et al.'s 'On the Desirability of Own-

Group Preference,"' *The Journal of Black Psychology* 19:3 (1993): 333–35.

Theisz, R. D. "Song Texts and Their Performers: The Centerpiece of Contemporary Lakota Identity Formation." *Great Plains Quarterly* 7 (spring 1987): 116–24.

Thornton, Russell. *American Indian Holocaust and Survival: A Population History since 1492.* Norman: University of Oklahoma Press, 1987.

Tooker, Elisabeth. "Women in Iroquois Society." In *Extending the Rafters: Interdisciplinary Approaches to Iroquoian Studies,* ed. Michael K. Foster, Jack Campisi, and Marianne Mithun, 109–23. Albany: State University of New York Press, 1984.

Tinker, George E. *Missionary Conquest: The Gospel and Native American Cultural Genocide.* Minneapolis MN: Fortress Press, 1993.

Torpy, Sally J. "Native American Women and Coerced Sterilization: On the Trail of Tears in the 1970s." *American Indian Culture and Research Journal* 24:2 (2000): 1–22.

Trask, Mililani. "Decolonizing Hearts and Minds: Interview with Mililani B. Trask." *Woman of Power: A Magazine of Feminism, Spirituality and Politics* (summer 1995): 32–38.

Travis, V. A. "Life in the Cherokee Nation a Decade After the Civil War." *Chronicles of Oklahoma* 4 (March 1926): 16–30.

Trennert, Robert A. *The Phoenix Indian School: Forced Assimilation in Arizona, 1891–1935.* Norman: University of Oklahoma Press, 1988.

Trosper, Ronald. "Traditional American Indian Economic Policy." *American Indian Culture and Research Journal* 19:1 (1995): 65–96.

Tucker, Norma. "Nancy Ward, *Ghighau* of the Cherokees." *Georgia Historical Quarterly* 53 (June 1969): 192–200.

Underhill, Ruth. *The Navajos.* Norman: University of Oklahoma Press, 1956.

U.S. Congress. House Executive Documents. *Annual Reports of the Commissioner of Indian Affairs.*

34th Cong., 3d sess., 1856. Serial 893.

56th Cong., 2d sess., 1899. Serial 3915.

57 Cong., 1st sess., 1901. Serial 4291.

Utter, Jack. *American Indians: Answers to Today's Questions.* Lake Ann MI: National Woodlands Publishing, 1993.

Van Kirk, Sylvia. *Many Tender Ties: Women in Fur Trade Societies, 1670–1870.* Norman: University of Oklahoma Press, 1980.

———. "The Role of Native Women in the Fur Trade Society of Western Canada, 1670–1830." *Frontiers* 7:3 (1984): 9–13.

Vaughan, Alden T. "From White Man to Red Skin: Changing Anglo-American Perceptions of the American Indian." *American Historical Review* 87 (October 1982): 917–53.

Vernon, Irene S. *Killing Us Quietly: Native Americans and HIV/AIDS.* Lincoln: University of Nebraska Press, 2000.

Villanueva, Victor. *Bootstraps: From an American Academic of Color.* Urbana IL: National Council of Teachers of English, 1993.

Vizenor, Gerald. "Dennis of Wounded Knee." *American Indian Quarterly* 7:2 (spring 1983): 51–65.

———. *Fugitive Poses: Native American Scenes of Absence and Presence.* Lincoln: University of Nebraska Press, 1998.

———. "Native American Indian Identities: Autoinscriptions and the Cultures of Names." In *Native American Perspectives on Literature and History,* ed. Allen R. Velie, 117–25. Norman: University of Oklahoma Press, 1994.

Warrior, Robert, and Paul Chaat Smith. *Like a Hurricane: The Indian Movement from Alcatraz to Wounded Knee.* New York: The New Press, 1996.

Weaver, Jace, ed., *Defending Mother Earth: Native American Perspectives on Environmental Justice.* New York: Orbis Books, 1996.

Weir, David, and Lowell Bergman. "The Killing of Anna Mae Aquash." *Rolling Stone,* April 7, 1977, 51–55.

Welch, Deborah. "Zitkala Scarona: An American Indian Leader, 1976–1938." Ph.D. diss., University of Wyoming, 1985.

White, Jack E. "Was Lincoln a Racist?" *Time,* May 15, 2000, 76.

White, Richard. *The Roots of Dependency: Subsistence, Environment, and Social Change among the Choctaws, Pawnees, and Navajos.* Lincoln: University of Nebraska Press, 1983.

*White Shamans and Plastic Medicine Men.* Native Voices Public Television (VCB Room 222, Montana State University, Bozeman, Montana, 59717). 1995. Videocassette.

Whitt, Laurie Anne. "Cultural Imperialism and the Marketing of Native America." *American Indian Culture and Research Journal* 19:3 (1995): 1–32. Reprinted in Mihesuah, ed., *Natives and Academics,* 139–71.

Williams, Teresa Kay. "The Theatre of Identity." In *American Mixed Race: The Culture of Microdiversity,* ed. Naomi Zack, 79–96, 318–19. Lanham MD: Rowman and Littlefield, 1995.

Williams, Robert A., Jr. "Gendered Checks and Balances: Understanding the Legacy of White Patriarchy in an American Indian Cultural Context." *Georgia Law Review* 24 (1990): 1019, 1036–43.

Williams, Walter. *The Spirit and the Flesh: Sexual Diversity in American Indian Culture.* Boston: Beacon Press, 1986.

Wilson, Angela Cavender. "American Indian History or Non-Indian Perceptions of American Indian History?" In Mihesuah, ed., *Natives and Academics*, 23–26.

Wilson, Dorothy Clarke. *Bright Eyes: The Story of Susette LaFlesche, an Omaha Indian*. New York: McGraw-Hill, 1974.

Wilson, Terry P. "Blood Quantum: Native American Mixed Bloods." In Root, ed., *Racially Mixed People in America*, 108–25.

Wise, Christopher, and R. Todd Wise. "A Conversation with Mary Brave Bird." *American Indian Quarterly* 24:3 (summer 2000): 482–93.

Witt, Shirley Hill. "The Brave Hearted Woman: The Struggle at Wounded Knee." *Civil Rights Digest* 8 (1976): 38–45.

———. "An Interview with Dr. Annie Dodge Wauneka." *Frontiers* 6 (fall 1981): 64–66.

———. "Women Fighting the Tide: A Conversation with Janet McCloud." *Turtle Quarterly* (summer 1990): 11–18.

Wright, J. Leitch, Jr., *The Only Land They Knew: The Tragic Story of the American Indians of the Old South*. New York: The Free Press, 1981.

Wright, Roy Dean, and Susan N. Wright. "A Plea for a Further Refinement of the Marginal Man Theory." *Phylon* 33 (1972): 361–68.

Wyler, Rex. *Blood of the Land: The Government and Corporate War against the American Indian Movement*. New York: Random House, 1982.

Yamamoto, George. "Interracial Marriage in Hawaii." In *Interracial Marriage: Expectations and Realities*, ed. I. R. Stuart and L. Edwin, 309–21. New York: Grossman Publishers, 1973.

Yellow Bird, Michael. "What We Want to Be Called: Indigenous Peoples' Perspectives on Racial and Ethnic Identity Labels." *American Indian Quarterly* 23:2 (spring 1999): 1–21.

Young, Mary E. "Women, Colonization, and the Indian Question." In *Clio Was a Woman: Studies in the History of American Women*, ed. Mabel E. Deutrich and Virginia C. Purdy, 98–110. Washington DC: Howard University Press, 1980.

# Index

females, Native (cont.)
  xvi; as feminists, xviii; as leaders,
  xix; roles of, xii, xiv
feminism, xviii–xx; definitions of,
  159–71
Fields, Jennie Ross, 63
Five Civilized Tribes, 104
Foreman, Minta, 66
Fort McDowell Recreation Center,
  150
Franklin, John Hope, 105
Frazier, E. Franklin, 108
Frazier, Ian, xii, 10, 14–18
Freeman, Edith, 93
fullblood: defined, 176 n.14

Gale, Mary (Hinnuagsnun), 46
Gans, Herbert, 95
Gaynor, Gloria, 103
Geronimo, 46
Ghost Dance, 48
Gila Rivers, 149
Girl Scouts, 146
Godfrey, Joyzelle Gingway, 81
Goshorn, Shan, 152
Grafton Hall, 144
Grandmother Turtle, 43
Greenpeace, 147
Guiterrez, Ramon, 35

Halsey, Theresa, 161, 162, 167, 207
  n.7
Hampton Normal and Agricultural
  Institute, 46
Handsome Lake, 48
Hansen, Lance, 24
Hanson, Jeffrey R., 103
Hapa Haole, 100
Harjo, Joy, 28, 30, 160
Harjo, Suzan Shown, 161, 162, 165
Harper's, 52
Harris, LaDonna, 145
Hauptman, Laurence M., 144
Healthy Babies Coalition, 152
Heap of Birds, Hachivi Edgar, 100
Hearon, Dora Wilson, 66
Hicks, Charles, 76

Highwater, Jamake, 197 n.40
Himmelfarb, Gertrude, 27
Hinnuagsnun. See Gale, Mary
Hinsley, Curtis M., 186 n.10
history: writing of, 3–8
History of America, 25
Hogan, Linda, 107, 205 n.30
homosexuality, 43
Hopi Pu'tavi Project, 152
Hopi Quilting Club, 152
Hopis, 35, 43–49, 152, 153, 154
Hopi Women's Coalition, 152
House Made of Dawn, 28
Hudson's Bay Company, 53
Human Genome Project, xi
Hunkpapa Lakota, 161
Hurons (Wyandots), 103, 108–9 n.15

I am Woman: A Native Perspective
  on Sociology and Feminism, 58
I Will Survive, 103
identity: appearance and, xvii; cul-
  tural ambiguity and, xv; defini-
  tions of Indian, 104; fixed, xv,
  xvii
Indian Act (Canada), 54
Indian and Pioneer Histories, 179
  n.5
Indian Arts and Crafts Act, 104
Indian Council Fire of Chicago, 146
Indian Country Today (newspaper),
  130
"Indian Girls" (poem), 19–20
Indian Maiden Art, 60
Indian Nations at Risk Task Force,
  192
Indian Religious Crimes Code, 48
Indian Rights Association, 52
Indian School Days, 96
Indigenous Studies, 19–20
Indigenous Women's Network, 147,
  204–5 n.15
Insane Cobra Nation, 91
Insta Maza (Joseph LaFlesche), 46
Institutional Review Boards (IRB),
  11, 14, 37

CPSIA information can be obtained
at www.ICGtesting.com
Printed in the USA
LVHW011034090721
692214LV00013BA/606

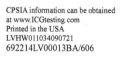

9 780803 282865